Awful Awesome Action: Volume 2

Jacob Gustafson

Copyright © 2022 Jacob Gustafson
All rights reserved.
ISBN:
9798398367782

DEDICATION

This book is dedicated to my wife Vida. She watched most of the films in this volume with me. Thank you for being patient, willing, and fun to watch sweaty men punch each other. I'm glad you spin kicked your way into my heart.

Introduction

Awful: extremely disagreeable or objectionable
Awesome: an emotion variously combining dread, veneration, and wonder that is inspired by authority or by the sacred or sublime

Welcome dear reader back to the wild, wonderful, and weird world of Awful Awesome cinema. In volume 1 of Awful Awesome Action, I covered over 100 films that were so awful, they were awesome and I'm back again to cover over 100 more! At this point I've published over 500 reviews of films that were often called "so bad, they're good", but as stated in the previous volumes, I don't think most of these films are bad at all. They are alternatively entertaining in ways the filmmakers didn't intend, but are still entertaining nonetheless.

As I said in the previous volume, no matter who you are, filmmaking is a very difficult pursuit. It's very time-consuming, stressful, expensive, and can be very disappointing and discouraging. It's very hard to get a film distributed and even harder to make any money at it. Most films that are released are met with apathy and are quickly forgotten by viewers. Some films rise to the top and become hits or maybe even classics. Here we are talking about films that have attained that rarefied air of being successful in their failure but make no mistake: I respect each and every filmmaker in this book and in all the other volumes. It's very hard to complete a film and even harder to have it be critically maligned when it's shown to the world (imagine really putting yourself out there and getting laughed at, that's a helluva gut punch). I am trying to suggest an alternative way of viewing the films to enjoy them, which is ultimately what every filmmaker wants: to entertain their audience and be remembered. I feel that it is my duty to bring these films to you lest they be forgotten by cinema fans or, even worse, written off. It has never been my intention to present these reviews in a way that would place me above them or their creators. I love them. I love them so much I wrote about them, and I want to share them with the world. I want you to watch them and love them too.

This journey of digging deep, scouring resources and paying attention to word-of-mouth has been such a fun, wild ride that I don't want it to ever end! I love the underseen, unloved, and unappreciated films that are buckets of fun to watch with friends. Keep your peepers peeled as I will be publishing another volume of Horror movies and another volume of Sci-Fi films too. This will bring my published review count up to over 600! I believe at that moment I will have (hopefully) earned the crown of the king of Awful Awesome cinema! Will there be a 3rd volume of Awful Awesome books? I certainly hope so! I'm not ready to quit watching and reviewing Awful Awesome movies, so my plan is to eventually have 3 volumes of each genre in print! Will I make it? Only time will tell. One thing's for sure: there are still plenty more films to find creeping under the darker and forgotten corners of cinema. I enjoy the hunt and the quest to find new pantheon-level films and sure-fire winners. You would think after watching so many already that I would be fatigued, but my thirst is far from quenched. How many hidden gems are waiting to be discovered? I can't wait to find out and I hope you come along and join me.

With each volume I've been able to dig deeper and deeper and find more obscure and sometimes, more rewarding cinematic discoveries. I hope you'll find a larger number of films that are totally unknown to you that you'll want to track down and enjoy with friends. You'll notice that with this volume I have cut out the Awful Awesome Night tips and the Awful Awesome All-Stars. I didn't want YOU dear reader to think that I was padding this volume out by repeating material already published in the preceding volume. If this is your first volume, I recommend picking up Volume 1 so you can get access to not only more reviews but my tips on how to have a fun night with friends and some guaranteed Awful Awesome Auteurs to keep your eyes out for. I hope you enjoy this volume. I think it has stronger selections, the films are deeper cuts, and I hope it's even more fun to read. So, get ready to dive into another wild selection of Awful Awesome films!

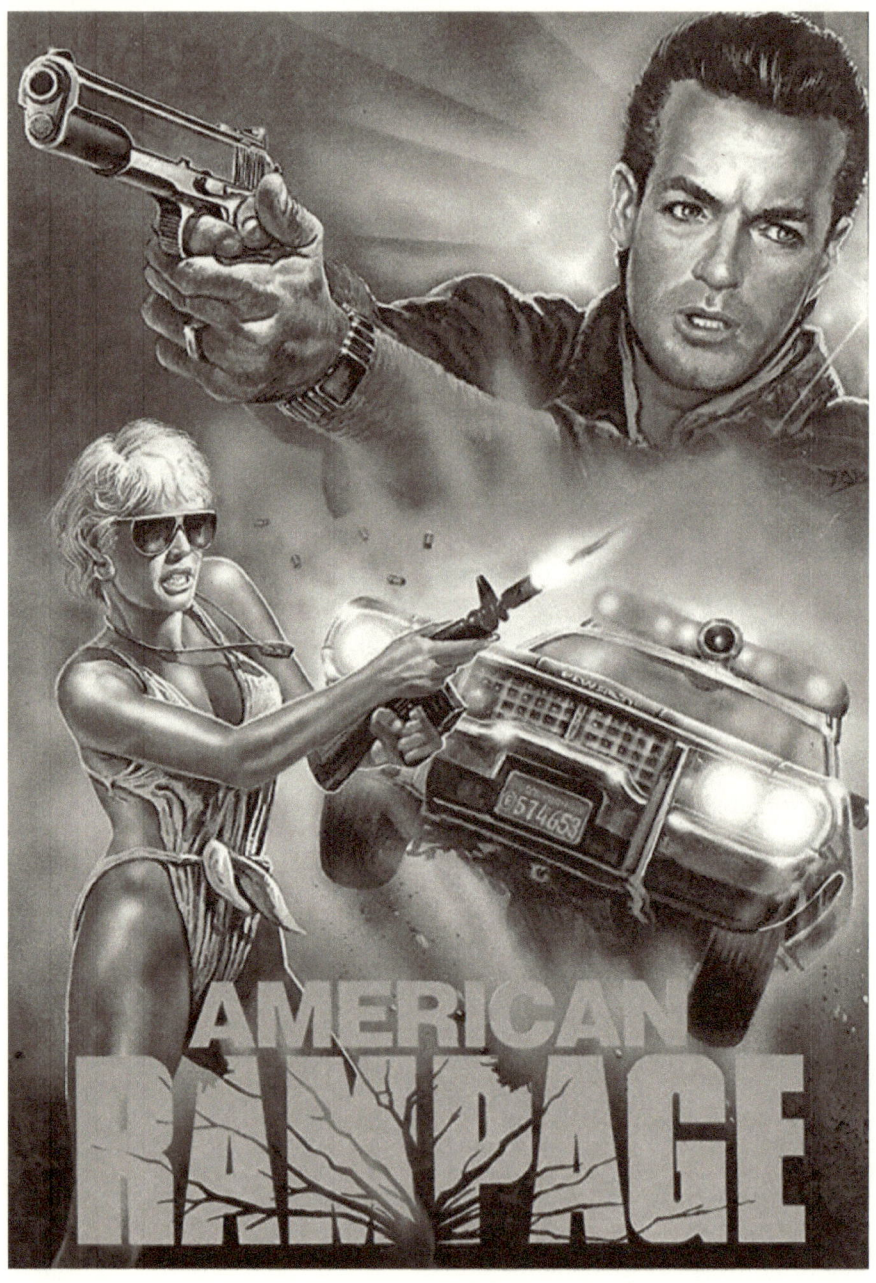

American Rampage (1989)
Directed by David DeCoteau
Runtime 86 minutes

David DeCoteau is a name that is no stranger to the pages of my books. A filmmaker that has cranked out a staggering number of films during his career, his films are very dicey when it comes to enjoying with friends. True his filmography is filled with low-budget films of every stripe, but I've gotten my fingers burned several times by his films. I decided I'd roll the dice and check this one out with my Awful Awesome crew.
The basic plot of American Rampage is the planned takedown of a crime kingpin by hot-shot cops. Our heroes are cops that are loose cannons but get the job done (you can almost smell the testosterone). Our male protagonist gets a new female partner after his old partner bites the dust. She's green and needs him to show her the ropes. He shows her *his* rope too and they fall in love. Meanwhile the crime kingpin doesn't like their attempts to foil his empire and so our heroes have to fight it out with a bevy of bad dudes. A lot more happens in this film, but I'd be lying if I told you I followed the details. My friends were just as mystified by the film as I was. It took several people to write this bad boy and I think rather than one writer improving on another, they all turned in partially done scripts, smashed em together and decided it was good enough. It wasn't.

American Rampage stars no one of note except maybe Troy Donahue, who gets top billing but only appears in the film briefly. We get double denim, bloody squibs, weak car explosions, far too many characters, extended scenes of women putting lotion on their nude bodies (including Linnea Quigley), hot guitar licks, violent female stripping, and sloppy fights. It also features extended scenes of dialogue and one scene where a character is secretly following another character that lasts for thirteen minutes with no dialogue American Rampage might be the best non-Puppet Master movie David DeCoteau ever made. It's fun, trashy, inscrutable, and cheap but not as cheap as his recent work.

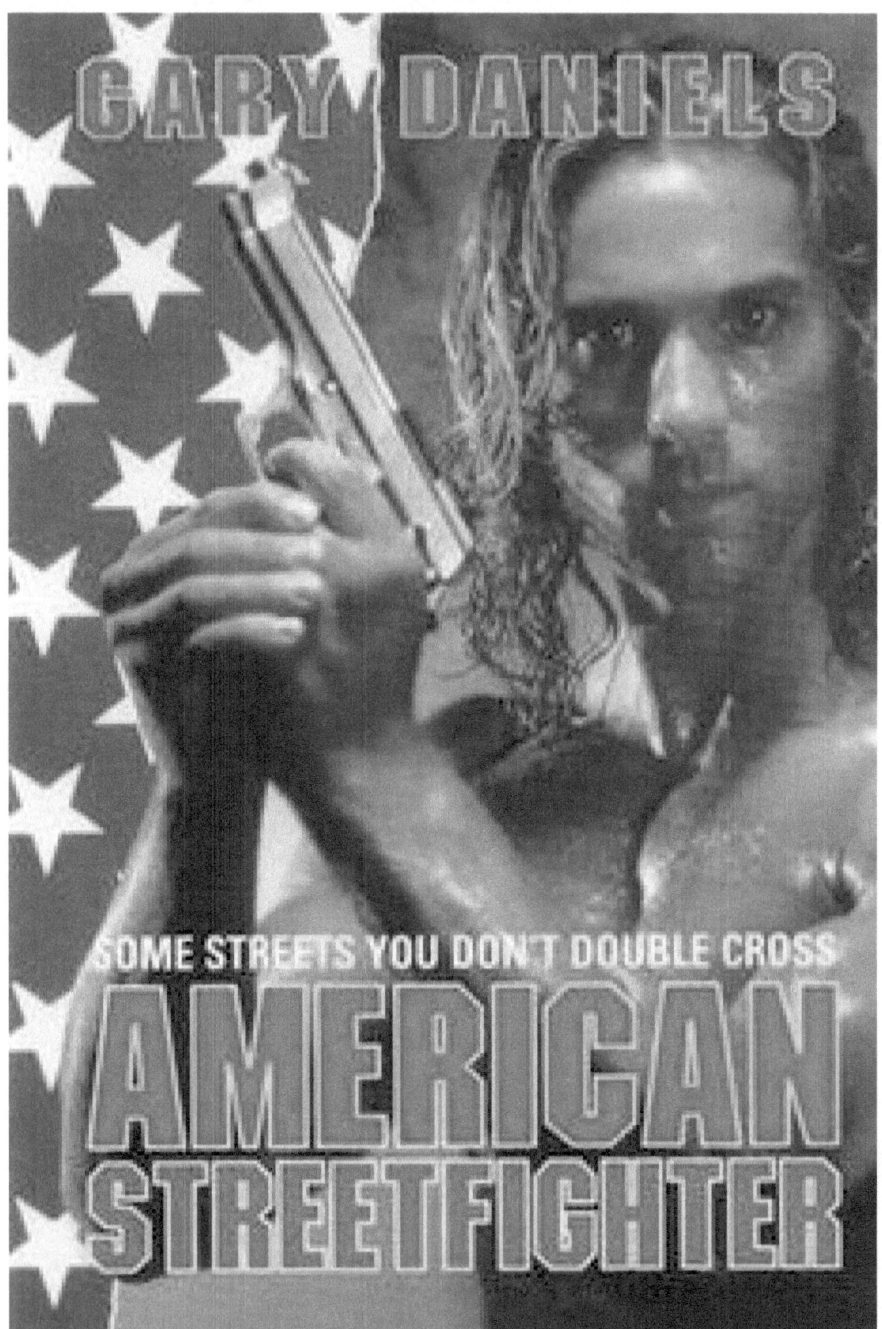

American Streetfighter (1992)
Directed by Steve Austin
Runtime 85 minutes

Produced by Cine Excel, American Streetfighter begins with Gary Daniels and a friend setting up some casual arson. They've been hired to damage a restaurant so the owner can collect on insurance money. Decked out in a black leather jacket with so many tassels it made Lorenzo Lamas jealous, he sets up a bomb inside the business. Just before the bomb is about to go off some off-duty employees decide to go hang out inside, because that's what you do when you're not working, hang out at work right? Daniels' partner gets shot and killed while Daniels beats a hasty retreat. He flees the country and becomes a captain of industry in Hong Kong. After 10 years of exile, he gets word from back home that his little brother has gotten mixed up in illegal pit fighting. Daniels tries to pay off the nefarious man in charge of the pit fighting (played by Gerald Okamura) but it's no good. The only way Daniels can get his brother out by taking his place and becoming a pit fighter himself! Gary Daniels is the titular American Streetfighter, despite being VERY obviously British. At one point someone says, "Oh you're a Limey," to which Daniels says, "no, I'm American" (welp, I'm convinced...).

The movie features some of the worst set decoration I've ever seen. It's obvious that they had access to only one or two locations and so they had to redress the sets to "fool" the audience. It didn't work. At one point there's sheets hung up on walls with random paint sprayed on them. Another time the location is filled with empty boxes. The music is full on cat-on-a-keyboard style which is always a trashy treat. The action is very sloppy and unconvincing, as is the acting. The plot hums along at a nice clip with little time wasted. We get a protagonist with an eyepatch, a weak motorcycle stunt, and even a carsplosion. American Streetfighter is as fun as the other Cine Excel Gary Daniels films like Full Impact and Capital Punishment. I would recommend it for a bottom-of-the-barrel action trash evening with friends.

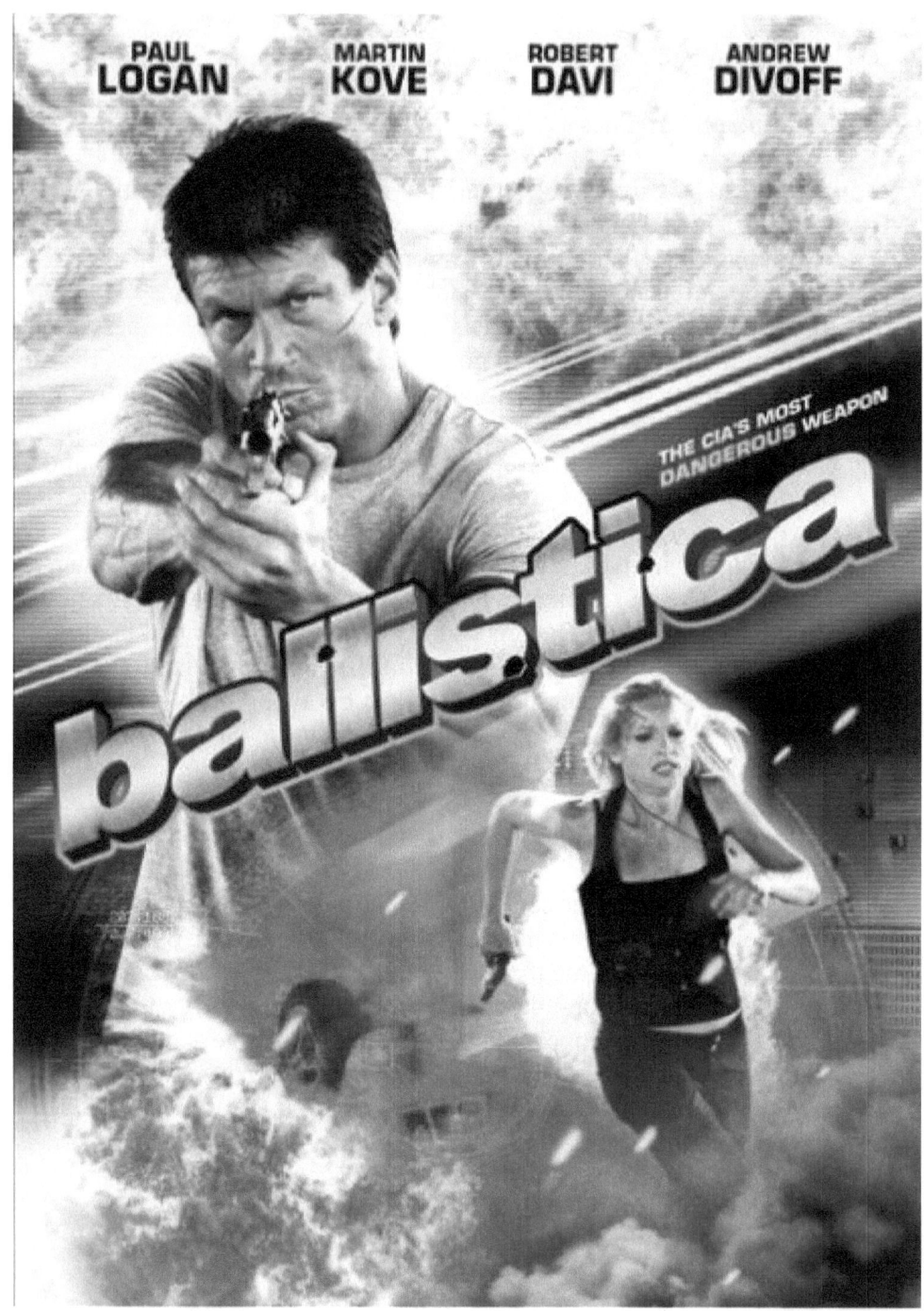

Ballistica (2009)
Runtime 90 minutes
Directed by Gary Jones

Ballistica is about Damian Sloan (Paul Logan), he's an ultra-elite special ops guy who has been trained in the ancient art of Ballistica. He states in the movie that a person can train in Ballistica their entire lives and never understand what it really is. Sounds great right? He works for Riley (Martin Kove), pulling clandestine jobs that no one else could pull off. The film begins with Damian landing in Russia on a secret mission to infiltrate a science lab that's supposed to have top secret stuff in it. He finds a young woman named Alexa, who he believes to be kidnapped by the Russians. Damian scoops her up, and using his fancy Ballistica moves, he gets her back to the loving embrace of Uncle Sam. There we find out that there's a crazy new bomb that the Russians have developed at the facility where Alexa was being held. Now Damien and Alexa have to work together to locate the bomb and get it out of Russian hands.

There is plenty of action within the runtime and even when no one is getting punched or shot, our main characters are swapping hammy lines with wooden performances. The action itself is very sloppy. I believe Ballistica was supposed to look Matrix-esque, but instead looks like kids playing cops and robbers. Our hero twirls around like a ballerina shooting indiscriminately but still hitting his targets. He tactically rolls when there is no need to, shoots behind him without looking and generally flops around like a fish trying to look really cool but failing miserably. It's clear if there was any real choreography going on, they had little time to design it, let alone practice it. Andrew Divoff plays a Russian and he and our hero rub the tips of their guns together in a scene that feels like a joke but is played totally straight. Robert Davi is in a sit-down role as Martin Kove's boss but it's still nice to see him. The film also uses poor green screen and CGI to create explosions and locations that they clearly couldn't pull off.

Ballistica is a hoot. It has enough action to keep the party going, some fan favorite actors, and a very silly and poorly executed style of martial arts that never stops being hilarious. I whole-heartedly recommend Ballistica.

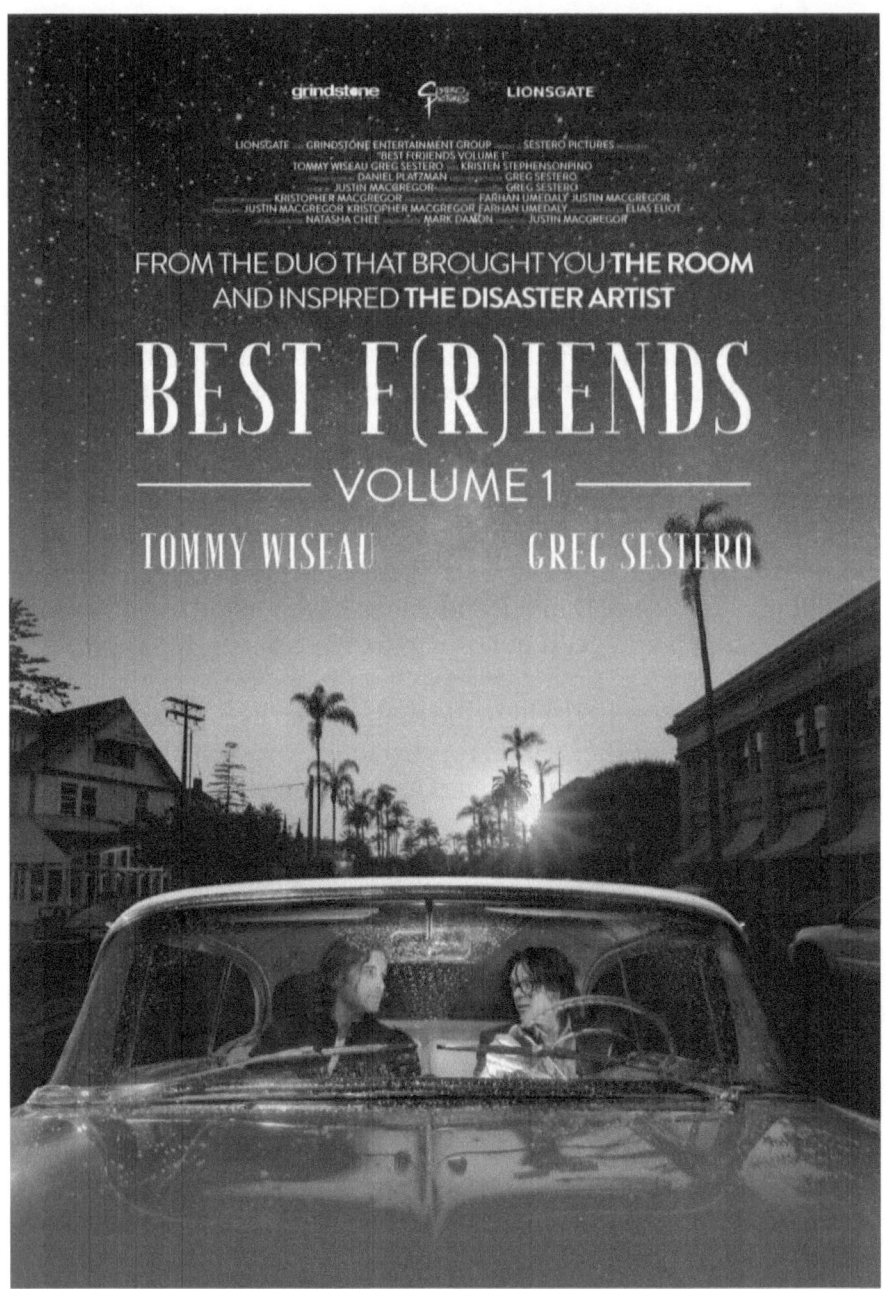

Best F(r)iends Part 1 (2019)
Runtime 104 minutes
Directed by Justin MacGregor

Best Friends stars Greg Sestero as a homeless man, injured, bearded, and alone (so sad...). One day he stumbles across a mortician, played by Tommy Wiseau. Greg is offered a job and he begins helping out in the artful mortician's office. Each victim is given a new mask which hides their dead face, and their gold dental work is extracted and secreted away. Turns out the mortician has boxes and boxes of dead folks' teeth. The apprentice begins stealing it and selling it clandestinely. With a fat wallet and better clothes, he strikes up a relationship with a barmaid and all seems well until the mortician finds out. They agree to split it 50/50 because the apprentice finds the buyer and the mortician has the goods to sell. The mortician starts to spend the money however and this doesn't sit well with the apprentice because it will draw attention to them. Plus, he believes his half is being spent too. The apprentice and his barmaid girlfriend hatch a plan to get rid of the mortician and live happily ever after but will they get away with it?

It's clear that Tommy was given an outline of what he was supposed to say as opposed to actual lines, so he ad-libs. His ad-libs are JUST as bizarre as you might expect and help to elevate a film that honestly would have been very forgettable, to something that approaches a unique blend of The Room with a somewhat Lynchian vibe. It takes at least an hour of the runtime for the conflict to be established, instead we just hang out with these oddball characters as they go about their days. This was clearly meant to be watched in one sitting (I didn't) and Part 1 is not meant to stand on its own. It ends on a cliffhanger, compelling the viewer to watch Part 2. I enjoyed the film for its oddness of characters as well as plotting. It's hard to review just this one part but I will say that either it's going to leave you very bored, or you'll be very eager to find out what happens next. I'm in the latter group. While it may not be 100% Awful Awesome territory, there are enough odd choices to lend itself to conversation and is truly a singular viewing experience due to Tommy and his performance.

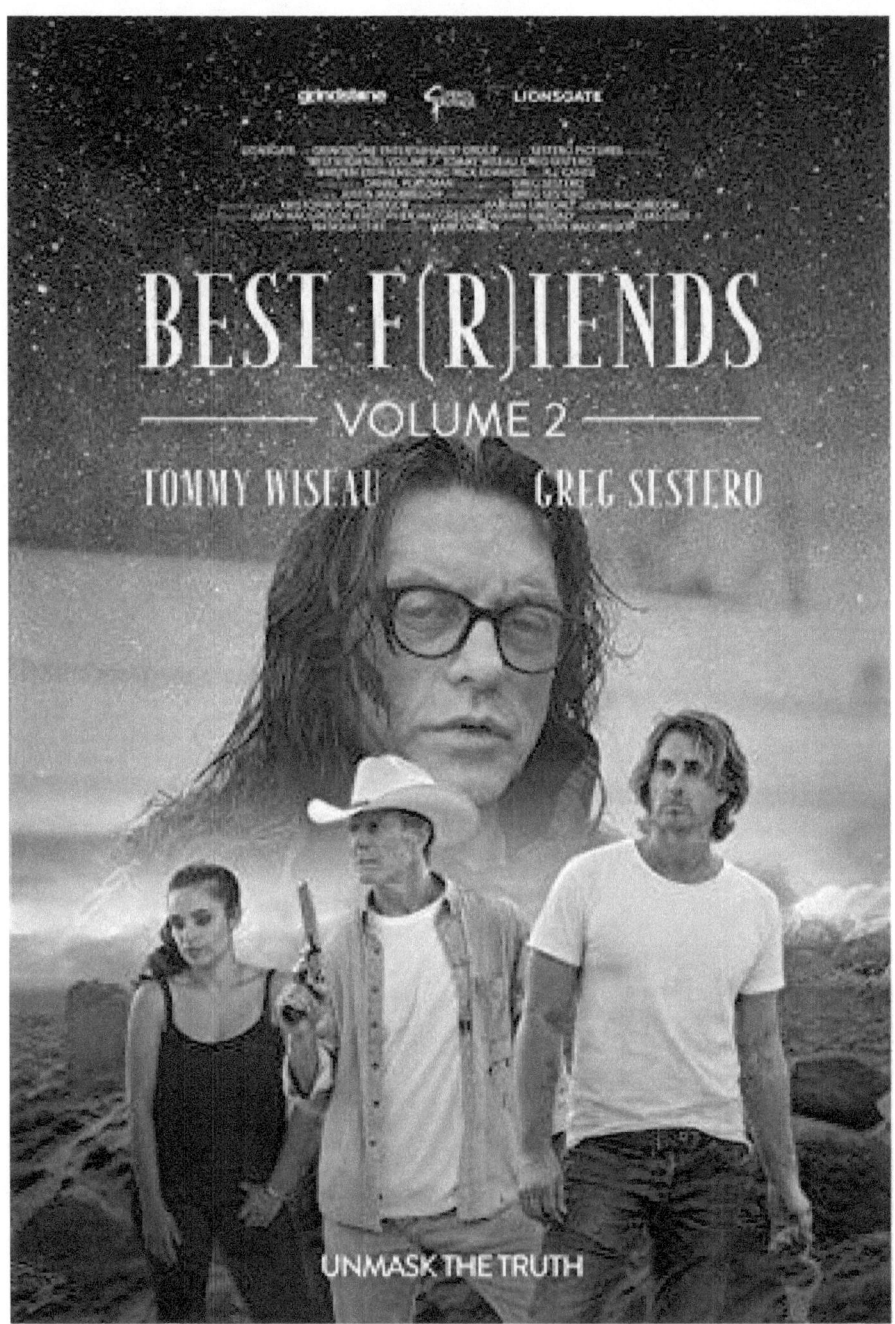

Best F(r)iends Part 2 (2018)
Runtime 93 minutes
Directed by Justin MacGregor

Part 2 picks up with Tommy wearing what can only be described as a Knights Templar helmet, and Greg Sestero handcuffed to a staircase. The film then backtracks to events that happened earlier and thus the film language of this edition is born: flashbacks cut with mysterious footage of what is (apparently) present time in the film's story. We learn that Tommy did fall down the cliff and that our shady couple fled the scene. Later they try to get into the ATM with the purloined keys but as it turns out the wrong keys were stolen (ruh roh!). Why weren't all the keys taken off the dead mortician? Who knows? Now the pair have to make their way to the barmaid's uncle who lives way out in Arizona. The hope is that either he can get it open, or that he knows someone that can. All is not what it seems however, and we are handed some obvious twists and a strange ending befitting what we would expect from a film starring Tommy.

Part 2 is unfortunately not the action-packed follow-up to Part 1 that one might desire. I was hoping that the meandering pace would be tightened up for the second half but no, it is just as slow, if not slower. It also suffers from a distinct lack of Tommy. Sure, he's in the film but not nearly enough. The uncle character is quite fun however, and constantly refers to male genitals in unique and hilarious ways, terms like "pink steel" abound and help to keep interest in the film. We also get a bed and breakfast owner played by an actor that is doing his damndest to out-act everyone. The film is trying earnestly to create a fascinating crime/thriller story but fails miserably because the plot feels like a rough draft hastily assembled the night before. Put together, the entire story clocks in at over three-hours long which is a very tough sell. Having seen both parts, I appreciate that the film was at least presented as two parts so I could take a break in-between. I have to wonder why the two feature-length halves weren't cut down to create a more reasonably length for the film, especially since there are long stretches where not much is happening. The entire film feels like a rough copy. I'm glad I watched both parts, but I can't wholeheartedly recommend it except to those who love Tommy.

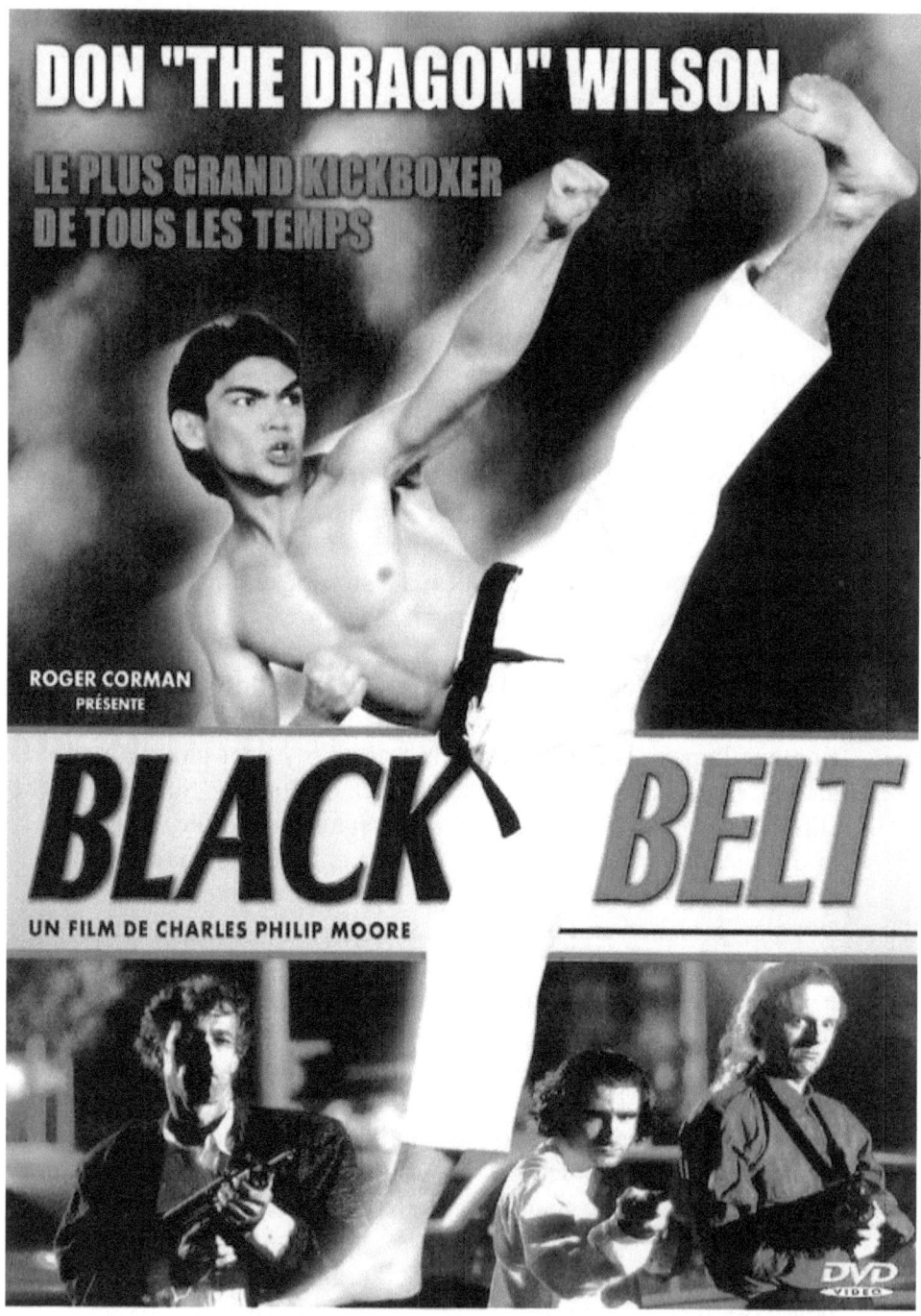

Blackbelt (1992)
Runtime 86 minutes
Directed by Rick Jacobson, Charles Philip Moore

Jack Dillon (Don "The Dragon" Wilson) is a martial arts instructor that used to be a cop. He left the force to escape the madness of the thin blue line but not before making quite a reputation for himself. After a pop star gets a severed finger as a "gift" from an admirer, she's sent to Dillon for protection. His cop senses begin to tingle and soon it's discovered that the severed finger belonged to a recently murdered prostitute who was found next to a room filled with dead bad guys. The carnage was wrecked by ironically named John Sweet (Matthias Hues). He's a hired killer, hence the room full of dead bad guys, but he's also a serial killer of women (kind of a two-fer). The pop diva is next on his list so it's up to Dillon and his former partner to both protect her and track down Sweet to end his killing spree. It's rare for Matthias Hues to get more than a bit part, so I was very happy with his suitably meaty role in the film. Don "The Dragon" Wilson always strikes me as a genuinely nice guy and I find his performances oddly comforting, it's like getting wrapped in a safe blanket that can also kick some serious ass. We get some terrible pop music and performances by our pop diva, which is always welcome in action trash like this. She has an abusive boyfriend which Wilson gets to man handle throughout the film (which is also fun to watch). There's no mystery however, we know who the killer is and surprisingly so do the authorities. For some reason they have trouble tracking down a super muscular man of 6'5" with a mane of blonde hair. The serial killer plot device adds a certain amount of sleaze to the proceedings as well as a bit of a horror vibe. Blackbelt was made at a time when horror's grip on video stores was waning and action was beginning to take over, so it's an interesting way of bridging the two genres.

I won't say that Blackbelt is a must-see action movie for awful awesome fans, but it is a must-see for fans of Don "The Dragon" Wilson and Matthias Hues. The film moves along at a good clip, has enough action to keep viewer attention, and features some really terrible music. It's a fun film and worth your time.

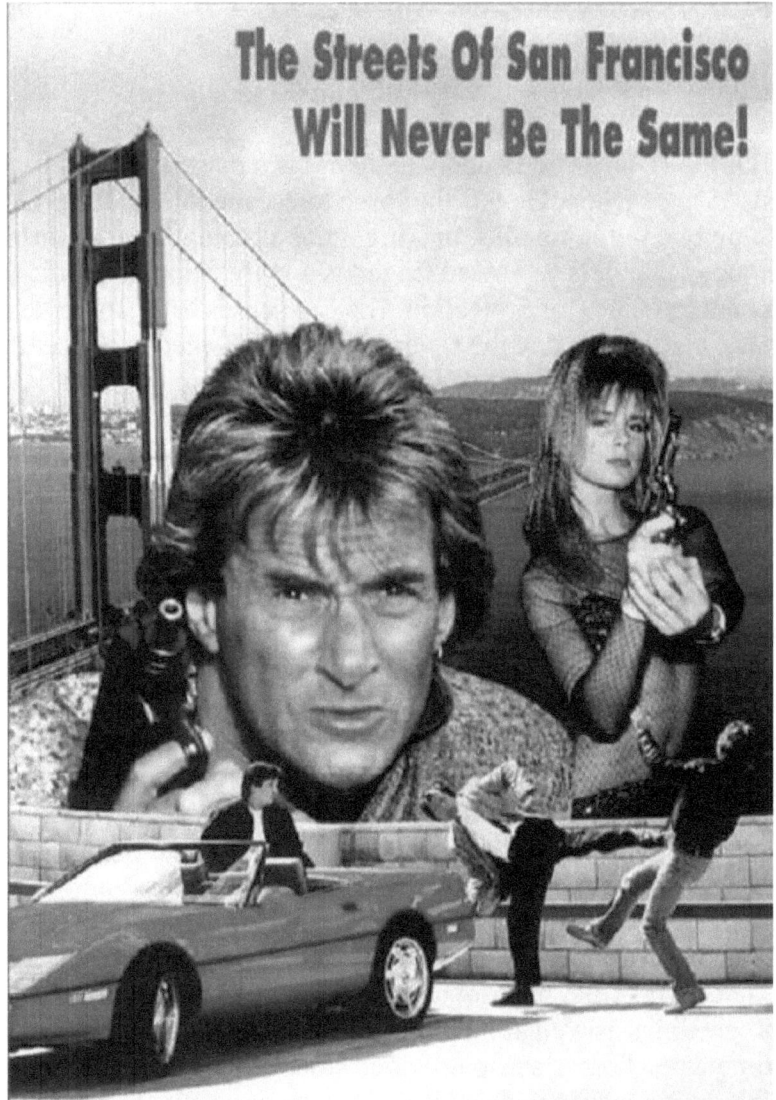

Blood Street (1988)
Runtime 80 minutes
Directed by Leo Fong, George Chung

Blood Street is a sequel to Low Blow, which is one of the more fun movies I've ever watched with my bad movie crew. Excited, I knew I had to get my friends together and witness the continuing adventures of Joe Wong, Private Detective. Joe Wong, now sans secretary, is approached by a pretty lady looking for her missing husband. She offers to pay him in sex and even offers to give him a freebie to get the job going. He declines the offer but takes the job and sets out to find her hubby (what a class act). Detective Wong starts his search and finds himself in the middle of a viper's nest of drug dealers, suppliers, thugs, and kingpins. He quickly realizes that this search is going to lead him to some seriously big fish to fry and punches his way to the truth. We also learn that our hero once had a family until they were brutally murdered in Texas. On a path of vengeance, he then journeyed to Mexico and found the killer and beats him to death. In the two years between this and Low Blow, Leo Fong did not learn how to act and quite frankly, that's a good thing. He's monotone and I wouldn't have it any other way. He did, however upgrade his car considerably. Now he has a sweet lipstick-red convertible corvette that he drives very sensibly throughout the whole film. It doesn't get smashed, it doesn't get in any high-speed chases, and he parks it safely. Bummer. Wong sports a sweet sawed-off single-shot shotgun that he uses frequently in the movie. We also get a fantastic dummy drop, death by dart, Richard Norton slumming it, and a cameo by George Chung. The film begins with a cocaine and sex party that goes to hell long before they all get shot: there is zero passion from any participant in this part. It's hilarious. While never reaching the high highs of Low Blow, Blood Street does deal out plenty of low-grade action that keeps the film humming along and fun to watch.

The short runtime helps considerably as well. If you're a fan of Low Blow or Leo Fong in general, Blood Street is a fun watch. While it isn't essential like Low Blow is, it IS fun, if a bit confusing. There's lots of action peppered throughout the film, which keeps the fun flowing.

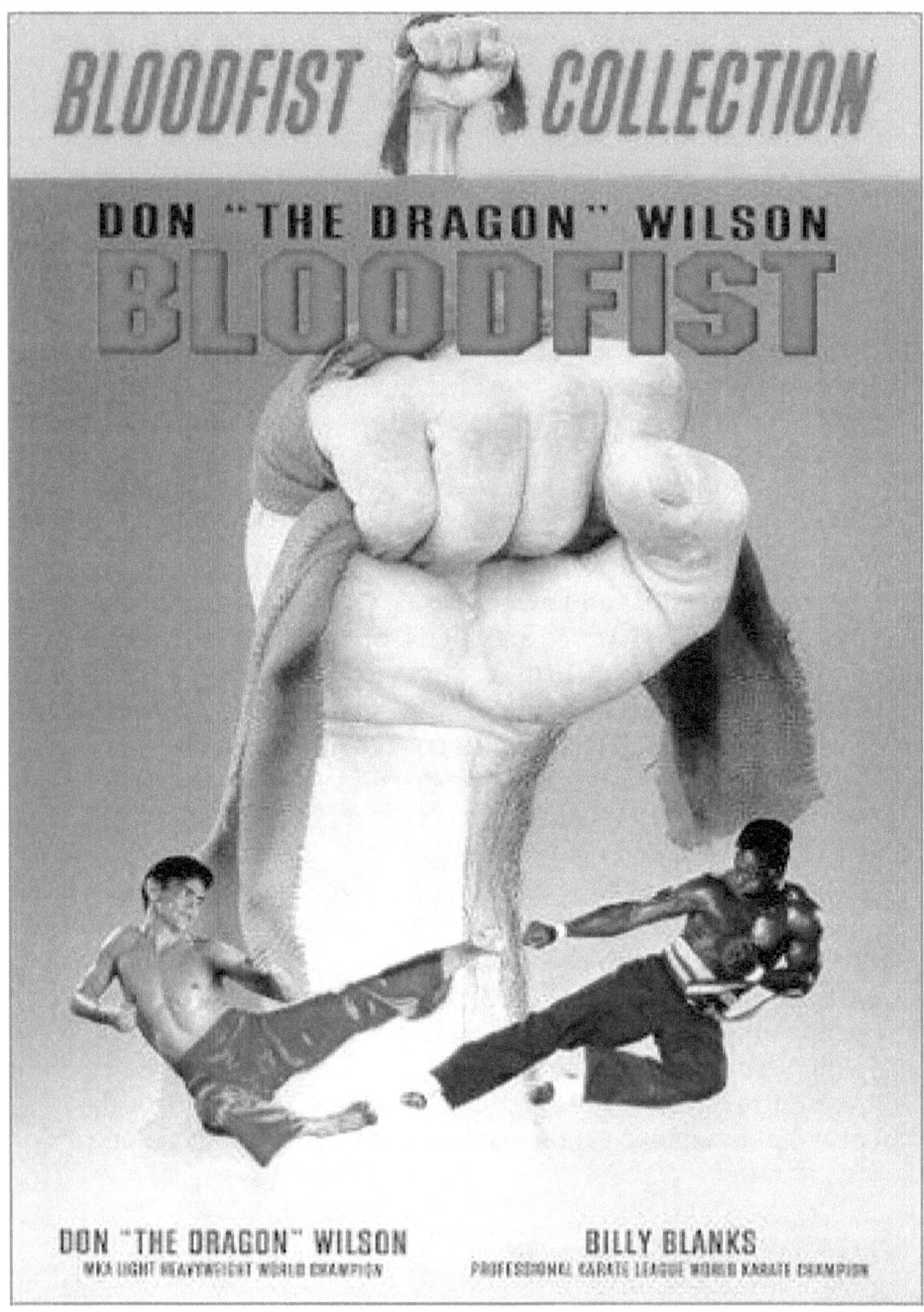

Bloodfist (1989)
Runtime 83 minutes
Directed by Terence H. Winkless

Bloodfist is about Jake Raye (Wilson); he's co-owner of a martial arts/boxing studio in the U.S. where he trains children to beat the hell out of each other using his sweet boxing moves. He doesn't compete because he's only got one kidney... You see, the other one is inside his unscrupulous brother. Said brother gets up and leaves the studio to go fight in an underground martial arts tournament in the Philippines. He doesn't win however, instead, he's killed. Ever the faithful brother, Jake flies to the Philippines to pick up his sibling's ashes and track down the killer. As it turns out, the only way to do any real investigating is to enter the tournament and... FIGHT for the truth. He meets American ex-pat Baby (a dude with a "boy named Sue" thing going on), who plans to enter the illegal tournament. Jake is also introduced to Kwong, an artist and trainer, who agrees to train Jake so he can find his brother's murderer and take him down! Oh, and Baby has a bodacious sister who Jake falls for. She's a stripper. It's complicated.

Bloodfist delivers on both the blood and the fist. The film is chock full of chop socky and big mouthfuls of fake blood. The plot moves quickly (even if it is cliché) and wastes little time. Heck the subplot involving Baby's sister and Jake is nothing more than an excuse to show her nekkid. The relationship isn't a focal point in the film, it's just there to deliver some T&A. These types of plot decisions can really drag a film down with needless bloated melodrama but thankfully that is not the case here. Wilson acquits himself well, or at least as well as he ever does. His acting has never been stellar, but I still appreciate his direct delivery of lines. His performance is rarely the reason to watch his movies anyway: it's about the action. Bloodfist delivers on that front too. We get numerous fight scenes, and even some stunt work with Wilson. Billy Blanks plays the unironically named Black Rose but isn't given much to do in the movie. Really, he's just like a mini-boss for Jake to fight but it's always nice to see Blanks pop up in a flick. Bloodfist is a solid entry in direct-to-video action cheese.

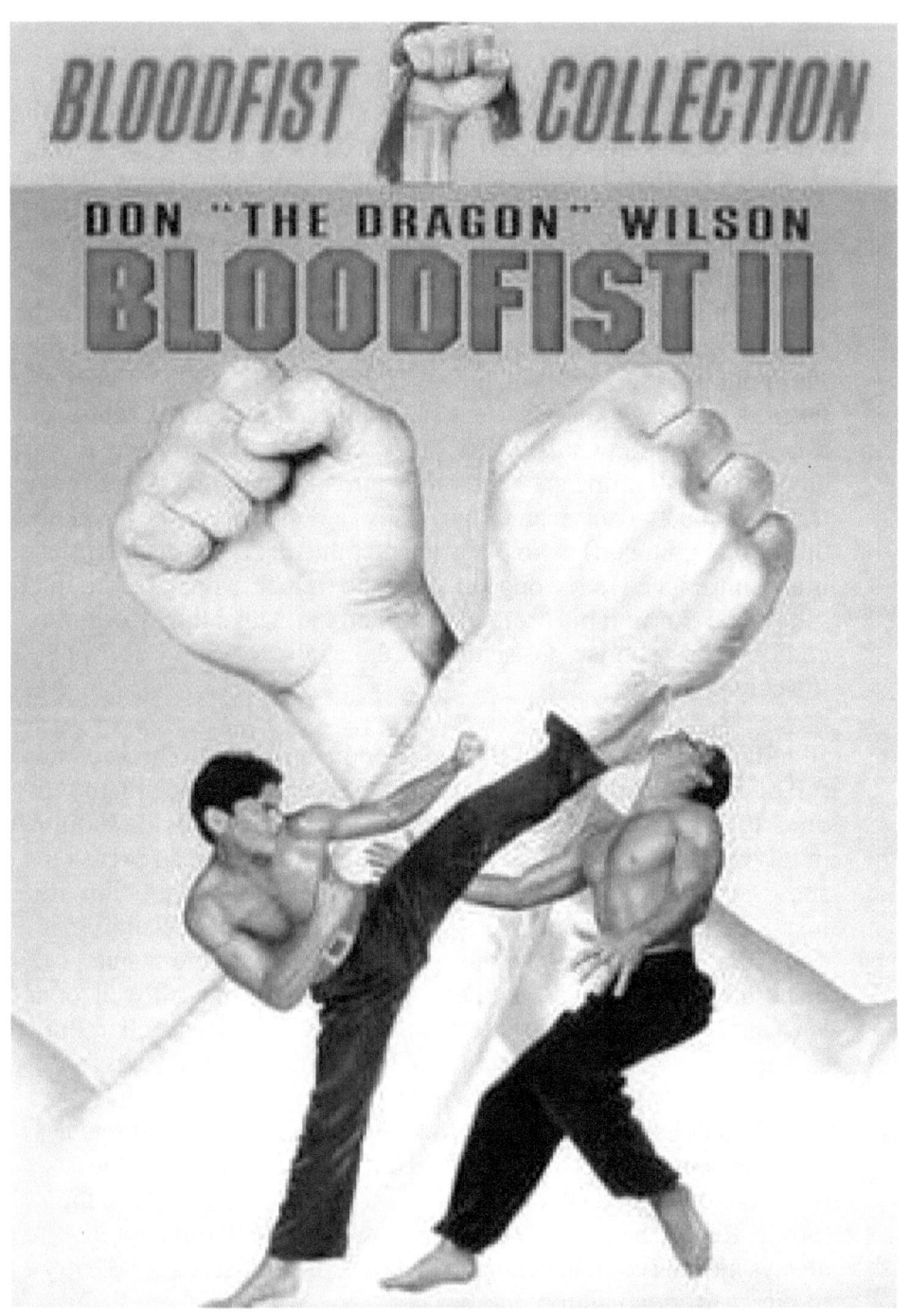

Bloodfist 2 (1990)
Runtime 83 minutes
Directed by Andy Blumenthal

After watching the first Bloodfist and realizing that there were eight films in the series, I knew I had to eventually watch them all (it was inevitable). Each film stars Don "The Dragon" Wilson and showcases his kickboxing abilities. Also returning for part two is Jose Mari Avellana who starred as Kwong in Bloodfist but inexplicably plays an evil bad guy Su in part 2 (they play it a bit loose with canon). Jake Raye (Don "The Dragon" Wilson) is in kickboxing match at the beginning of the film (just an average day in the life...). In order to end the fight, he fires off a fierce kick which accidently catches his opponent in the throat killing him. Crushed, Raye quits fighting and starts drinking. He's well on his way into a bender and we find him in bed with a hooker when his phone rings. It's an old buddy who is in trouble in the Philippines, turns out he needs to get out and needs Raye to help him escape. Begrudgingly Raye decides to help his friend and flies to the island. Upon landing the action kicks off: he's nearly beaten up and mugged before successfully being captured and drugged. He awakens, chained aboard a ship with other fighters who are in the same predicament. They've the best in the world in their various styles and have been kidnapped to fight in an illegal fighting tournament for the pleasure of evil rich dudes. Now it's up to Raye to free everyone before going home... presumably to get drunk and pay for more hookers. Bloodfist 2 does a good job of being close to its predecessor without completely copying it. There's enough variance to keep it somewhat fresh even if it really is just another Bloodsport clone. Wilson again is solid, dealing out plenty of Dragon Justice. We get some stunts early on in the film and again, everyone's mouths are full of blood. It's very strange to see Jose Mari Avellana play a completely different character in this sequel, as if viewers wouldn't notice? For half the movie I thought he was Kwong until I figured out his character was unrelated to the first film, even though Wilson plays the same character. Weird.

It's a solid flick that trims most of the fat and gives the viewer what they want: Wilson kicking fools in the face. The lean runtime helps to keep the movie going on what was obviously a limited budget.

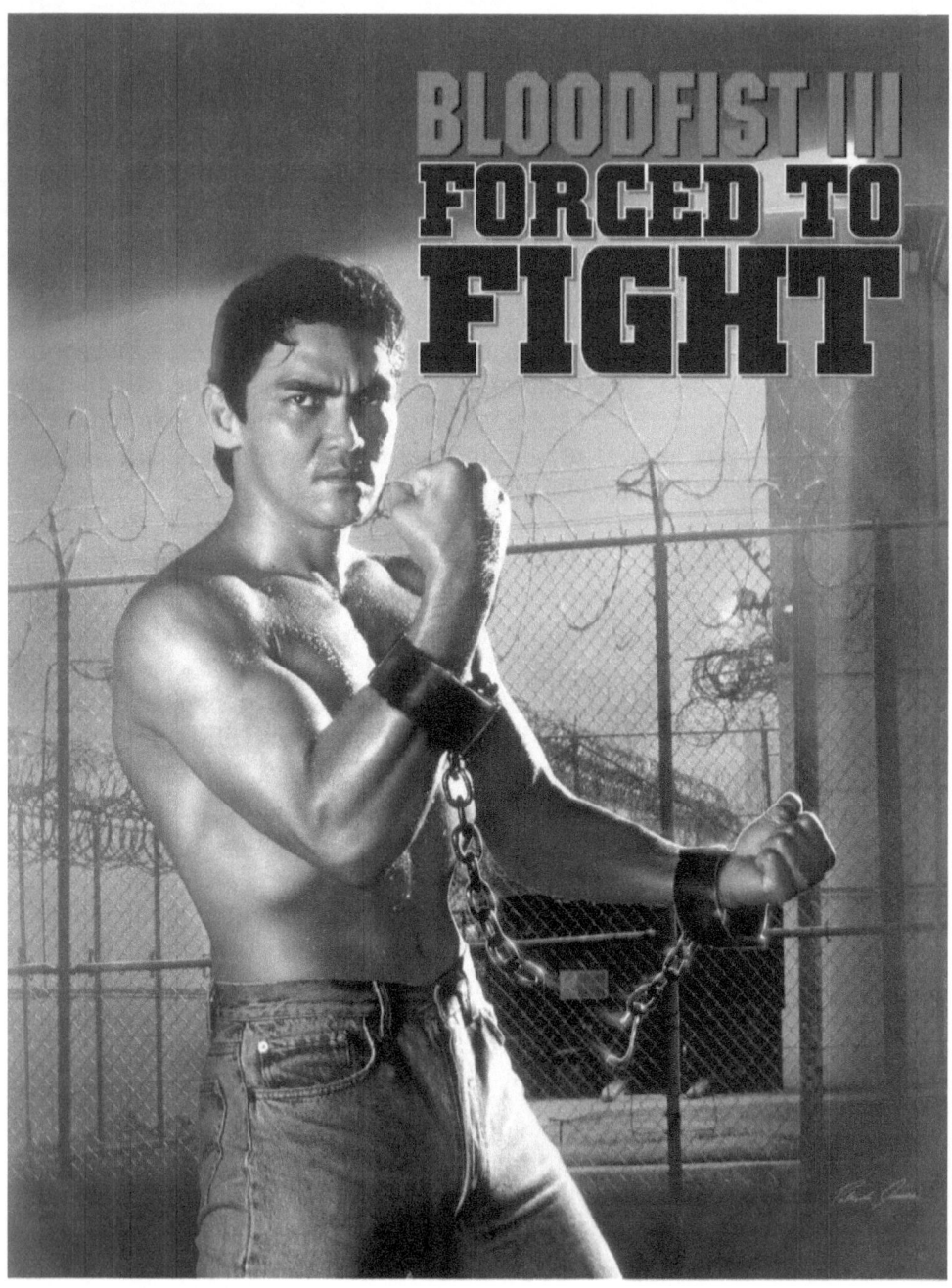

Bloodfist III: Forced to Fight (1992)
Runtime 88 minutes
Directed by Oley Sassone

Bloodfist III: Forced to Fight begins with Don "the Dragon" Wilson rotting away in prison. He plays Jimmy Boland, and we don't know why he's there, but we do know that he looks great in a tucked in white tank top and jeans. Dude may be in prison but that doesn't mean that he can't look neat and tidy. He stumbles upon the murder of his friend by another inmate, so of course he gets vengeance ...by killing the killer. Mistake. As it turns out this particular inmate was the connection a drug dealer inside the prison needed to score drugs (that's bad for business). After the incident he's moved to another place in the prison where he runs afoul of the seriously angry dude who can now no longer get drugs to sell. Boland is put in a new cell with Samuel Stark (Richard Roundtree) who is a prisoner that has become enlightened. He's your cliché educated prisoner who hold a lot of sway inside because of his impressive knowledge of the law. Boland spends the rest of the movie making enemies with the white prisoners (who are very racist of course) and is already the enemy of most black prisoners because the prisoner he killed in sweet vengeance was also black. His only friend is Stark, and he might not be enough to keep Boland safe. Good thing Boland can kick some serious ass on his own.

I'll be honest here: I'm not a big fan of prison movies in general. Sure, there are a handful of solid action flicks that take place in prison, but mostly they sort of bore me. Bloodfist III is no exception. We do get a fair amount of action but it's all pretty tame and uninspired. The film is also very preachy to an unbearable degree and while I had no trouble finishing it, I won't be returning to it any time soon or probably ever. Everything about the movie is mediocre. The acting, the music, the direction, the script. There's really nothing memorable about the movie. So far, this is the weakest entry in the Bloodfist series but then again there's 5 more official films to go and one unofficial entry as well, so there are plenty of more opportunities to make this one look good. Your enjoyment of this entry depends heavily on how you feel about Don "the Dragon" Wilson and prison movies. For me, it's a pass.

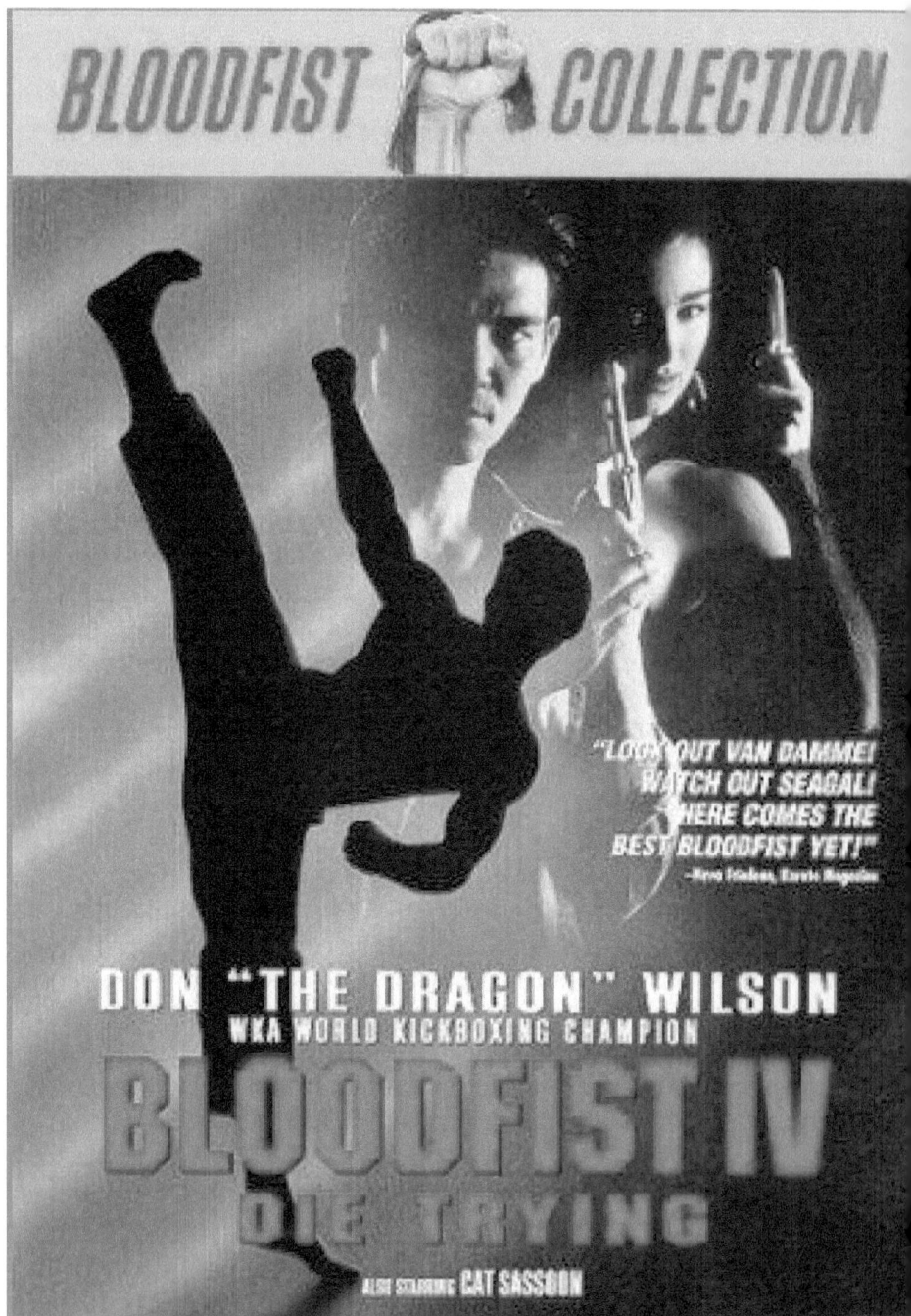

Bloodfist IV: Die Trying (1992)
Runtime 83 minutes
Directed by Paul Ziller

Part IV finds Don "The Dragon" Wilson playing Danny Holt. He's a repo man known to capture cars in difficult situations, and he can take out the owners with his fists and feet if need be. A BMW on the repo list gets taken, but it belongs to some seriously dangerous mafia-type guys. Inside the car is a box of Easter bunny chocolates... and inside those chocolates are secret items worth a huge amount of money! The repo office becomes a war zone when the mafia guys come to get their car (and their chocolates) back and decide to unload machineguns into everyone (no witnesses!). Nearly caught in the firefight, Danny escapes with the chocolates (a gift for his daughter). When the cops show up to investigate the crime scene, the obvious conclusion is that Danny did it. At the same time, the mafia guys kidnap Danny's daughter to force him to hand over the chocolates and Gary Daniels (playing Scarface, a mafia guy) is also on Danny's trail, just in case the kidnapping doesn't inspire him to cooperate).Bloodfist IV: Die Trying might just be the best in the series. It is action-packed from the very beginning of the film and doesn't let up. Danny can't go anywhere in this movie without getting into a fight and the constant melee never gets boring. Gary Daniels is sadly underutilized here, but his hair is so amazing it almost makes up for it, it's blown out and huge, wavy and tremendous. Getting to see the two of them go toe-to-toe is also especially fun. Cat Sassoon (Angelfist) shows up for a hot minute as a knife-wielding goon as well. Tough cops bust in and act tough until some Feds arrive... and then they all try to out-tough each other while Danny runs around kicking the hell out of everyone that gets in his way.

The film's conflict gets set up quickly and it doesn't get bogged down in any useless subplots, which can be the death knell for cheap action like this. The movie's short runtime and action-packed plot make this one a clear winner.

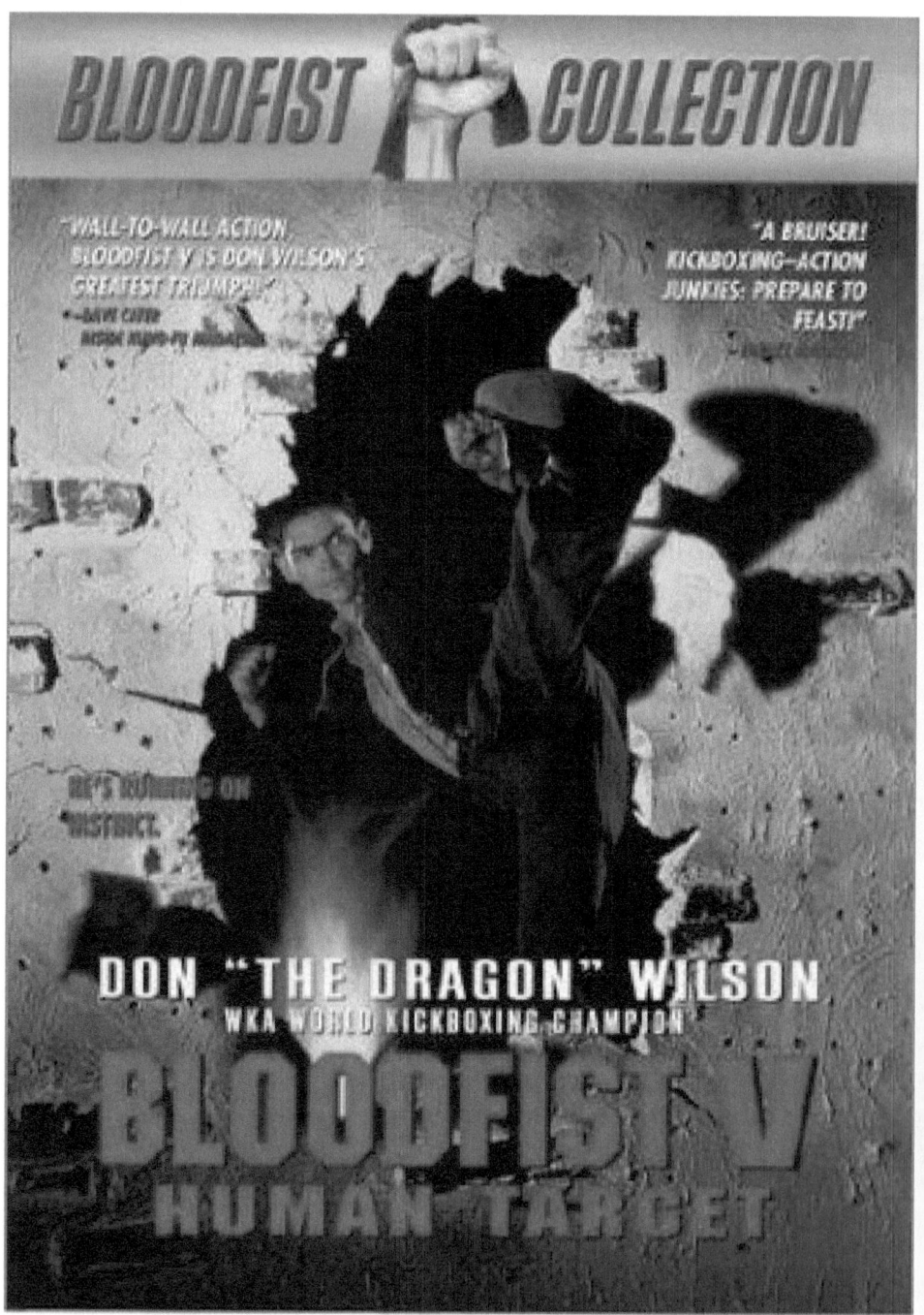

Bloodfist V: Human Target

Runtime 83 minutes
Directed by Jeff Yonis

Bloodfist V: Human Target once again stars Don "The Dragon" Wilson, this time playing Jim Stanton. He wakes up in a hospital bed with no memory of who he is, where he is, or how he got there. That's right: the Bloodfist series went full soap-opera and decided to do one with amnesia. When I was a kid, storylines involving amnesia were so common I figured it would probably happen to me one day. Every show seemed to have one episode on it. It seemed like amnesia was going to be a much bigger problem in my life than it has been. Stanton gets helped from a trashy woman who drives a pimp-mobile because it belongs to…her pimp. You see, she's a hooker and her pimp is no nice guy, and of course they have a fight... so Stanton steps in and helps her. From here on out the two try to piece together who he really is while some bad guys occasionally try to kill them. They find a suitcase full of money and realize he's supposed to buy some explosives, but they don't know why. It takes the entire film, up until the very end to finally piece together who Stanton is and what the heck he was doing before he was put in the hospital with a head wound.

I'm sorry to say that Bloodfist V: Human Target is a real slog to get through. It doesn't have enough action at all. I didn't want to see our hero make phone calls, drive around, talk to people, and not punch them. Sure, there are some action sequences but it's pretty clear that the budget was very meager here, even for a Bloodfist movie. The film trades high kicks for lots of dialogue, none of which I cared about. The mystery of Stanton didn't grab me at all. Who cares really? I only want to see him get into trouble and mess-up bad guys. I just watched the movie last night, as I'm writing this review, and I can't think of anything memorable from the film at all except at the beginning Stanton has a very long mullet, but it gets shaved in the hospital (it's a damn tragedy). Otherwise, this one is utterly forgettable. I suggest you skip it unless you are a Bloodfist or Don "The Dragon" Wilson completist.

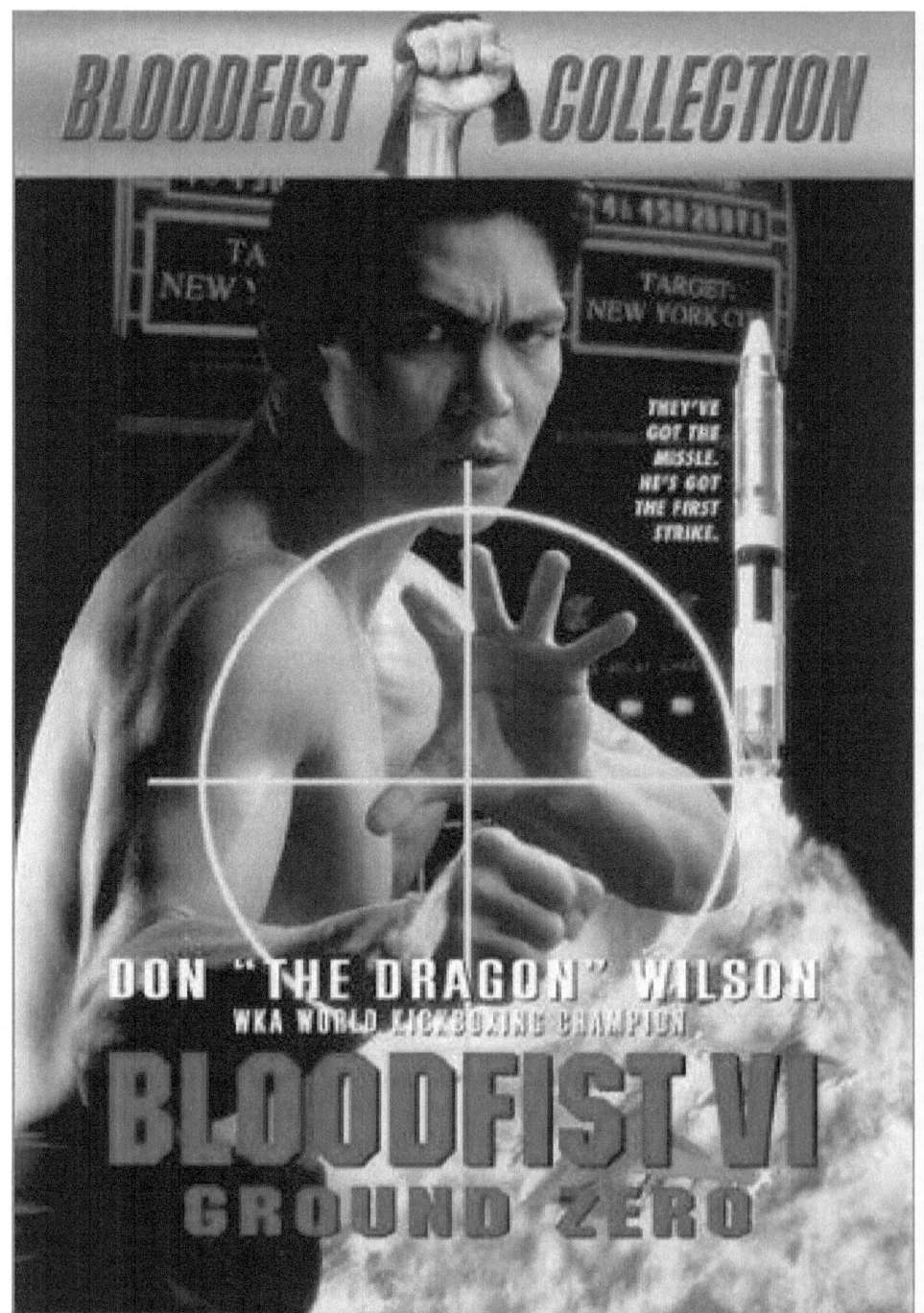

Bloodfist VI: Ground Zero (1995)

Runtime 85 minutes
Directed by Rick Jacobson

Bloodfist VI: Ground Zero finds Don "The Dragon" Wilson pulling duty as a military messenger. His job is to transport highly important messages and letters from military base to military base. He likes his job. He gets to drive a sweet Jeep with no top or doors, he doesn't have to answer to anyone and it's hard to screw it up. On the way to his destination, he stops to help a poor wounded bunny rabbit. He just walks over, scoops it up, and gives it some first aid. It's during this bunny rabbit rescue mission that his destination, a nuclear bunker, gets overtaken by terrorists. They kill nearly everyone except the only female officer in the bunker (Cat Sassoon, Bloodfist IV), but only because she's on their side! They have one key to launch a nuclear missile, but the other has been hidden. While they try to find it, up comes Wilson with his very important message. They let him into the base because they are afraid of being found out before they can locate the second key. Big mistake. Wilson isn't trapped in the bunker with them, they're trapped with HIM!
As always, Wilson is a total badass and knows how to take out the trash. Vastly outnumbered and stuck in a small location, he has to stop the terrorists before they blow up the world. Essentially this is Die Hard in a bunker. At some point Wilson takes off his shirt for no reason but John Mclaine did it in Die Hard so dammit, Wilson will too.

Bloodfist VI: Ground Zero is yet another Roger Corman cheapie that is lean, mean, and gets the job done, much like Wilson's Jeep in the film. The action is plentiful, but it's mostly shootouts as opposed to Wilson's usual martial arts excellence. The film once again promotes his kickboxing champion status and then puts a gun in his hand and has him mostly shoot everyone... which is a bit of a drag. The squibs are big and bloody, but I prefer my Wilson movies with hand-to-hand combat. Bloodfist VI: Ground Zero isn't nearly as dull as Bloodfist V but then again, most films aren't. It isn't as much fun as part IV but better than Part III. You can take that however you would like. It's a mediocre time waster. If you love Wilson, it's pretty good. If you don't, don't bother.

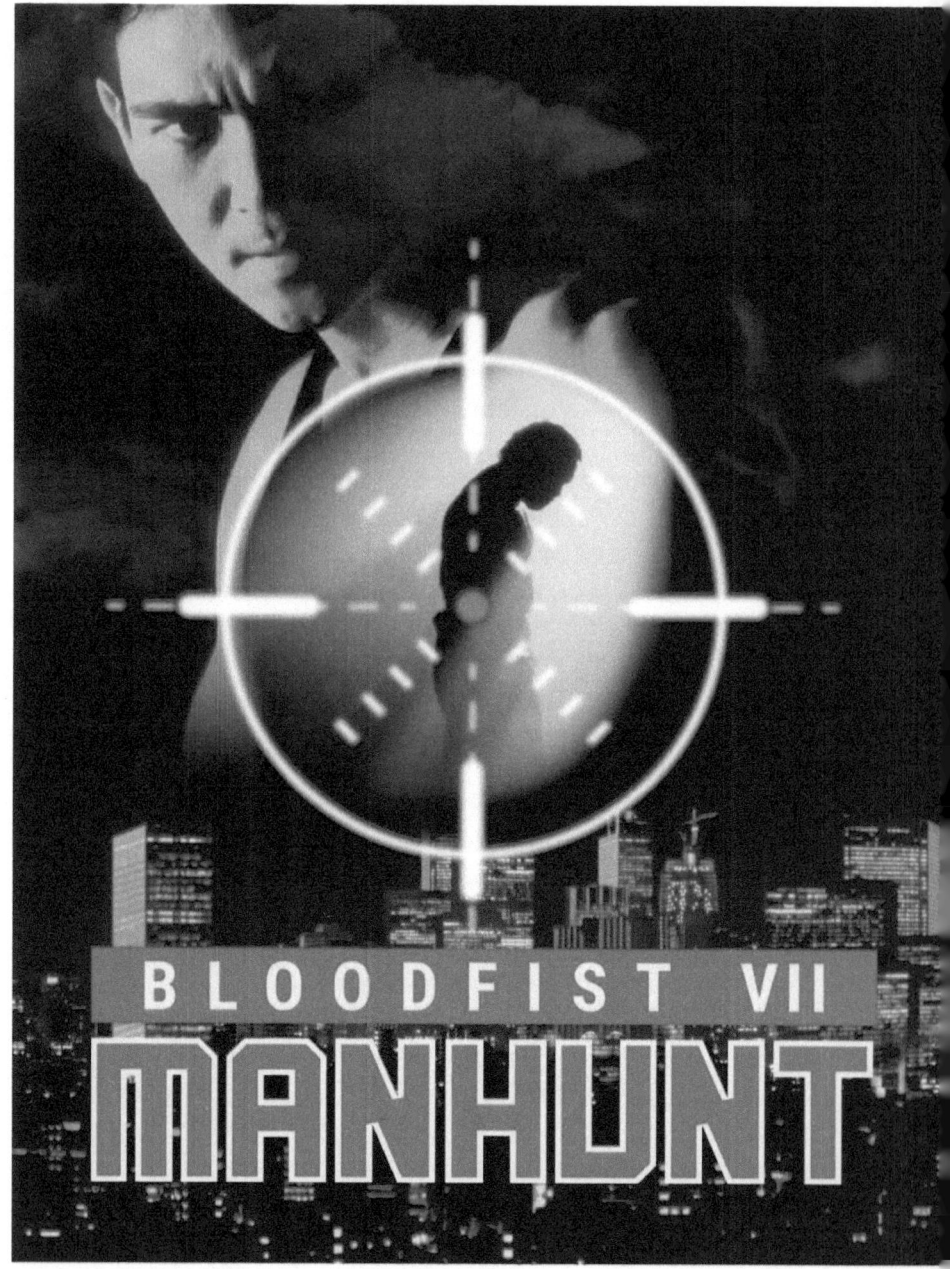

Bloodfist VII: Manhunt (1995)

Runtime 90 minutes
Directed by Jonathan Winfrey

The seventh installment of the unrelated Bloodfist series starring Don "The Dragon" Wilson finds Wilson as a bit of a drifter. He's driving a super sweet Cadillac, but he's troubled and broody. He stops at a bar to ask for directions, and wouldn't you know it, he gets involved in a bar brawl. He escapes with a yuppie woman who is also on the run. She's running from an abusive relationship and Wilson is heading to Mexico for reasons unknown. He awakes the next morning, and his Caddy is gone and so is the lady. She leaves him her keys to her sweet BMW though. He figures out where she lives and drives her beige yuppie-mobile to her house to confront her. The house has been ransacked by someone and a cop attacks Wilson. Big mistake. Wilson kills him but now he's on the run for being a cop killer (that escalated quickly!). Later he kills more cops and now he's really screwed. He has to find the lady, clear his name, and find out what the heck is going on.

Bloodfist VII: Manhunt isn't the best in the series as Wilson mostly shoots folks and doesn't get to use his sweet martial arts, which is kind disappointing. It isn't the worst in the series either though, as it has a fair amount of action injected in it. It also features Steven Williams (Jason Goes to Hell) who is always fun to watch on screen. The guy knows how to play intense and angry and gets many opportunities in the movie. If you really enjoy Don "The Dragon" Wilson's movies, this is a middle-tier effort. If you've never seen one of his movies or any of the Bloodfist flicks, don't start here. Wilson made a TON of films throughout the 90's and there are far better efforts like his Ring of Fire PM Entertainment movies. In the end, Bloodfist VII: Manhunt is a middling effort only worth seeking out if you want undemanding action or if you love Wilson. I can't blame you if you do, I know I do too.

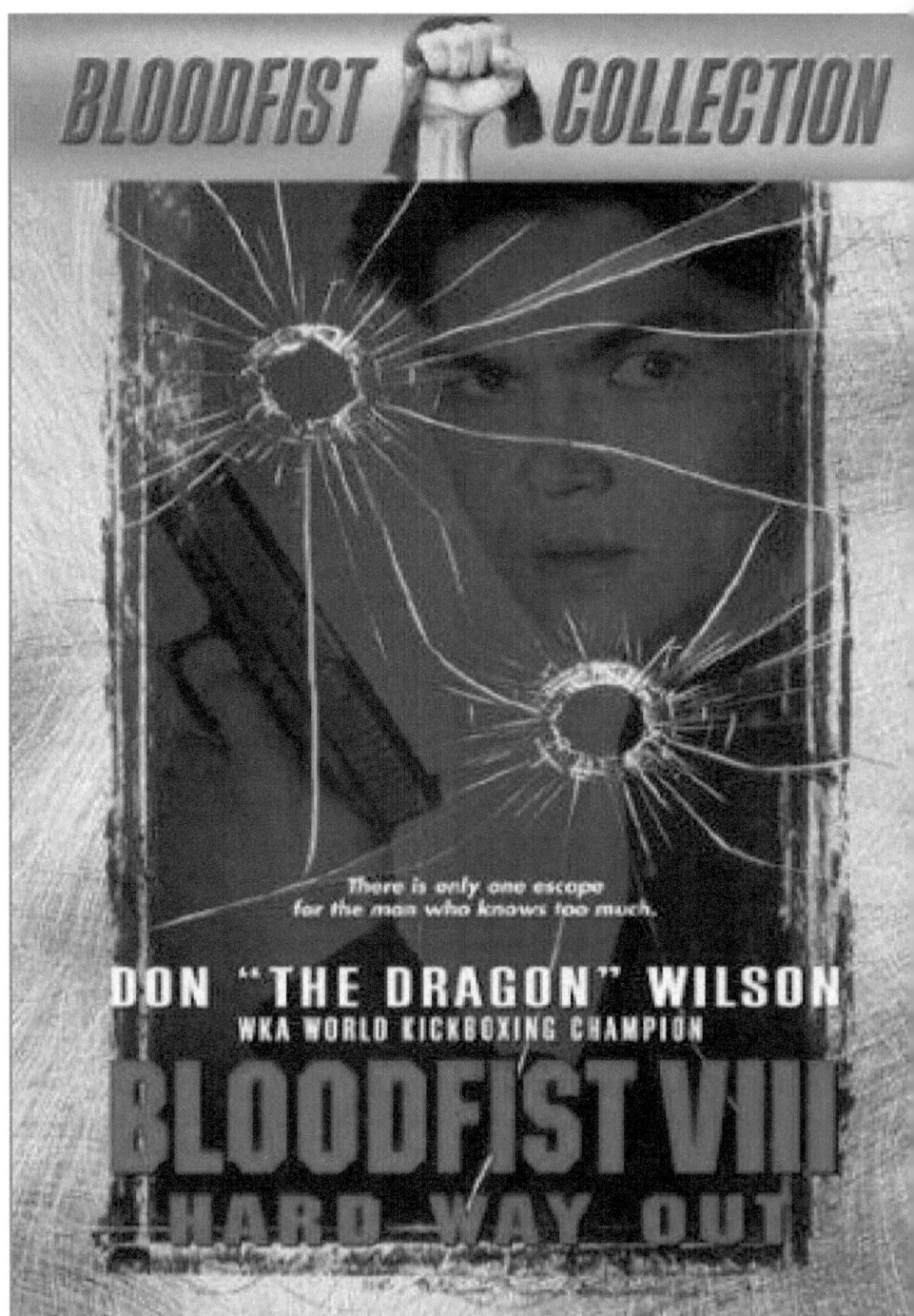

Bloodfist VIII: Trained to Kill (1996)
Runtime 84 minutes
Directed by Rick Jacobson

Bloodfist VIII: Trained to Kill begins with the assassination of a man in a liquor store staged to look like a robbery. We then meet Rick Cowen (Wilson), a high school math teacher. He's got a son that hates his guts because he was absent from most of his son's life. Cowen is a hunk (apparently), and the female teachers want a piece of his action. Later, Cowen and his son (who looks about 30) are arguing once again about how Cowen wasn't there and he's not a "real" dad. Suddenly the house is under attack and Cowen kills all of the attackers. Cowen's son is stupefied because he had no idea that Cowen was badass. You see, Cowen was once a CIA agent and now it seems that some of his enemies have found him and want revenge. Cowen's name isn't even Cowen, it's MacReady! He's actually Irish! Let that sink in a moment. Cowen/MacReady and his son travel to Ireland to get to the bottom of the plot against him and more action ensues on a cold beach and wet roads and on a ship.

Bloodfist VIII: Trained to Kill sees Don "the Dragon" Wilson looking more muscular than ever before, but he also has a truly heinous bowl cut hairdo that I found totally distracting throughout the whole film. Those of you that lived through the 90's knows what I'm talking about: parted in the middle, shaved in the back with the hair about the length of the ears on top. It's completely hideous. I should know, I had one! Thankfully the film has more of Wilson kicking and punching than shooting. The stunts are rather weak in this one, like a car crash on a beach that is so bland and unexciting it made me feel sad for the movie. The son character is pretty obnoxious early on, but thankfully his whiny "poor me" schtick takes a back seat after Act 1. The film is only 84 minutes but still manages to feel a bit padded out and also falls for the "wait there's more" trope that made many 90's action films feel overly long. Just when you think the movie is over, there's one last ditch attempt by a bad guy and it's almost always tiring and unwanted, such as is the case here.

Bloodfist VIII is a solid enough entry into Don's filmography. There's certainly worse Bloodfist movies in the franchise.

Bloodsport II

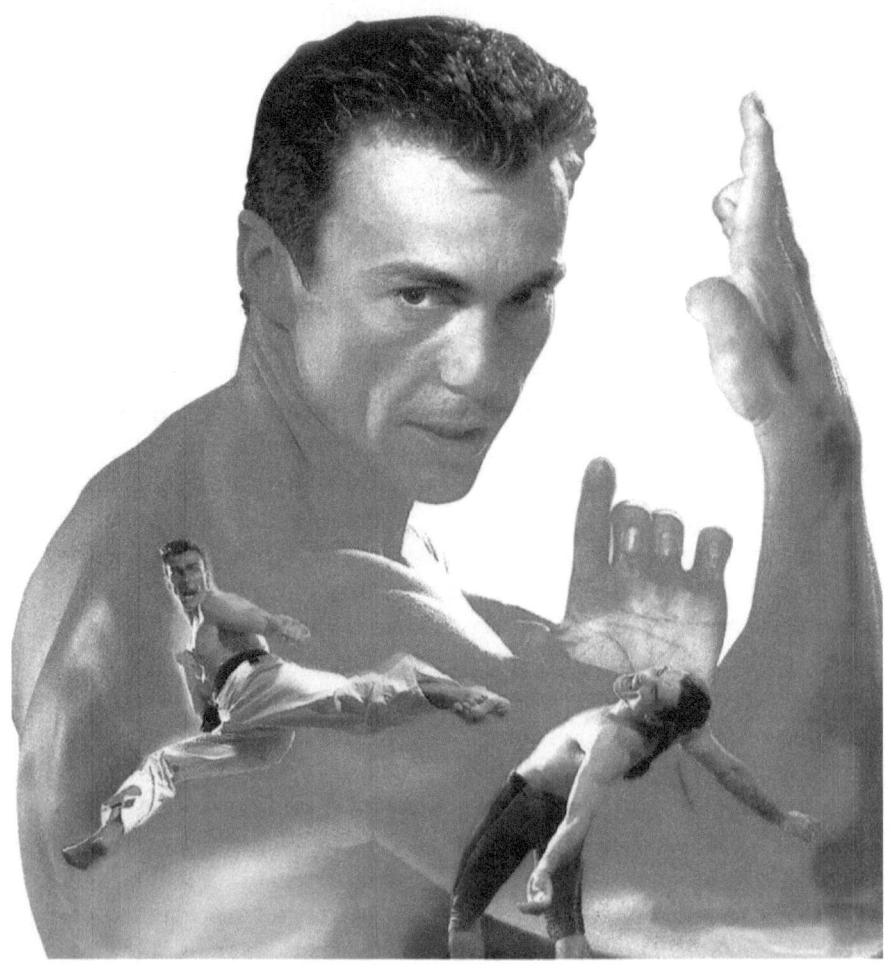

Bloodsport 2 (1996)
Runtime 80 minutes
Directed by Alan Mehrez

Bloodsport 2 seemingly has little to do with the original film except for one returning character, but I'll get to that in a bit. Swiss-born Daniel Bernhardt stars as Alex Cardo. He's tall, dark, handsome, and also a thief. He tries to steal an ancient samurai sword but gets caught and sent into a Philippine prison. He's the only westerner in the place and so of course everyone wants a piece of him. He's 6'2", so there's plenty of pieces to go around. After getting beaten by seemingly everyone in the prison, Sun (played by the always awesome James Hong), comes to his aid and scares everyone off. He's got the secret sauce when it comes to laying the smack down. He sees potential in Alex and agrees to train him using his sweet skills. One of the guards is a real pistol, nicknamed Demon, he's invincible. He's the champion at the underground Kumite. So essentially, he's the Chong Lee of this movie. Alex is also invited to fight at the kumite, and he accepts so he can mess up Demon's face. There he meets Ray Jackson (Donald Gibb, reprising his role from the first film). Jackson was JCVD's biker buddy in the first movie. Alex is also approached by Agent Leung (played by Pat Morita who must have seriously needed a paycheck) to try to get involved with an illegal sword dealing circuit. So, Alex has to help the agents bust the sword dealers and he has to bust Demon's head. All in 80 minutes.

Bloodsport 2, made nearly a decade after the first film, is a silly flick. It's really late in the game for a martial arts tournament flick. Remember, just 3 years later The Matrix would change the game completely when it came to action movies. The film has an even lower budget then the already modest first film and it shows, especially in the tournament. The fighters lack the individuality of the first movie but hell, this is just a cheap cash-in so who would expect more? On the other hand, the film does a good job of trimming the fat and delivering the goods. Bloodsport 2 won't win any awards for originality, but it's much better than I assumed it would be. The film doesn't overstay it's welcome, has plenty of action, and the lead is charismatic.

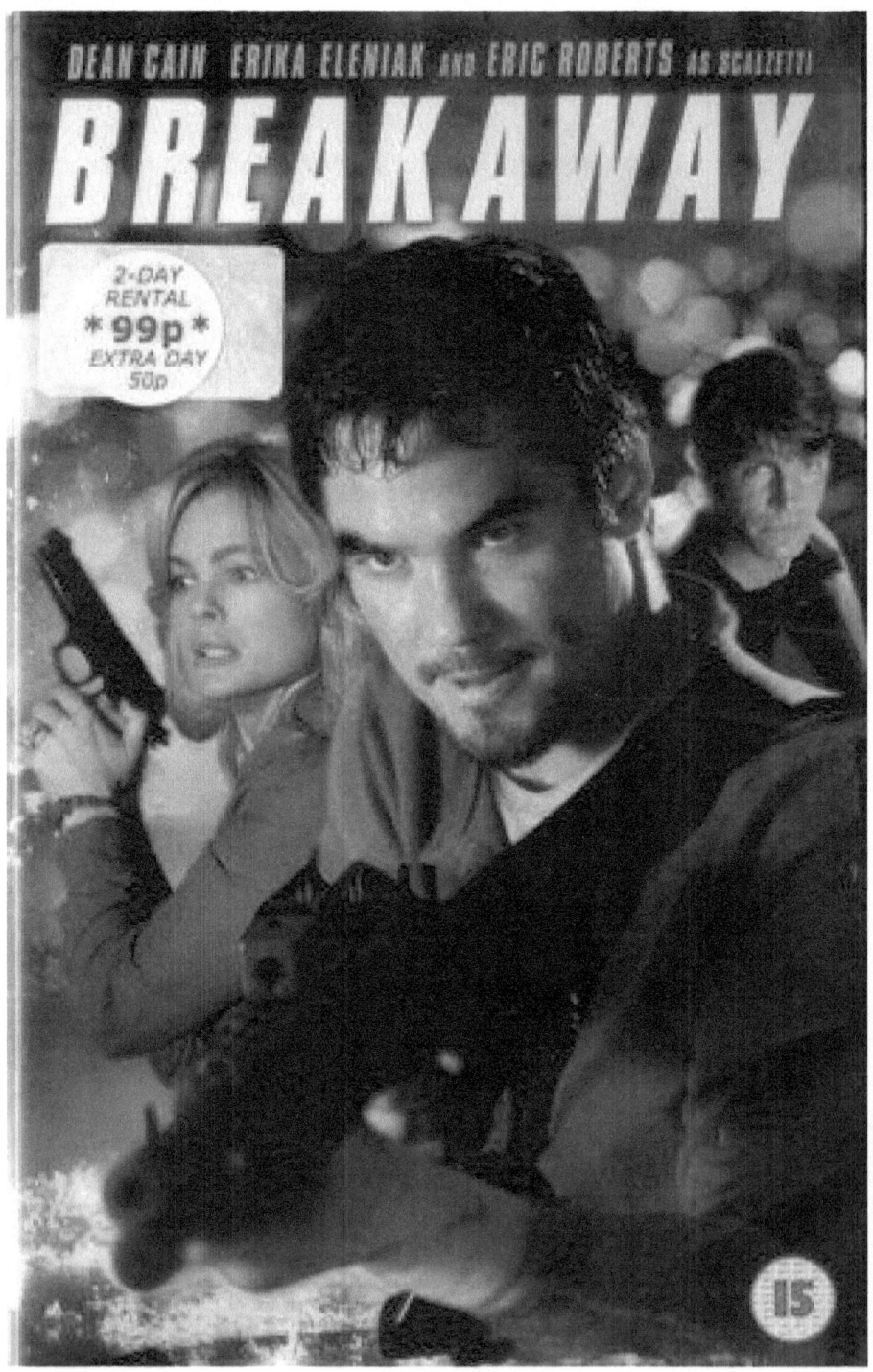

Breakaway (2002)
Runtime 90 minutes
Directed by Charles Robert Carner

Dean Cain stars as Cornelius Morgan, a tough cop who's a "loose cannon but he gets the job done". After a hostage situation that ended in a hail of police bullets, Morgan is suspended until a hearing on his actions that precipitated that shootout could be held. Frustrated, Morgan takes it out on his wife and later decides to apologize with a bouquet of roses. Morgan heads to the local shopping mall where his wife works to give her the roses and patch things up when he realizes that the mall is in the process of being robbed by an organized group of criminals led by Jimmy Scalzetti (Eric Roberts). Morgan's wife has been taken hostage while the crew works the job. The thieves quickly discover that Morgan is in the building and the rest of the film is spent with them trying to simultaneously kill Morgan and make off with the loot, while Morgan tries to stop them.

When watching Breakaway, I immediately got a vibe very similar to the best PM flicks: a simple story line with action around every corner and cartoony characters. The film starts with a bang and doesn't waste much time setting up the main thrust of the plot. After Morgan discovers the criminals, the film is non-stop shooting, punching, jumping, fighting, and chasing. Not only is Morgan a knock off John McClain, he's also crafty and devises some clever ways of taking out the bad dudes using what's available to him in the mall. So, Morgan has a bit of MacGyver's DNA too. Eric Roberts steals the show, as he often does. He's a born natural and plays Scalzetti as a villain, but a believable one. He even allows his audience room to sympathize with his character by the end of the movie. The film's high-stakes ending involves a giant tunnel and very tiny off-road go-carts, which never stops being funny.
While not as over-the-top as a PM Entertainment movie, Breakaway manages to encapsulate the fun vibe that make PM flicks so much fun to watch. Dean Cain is a good leading man, Eric Roberts a great bad guy, and the film is well paced with plenty of action to keep the pace moving rapidly. While not a "must see" flick, it is a whole lot of cheesy action fun well worth the runtime.

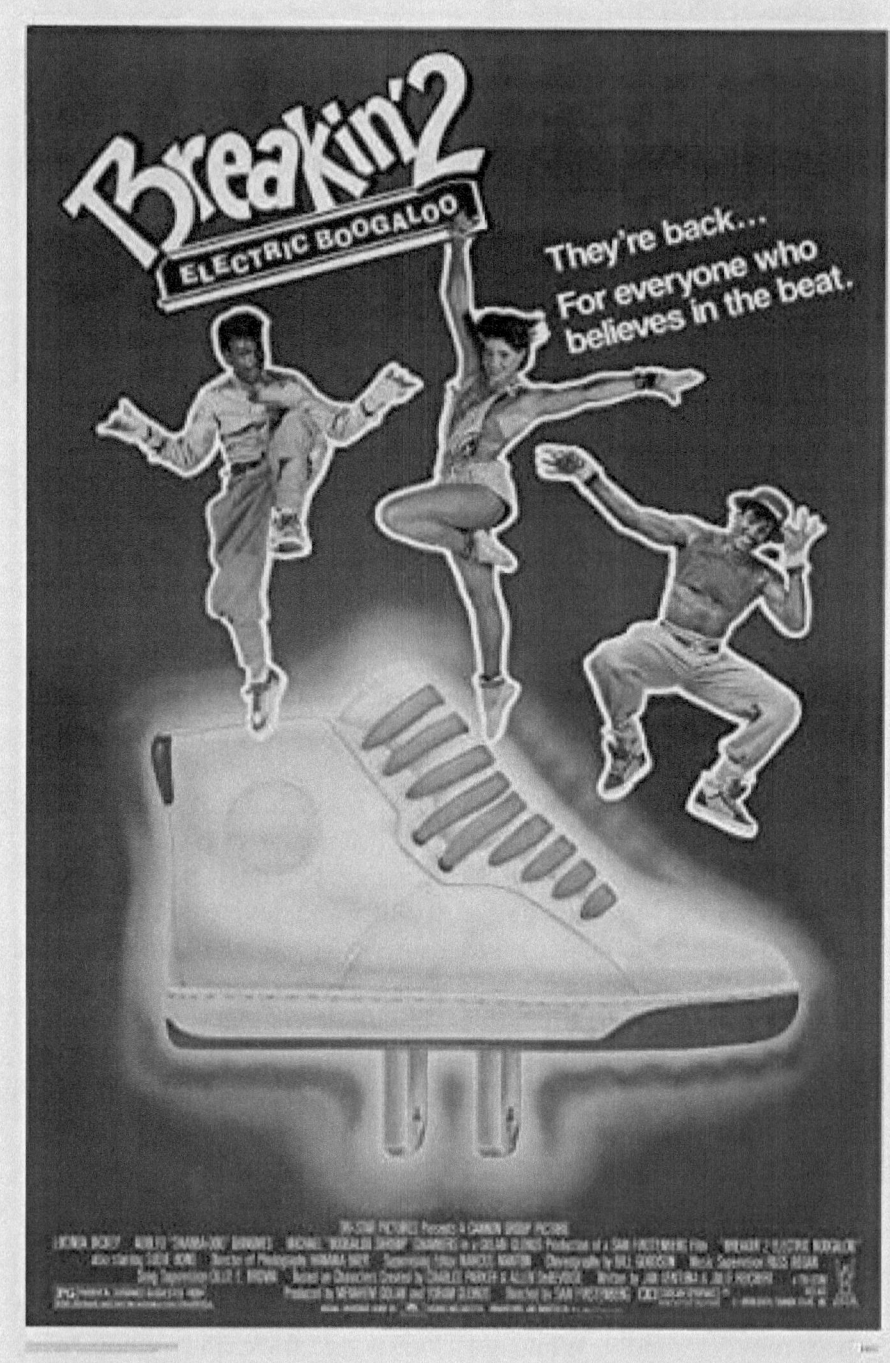

Breakin' 2: Electric Boogaloo (1984)
Runtime 94 minutes
Directed by Sam Firstenberg

Breakin' 2: Electric Boogaloo brings back all the principal actors from part one. They're all still poppin' and lockin' and enjoying life. Kelly, played by Lucinda Dickey, has made new strides in her dancing career and has been doing well with the highbrow dance world. Ozone, played by Shabba-Doo Quinones, and Turbo played by Boogaloo Shrimp Chambers, have set up a recreation center for poor youth in their neighborhood. There they dance and sing and have a great time. That is until they find out that the place is going to be torn down unless they can raise some serious cash to save it. Kelly ditches her life of fancy dancing to help Turbo and Ozone hatch a plan to save the rec center.

Breakin' was a huge hit for Cannon. So much so that production began on this film very quickly and the sequel was pumped into theaters less than a year after the first film came out. The prior movie was a bit grittier and "real", but this one is just a straight-up cartoon. All the colors are bright and loud. There's more dancing, and less plot. Turbo dances on the ceiling using the same room that Wes Craven utilized in A Nightmare on Elm Street. Ice-T returns to spit more rhymes and his outfits are even more ridiculous than before. The film also features a fantastic and hilarious dance number in a hospital that rivals the McDonalds dance number in Mac and Me. The plot of this flick is highly cliché, and the characters are living cartoons wearing fabulously 80's outfits. How could I not love this film? It's so fun, silly, and stupid. The movie has great pacing, with much of the melodrama from the first one dropped in favor of more dancing.

Breakin' 2: Electric Boogaloo lived up to the hype. It's colorful, ridiculous, and fun. This movie put a giant smile on my face. I wish they had made Breakin' 3: World War III where Turbo and Ozone have to break dance-fight zombies and toxic mutants while Lucinda Dickey tries to learn the finer points of killing while doing the robot. Ice-T could have reprised his role and entertained the human survivors while wearing pretty much what he wears in Breakin' 2.

Bruce's Deadly Fingers (1976)

Runtime 91 Minutes

Directed by Joseph Kong

Bruce Lee was such a huge phenomenon at the time of his death that fans didn't want to admit that he had died. There were rumours that his death was faked and that he had instead escaped the limelight, much like with Elvis (or Andy Kaufman). This opened the door for the concept of faux Bruce Lee movies starring actors that were able to emulate his style and look. Low-budget hucksters in Hong Kong capitalized on this fad by pumping out lots of these types of films in the hopes of deceiving a paying customer into thinking they were getting a new or "lost" Bruce Lee film. Heck, this method was even used to help launch Jackie Chan's career. Bruce's Deadly Fingers is one such film starring Bruce Le (note the missing "E" from the last name). Le made a career cranking out these types of movies but was talented in his own right. Bizarrely he can be seen in the horror film Pieces briefly after he nearly gets run over by a motorcycle.

The plot of Bruce's Deadly Fingers is simple. The film acknowledges the death of Bruce Lee but posits that he had left a book that detailed his Five Finger style. The style as the title suggests is deadly and all sorts of criminal kung fu ne'er-do-wells want it. Our hero is Bruce Wong, Bruce Lee's friend. Distraught over the death of his friend, Wong returns to Hong Kong only to find that some seriously bad dudes are trying to find the mysterious Five Finger Kung Fu book. They've also kidnapped Bruce's sister and forced her into prostitution! Wong has to stop the bad guys, find the book, and rescue the girl.

For fans of 70's kung fu, this movie is a treat! The film begins with a fight and then shoehorns fights into the plot every 5-7 minutes, making this movie about as action-packed as a plot will allow. The fights themselves vary in quality but the film overwhelms the viewer with the sheer volume of punches, kicks, and tosses. The visuals also explode with 70's fashion. We're talking bell bottoms, platform boots, and colorful button-down shirts with wild prints, and these are all worn by the male characters. This film was made at the height of what we consider 70's style so the fashions and room decorations are entertaining all on their own. Bruce Le does a good job of carrying the film. He's charismatic and energetic in his fights. It's obvious he's giving his all and for my money, it's a lot. Aside from a rather disturbing scene involving torture by snake, the film isn't particularly memorable but it sure is fun.

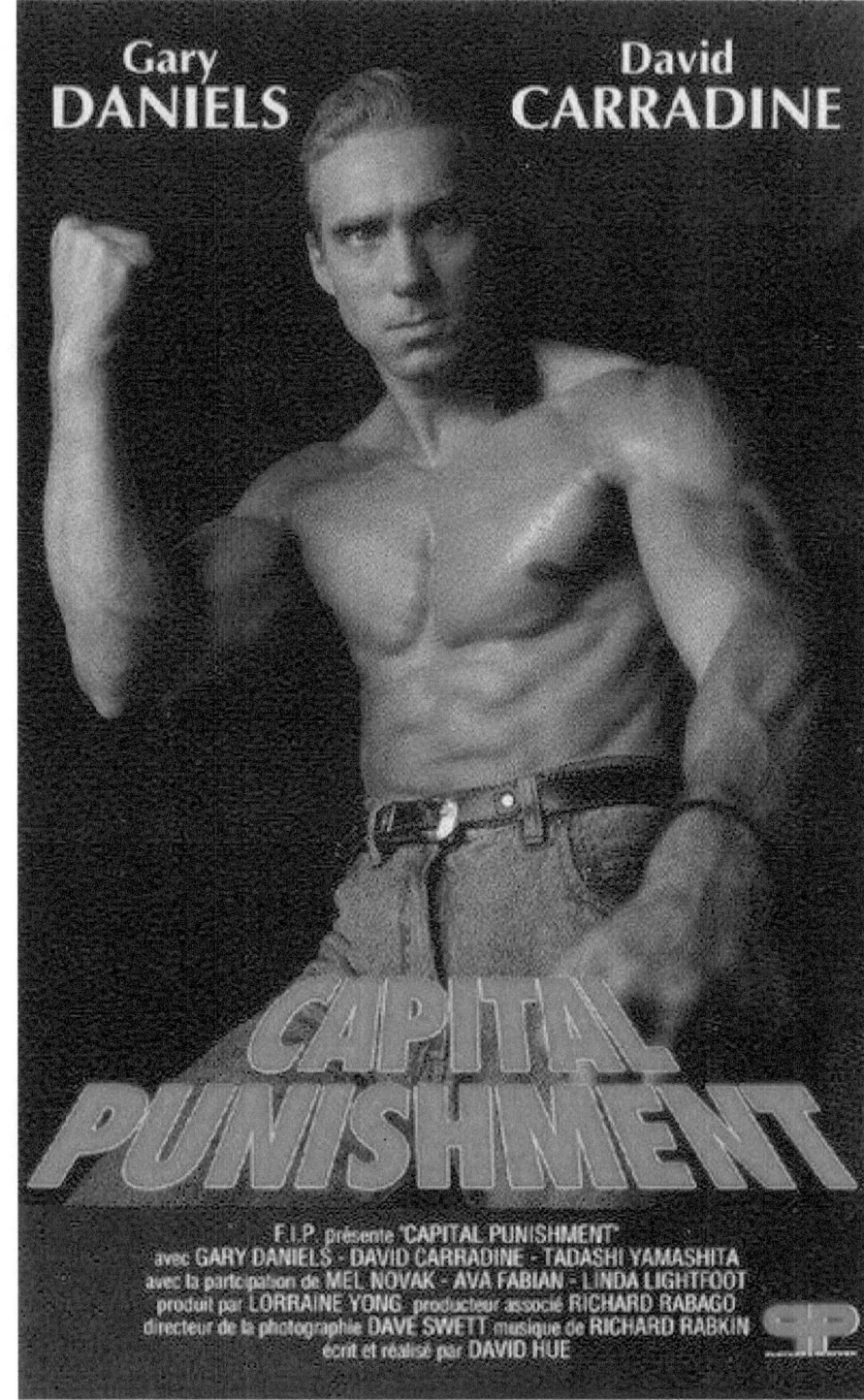

Capital Punishment (1991)
Runtime 86 minutes
Directed by David Huey

Gary Daniels stars as James Thayer, a kickboxing champion whose sensei Nakata (Tadashi Yamashita, American Ninja) has turned down a dark path. Nakata has developed and distributed a new drug called Kick. It gets you high as hell... but it causes significant birth defects in 9 out of every 10 women. The DEA wants to shut Nakata down, so they hire Daniels to pretend to beat a kickboxer (close to Nakata) to death in the ring so that the kickboxer can be put into protective care and provide testimony against Nakata. The trouble is, the DEA set Thayer up! He really does kill the kickboxer and now he's on the run from the law and trying to clear his name.
I really enjoyed the other Daniels/Huey vehicle, Full Impact, and this film did not disappoint. Capital Punishment lived up to my own hype. The film is very hard to follow with unlikely (and often unintelligible) plot twists around every corner, but that only adds to the fun. It doesn't help that the audio is bad in the film and yet the audio issues only endeared the movie to me more. David Carradine shows up in the film in a sit-down role for the ages. He smokes, talks on the phone, and reads his lines taped to a computer screen. Fight scenes erupt in the film every ten minutes or so, keeping the action high, and the sense low. At one point in the movie, he's riding a motorcycle, chasing a goon in a car... when inexplicably the goon's car explodes. It's hilarious. That isn't the only over-the-top and nonsensical explosion in the film either. One malicious character is crushed by a waist-high slab of ice knocked over by Thayer that somehow manages to crush his chest. Did the ice jump? Mel Novak plays one of the DEA agents and it's clear he's never held a gun, a badge, or been in a fight, but does all three in this film as best as he can... which to be frank, is terribly. The music is often obtrusive, utilizing multi-layered and confused synths, and what could be the most bored sounding guitar work in the history of bad movies.

Capital Punishment is a winner. The short runtime, high action content, low-budget, and nearly indecipherable plot make it a blast to watch with friends. I highly recommend it to fans of bargain basement action trash.

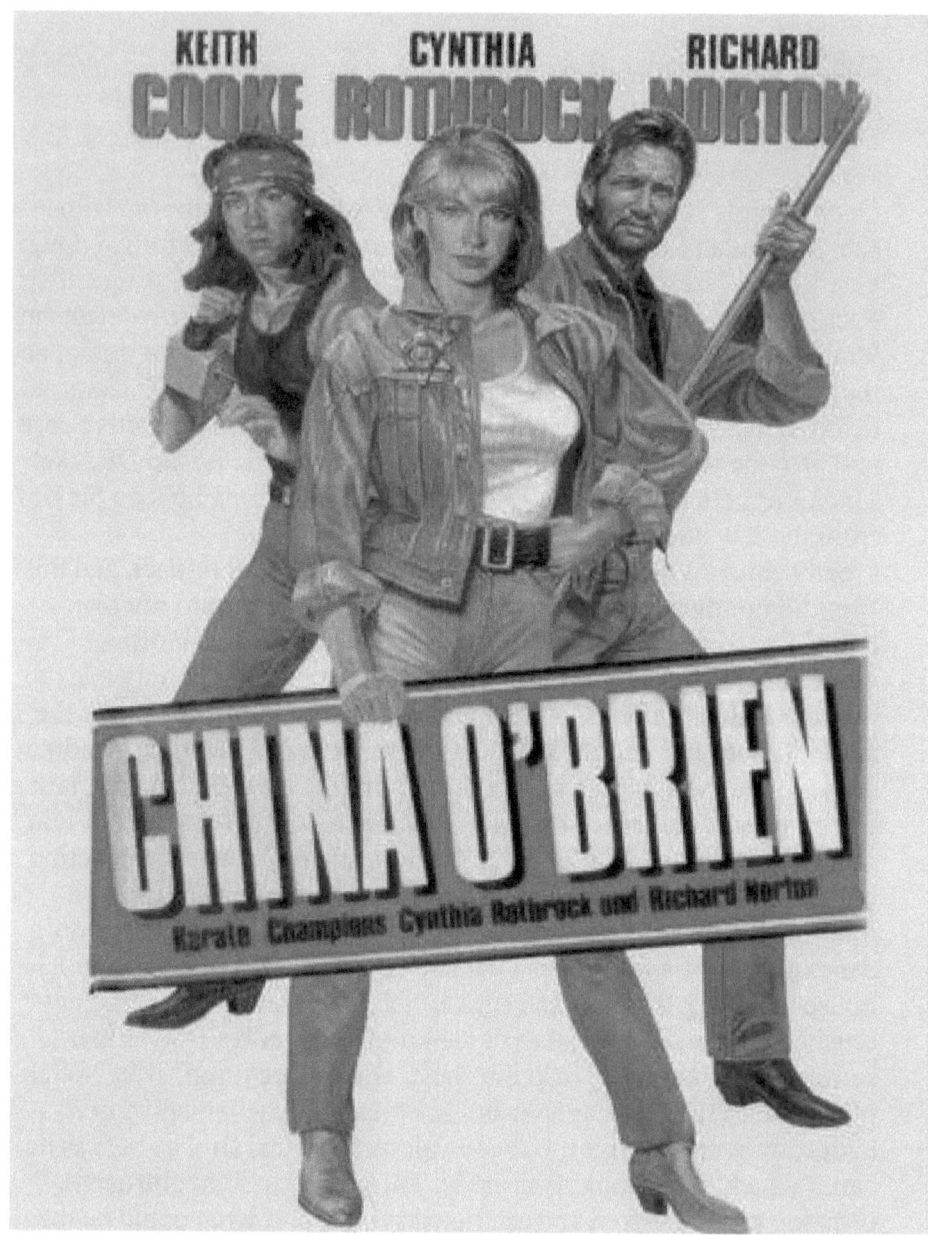

China O'Brien (1990)
Runtime 84 minutes
Directed by Robert Clouse

China O'Brien (Rothrock) is an inner-city police officer/martial arts instructor. She's challenged to an exhibition by a dude who doesn't believe she's legit. He sets up a meeting in a dark alley after her classes are over and she accepts. Wearing salmon parachute pants, a purple blouse, and a turquoise/pink neckerchief, she's ready to kick some ass *in style*. China stops with the teaching and kicks some ass in *earnest*. A shadowy figure steps behind the challenger armed with a pistol and China kills the assassin. China gives up her badge and heads home to the country to figure out what to do next. Her daddy is the sheriff, and she discovers that the whole town was bought and sold by dirty businessman. After her daddy's car is blown up, she decides to run for sheriff and get rid of the scum that has infested her small town. Along with the help of local stud Matt (Richard Norton), and mysterious young rebel Dakota (Keith Cooke), she's ready to scorpion kick the crap out of the bad dudes. I had quite a bit of fun with this one. China can't go anywhere without some surly dudes trying to fight her and she's always game for a tussle. She wears a lot of denim which is always a plus for me. Richard Norton rocks not only denim pants but a denim shirt, thus making him double denim (the legendary Canadian Tuxedo). He starred in several films alongside Rothrock, making them the direct-to-video action power couple of the 90's. Norton is Australian, and it's never explained why he has an Aussie accent, since they play it like he and Rothrock grew up together in the town. Rothrock's mom doesn't seem to care much about her husband being blown to smithereens, she's too busy being a cheerleader for her daughter. It's weird and funny and sad all at the same time. Dakota wears a weird box on his wrist along with a black glove. It gives his hand the appearance of a comically large microphone. Apparently, his character had his hand stomped and now he has to wear the glove and box.... because...reasons. Everyone in town disbelieves' China's skills as a fighter and they all live to regret it.

It isn't as much fun as Undefeatable but there's something nice about watching a tightly made film.

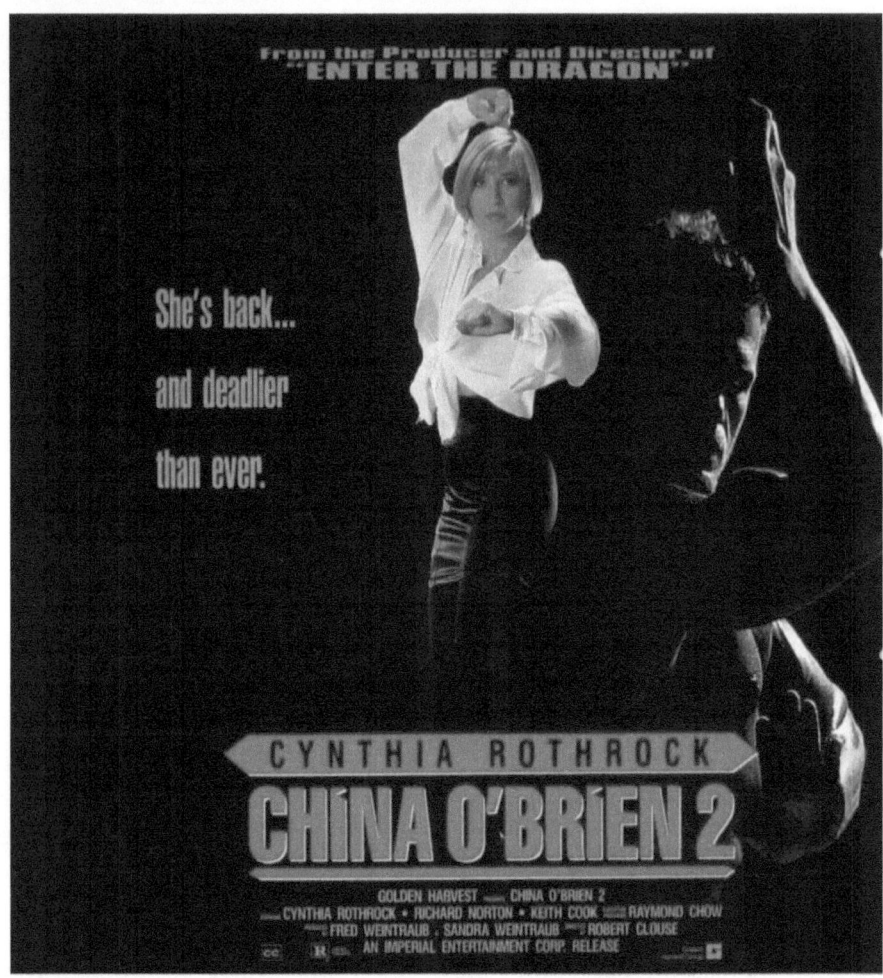

China O'Brien 2 (1991)
Runtime 90 minutes
Directed by Robert Clouse

China O'Brien 2 begins with a series of assassinations of people we know nothing about. We then watch a prison break by a skinny dude with a big mustache named Baskin. After that we reconnect with China. She's still Sheriff and everyone loves her. She's responding to a report at a bar where a wild mountain man came and drunkenly tore up the bar. She then goes to his mountain abode and whips his ass while Matt (Richard Norton), clothed in 100% pure denim, sits on China's squad car and laughs (what a boss). Assault and Battery is funny right? The town is enjoying Fourth of July festivities later and while the whole town watches the fireworks, a gang of bad guys (in worse suits) kidnap a family at gunpoint. China nearly misses the whole thing because what businessman would brandish a pistol? Surely that wasn't a gun in his well-manicured hand, right? Turns out they're Baskin's goons. The family was in the witness protection program, and he's got a bone to pick with them on account of their testimony putting him in prison. After China stops the kidnapping, the family contacts the FBI who just shrug at the near kidnapping. It's up to China, Matt, and Dakota (Keith Cooke, Heatseeker) to find out where Baskin is hiding and take him down to justice. Much like the first film, there is plenty of action in this installment. Rothrock gets to use her signature scorpion kick and Dakota still has his weird box/glove combo on his hand. Norton is as swarthy as always. Baskin looks like a dude who would always have a really thin joint behind his ear and talk a lot about getting laid while being eternally high/drunk. He does not look like a crime boss. He sports one gold hoop earring and likes to wear a bejeweled straw hat. Despite all this the actor acquits himself well as a scumbag. China wears a denim jacket with her badge pinned to it. My guess? They didn't have the budget/time to get her a real uniform.

This sequel takes a while to get started, but once it does its wall-to-wall fights, especially in the last 20 minutes or so. Billy Blanks shows up as a goon wearing zebra pants. China O'Brien 2 would certainly be fun to watch with a bunch of friends.

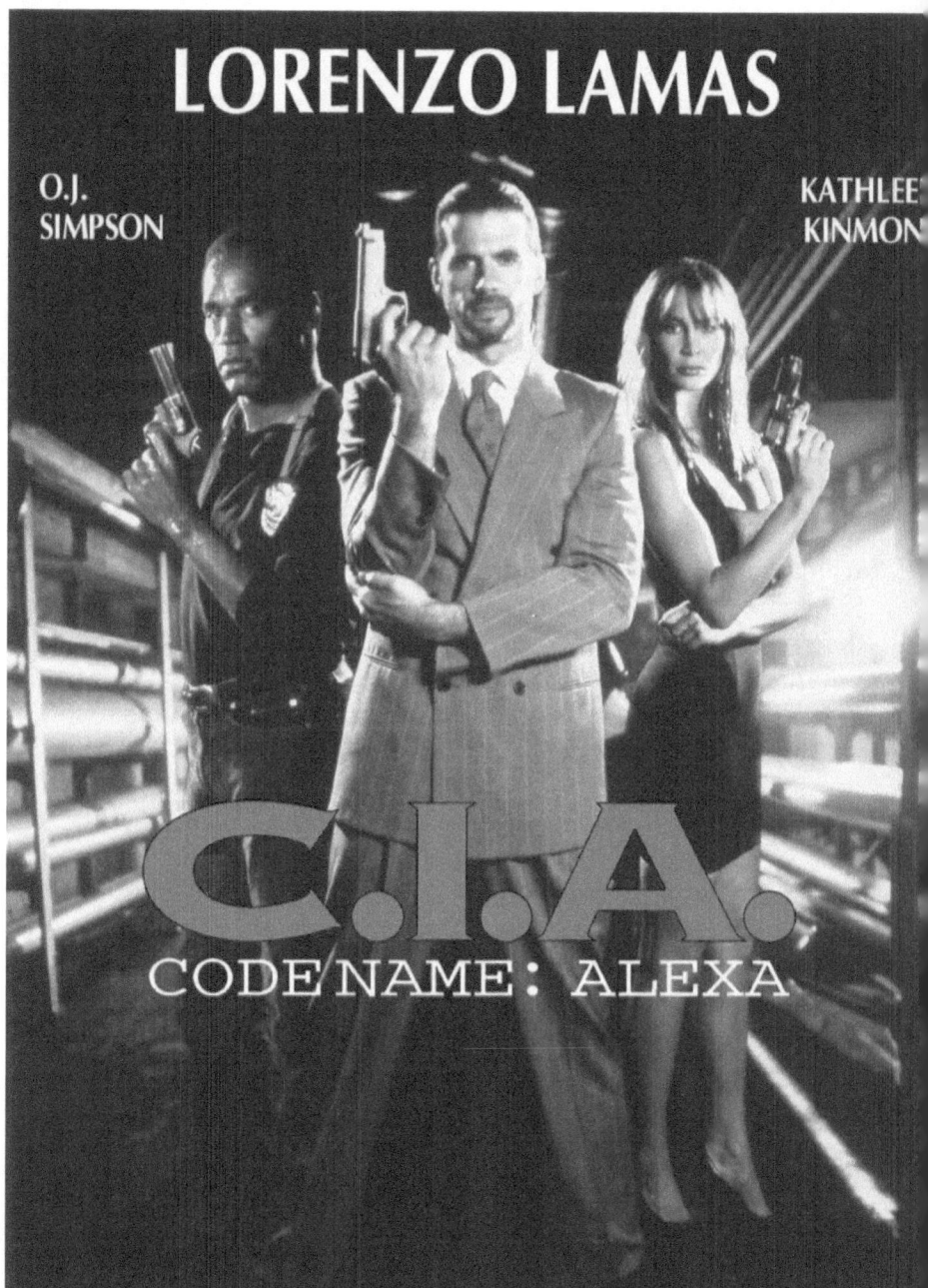

CIA Code Name: Alexa (1992)
Runtime 90 minutes
Directed by Joseph Merhi

CIA Code Name: Alexa is a PM Entertainment film that is considered one of the better films the studio produced during its existence. It stars Lorenzo Lamas which is an extra bonus in my book. Plus, it also stars O.J. Simpson, which is just plain weird.

The film begins with terrorists who have taken hostages inside a building. The police are under fire while special agent Mark Graver (Lorenzo Lamas) shows up to fix the problem. He's a loose cannon but he gets the job done. He steals a police motorcycle, drives it into the building and shoots up the place. Not before one of the terrorists swallows a very important microchip. This microchip is the reason for their assault on the building to begin with. One of the terrorists kills the partner of Detective Nick Murphy (O.J. Simpson) and gets captured. Turns out she's the titular Alexa. Then she's secreted away to a clandestine high tech federal building where Graver tries to get her to talk. Detective Murphy shows up looking for answers but is instead detained. Meanwhile the head of the terrorists wants his microchip and schedules an assault on the slain man's funeral. The chip is recovered by the good guys, but of course the bad guys get Alexa's daughter. Now Graver and Alexa have to fight the bad guys, get the daughter and save the world. All in a day's work for Special Agent Graver and his new buddy Detective Murphy.

CIA Code Name: Alexa is a lot of fun. PM Entertainment stipulated that their action films had to have action every 7-10 minutes and this film manages just that. The writer brilliantly shoehorns in conflicts and fights throughout the film, so the movie never drags. Lamas' performance is odd in that he perpetually whispers throughout the entire film, making his dialogue hard to hear. While the film may not feature the extreme over-the-top destruction, we expect from a PM film it does deliver plenty of action to satisfy viewers. I had a ball watching it and I agree: it is one of the better films PM Entertainment released.

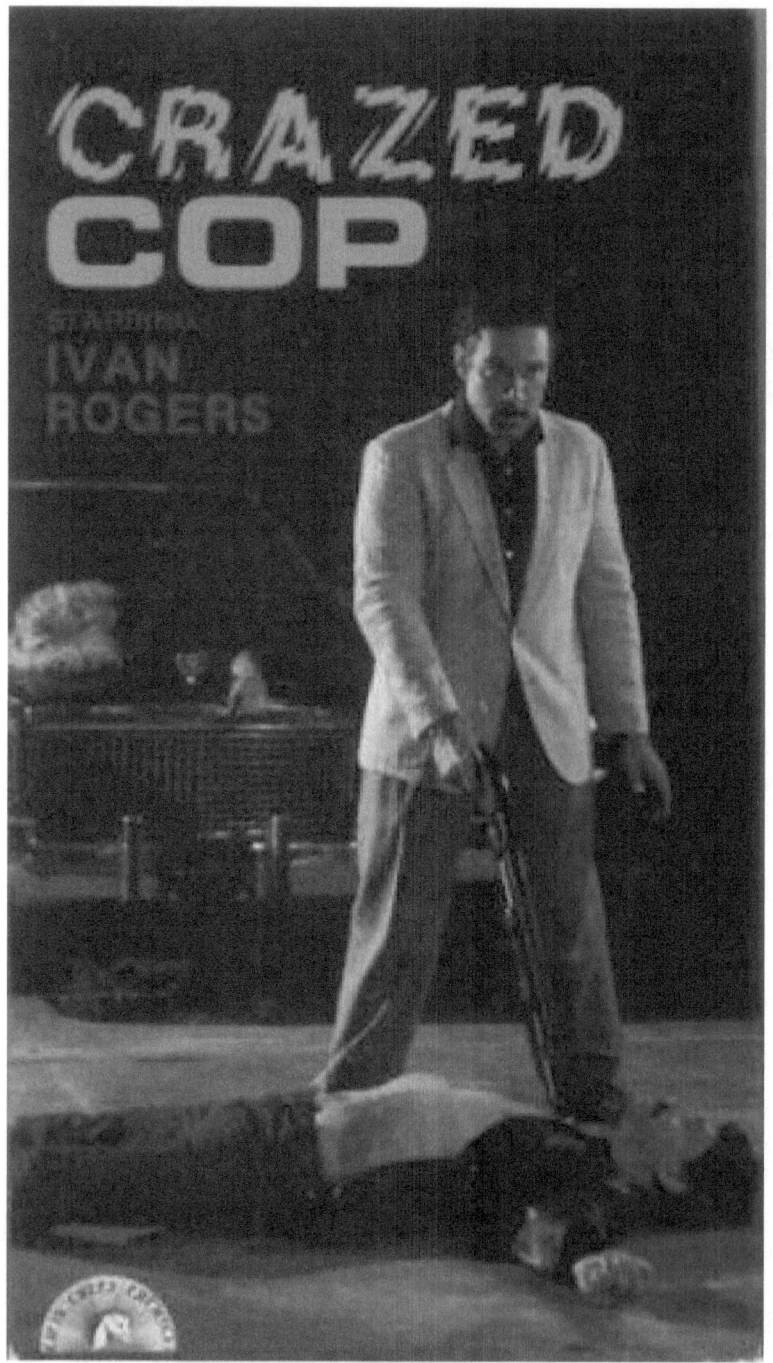

Crazed Cop (1986)
Runtime 81 minutes
Directed by Paul Kyriazi

Directed by Paul Kyriazi, who also directed the awful awesome film Omega Cop, I'm glad I stumbled upon this one while doing "research".
Ivan Rogers stars as Joe Weeks, a suicidal police detective whose sanity is hanging by a thread. He's a loose cannon and he plays by his own rules, which usually results in the death of bad dudes. In order to rein him in he's given a new partner, female detective Waite. Together they're tasked with busting Frank Hanna, a local drug kingpin. Weeks' wife was brutally murdered by one of Hanna's men when Weeks got too close, and so now it's personal (SUPER personal). The duo may have also stumbled upon corruption that goes up to the highest levels, so they'll have to not only dodge bullets from the bad guys but from the boys in blue too!

Crazed Cop is fun in a very low-budget and grimy kind of way. The film begins with Weeks' playing Russian Roulette at the beginning of the day, a routine he goes through repeatedly throughout the film. We're given no context but through this scene we learn that A) Weeks is a man on the edge and B) this film has no subtlety. Ivan Rogers tries to play Weeks as a stoic man who has seen too much and has no emotion left, instead he's pretty stone-faced and almost entirely lacking in charisma. Everyone else wades through the heavily expository dialogue as best as they can with often funny results. We get some shootouts (including one where Weeks hides in a sewer and pops out like a ninja turtle), an explosion, and a climactic car stunt involving an actor on the roof while the car is moving (though I suspect that this was filmed with a projection screen rather than filmed live). We get a decent bar fight that goes from a dust-up to a murder really quickly and some intimidation with a chainsaw (ala Scarface). The music is memorable and repetitive with just a few chords played on a cheap keyboard, and yet I kind of liked it. I could see myself listening to it while working in fact. Crazed Cop is short, has a decent amount of action, bad line reading, funky music, and a very low budget. if you like cheapjack cop films, especially if you enjoyed Omega Cop (Sci-Fi Vol. 1), this one is worth checking out.

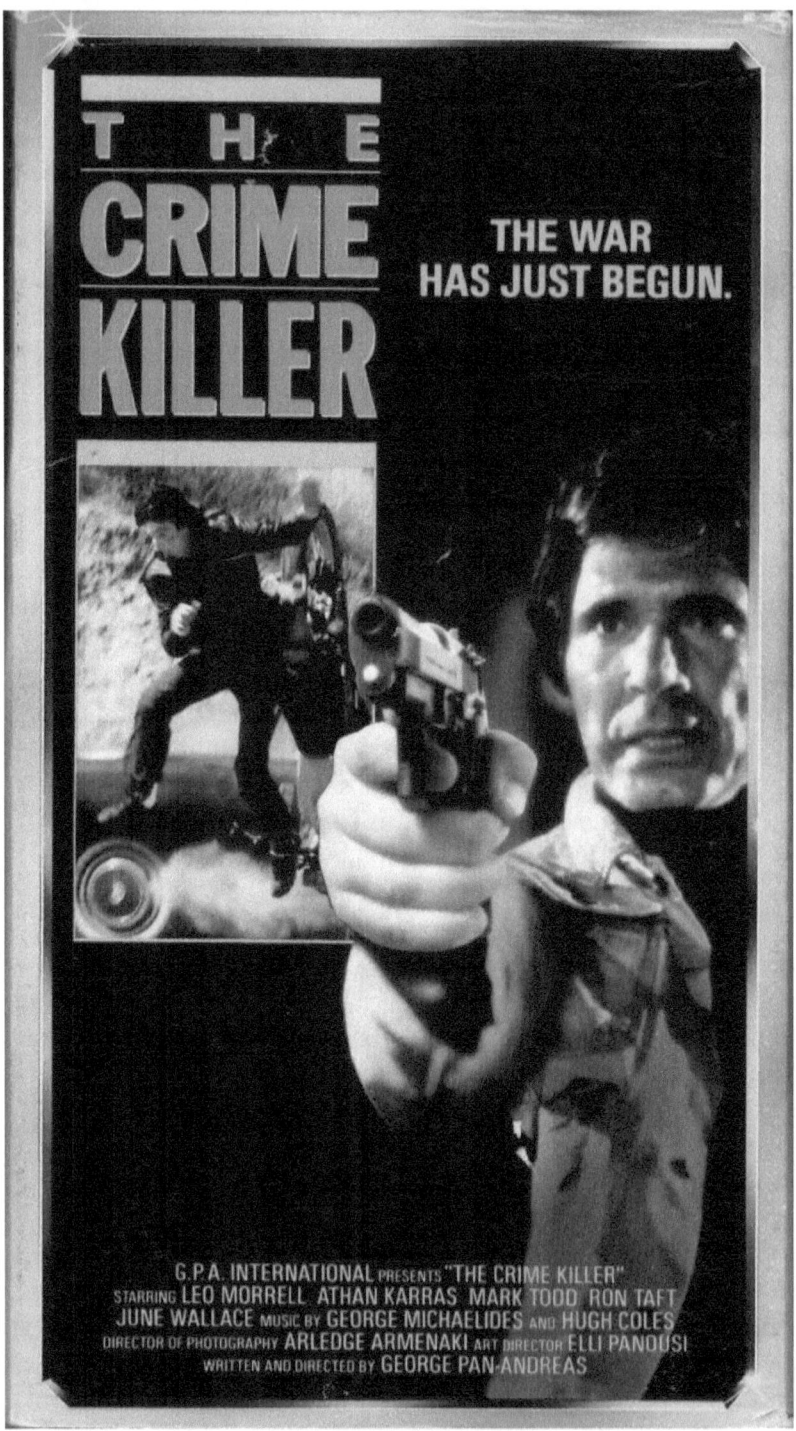

The Crime Killer (1985)
Runtime 90 Minutes
Directed by George Pan-Andreas

The Crime Killer is about Zeus (but not THAT Greek guy). He's a cop and a loose cannon but he gets the job done. The film begins with a shootout where his partner is killed and Zeus gets away, but he is also wounded. Two other cops find him and realize they could make some serious cash if they killed Zeus, because he's got a price on his head from the local crime syndicate. Realizing the danger, Zeus kills both cops (good luck with Internal Affairs on that one...). He's kicked off the force and now Zeus is nothing but a vicious dog that's been let off its chain. At some point the FBI decides to hire him as a covert agent to help them destroy the crime syndicate and Zeus eagerly agrees. He's willing to do anything to take out the criminals and clean up his town, even if it means dressing up as a gardener and pretending to be a Mexican... which he does in this movie. For real.

The Crime Killer is a vanity project for director/star George Pan-Andreas, who I believe IS Greek. This is important because he has a heavy accent and some of the dialogue gets jumbled up a bit and makes little sense when he says it. It also adds a bizarre layer to his performance as a Mexican gardener. He's a Greek guy with a heavy accent, pretending to be a Mexican guy with a heavy accent. It's strange for sure. Clearly, he wanted to make a movie that showed off how badass he is, and these are the films that I love. Movies that exist solely to stroke the ego of the (usually) director/star of the film. They often have no filter as well as being so outlandishly over-the-top that they become hilarious as well as a little bit sad. The Crime Killer has plenty of action, including a particularly nasty run in with a dirt bike and a goon's face. It's clear however that George can't really fight. He's pitted against stunt men who can fight, and he looks hopelessly sloppy. It's obvious he wouldn't actually win these fights, and this only adds to the vanity flavor of the movie. That being said, it didn't go over as well with my friends and I as I thought it would. I was expecting another Miami Connection, and unfortunately The Crime Killer is far from those lofty heights.

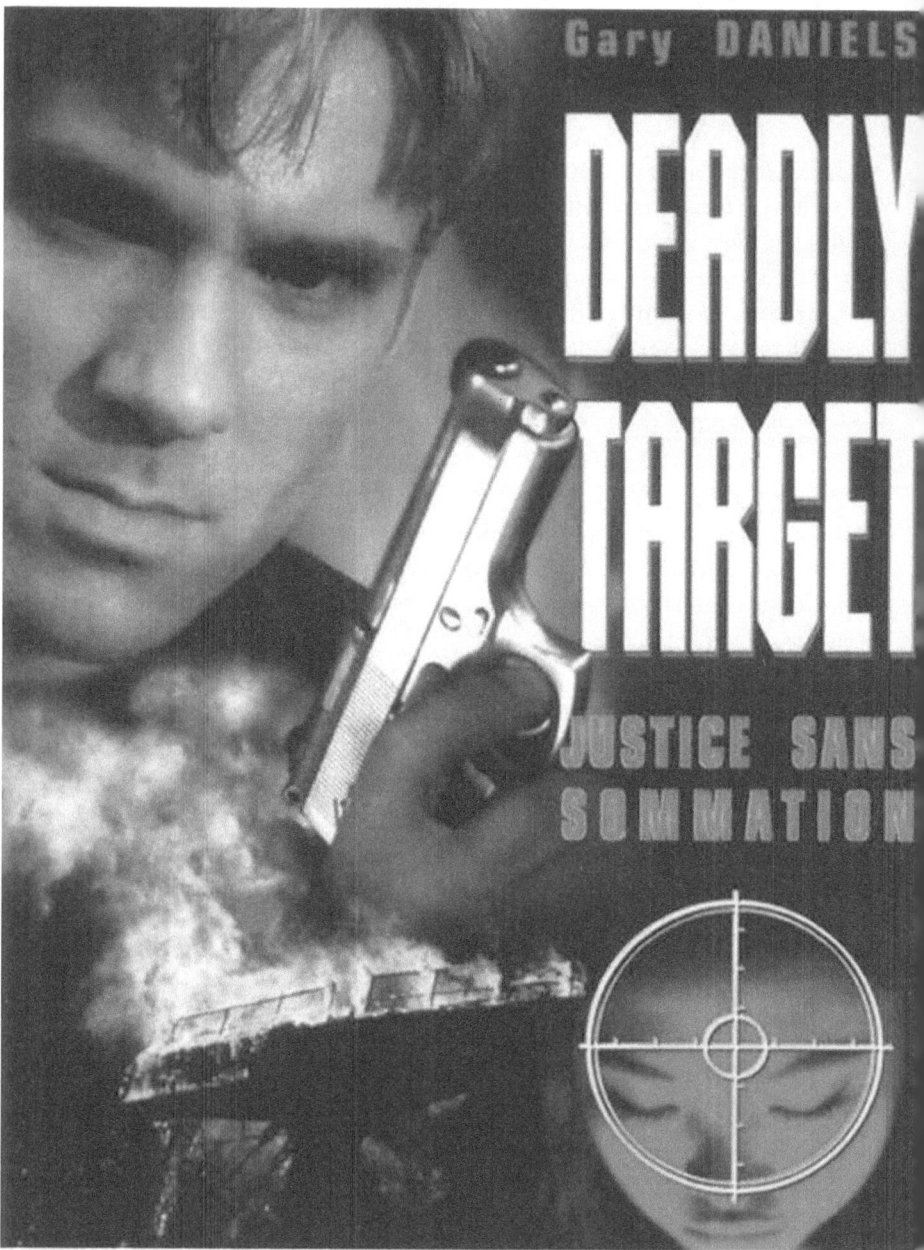

Deadly Target (1994)
Runtime 100 minutes
Directed by Charla Driver

If there's one thing, you'll learn from reading this book it's that PM Entertainment films are a great place to find awesome over-the-top silly action. Deadly Target is about Charles Prince (Gary Daniels), a Hong Kong detective tracking down Chang, a mobster responsible for a whole lotta crime and a whole lotta death in Hong Kong. He's followed Chang to the United States where he hopes to finally bring him into sweet justice. See Chang is trying to break into the American Triad world by selling his filthy drugs, something that the Triad don't want to do. Chang doesn't care however, he's got the horse, he's got the manpower, and he's got the homicidal rage to complete the package. The American cops want to bring down the Triad and stop Chang from selling his junk, so they allow Detective Prince to assist, what they didn't bargain for was Prince's wild ways. Furious about his blatant disregard for protocol he becomes persona non grata with the boys in blue, except one detective who wants to stop Chang at any cost. The two team up and "cowboy" it up with lots of kicking, shooting, and general outrageousness.

Deadly Target is a fun flick. Gary Daniels has some very broad shoulders. In fact, my wife and I assumed he was wearing big shoulder pads in his biker jacket he frequently wears in the movie. He wasn't. he really does have very big shoulders (I'm talking MASSIVE). He hooks up with what could be the most generous and pleasant card dealer ever in the history of cinema. She drags his enormous weight back to her place after he's beaten up by a triad and lets him stay in her house throughout the rest of the movie. Then again, Daniels is a hunk so I can't blame her really. The film features many of the favorite PM Entertainment hallmarks: a helicopter explodes, someone is thrown out of a window in a high-rise building, cars explode, and there is a lot of shooting and fighting. The plot revolves around fitting in lots of violence and I approve. It is perhaps about ten minutes too long and suffers from some slumps in the beginning third of the movie, but overall it delivers on what I expect from a PM Entertainment flick.

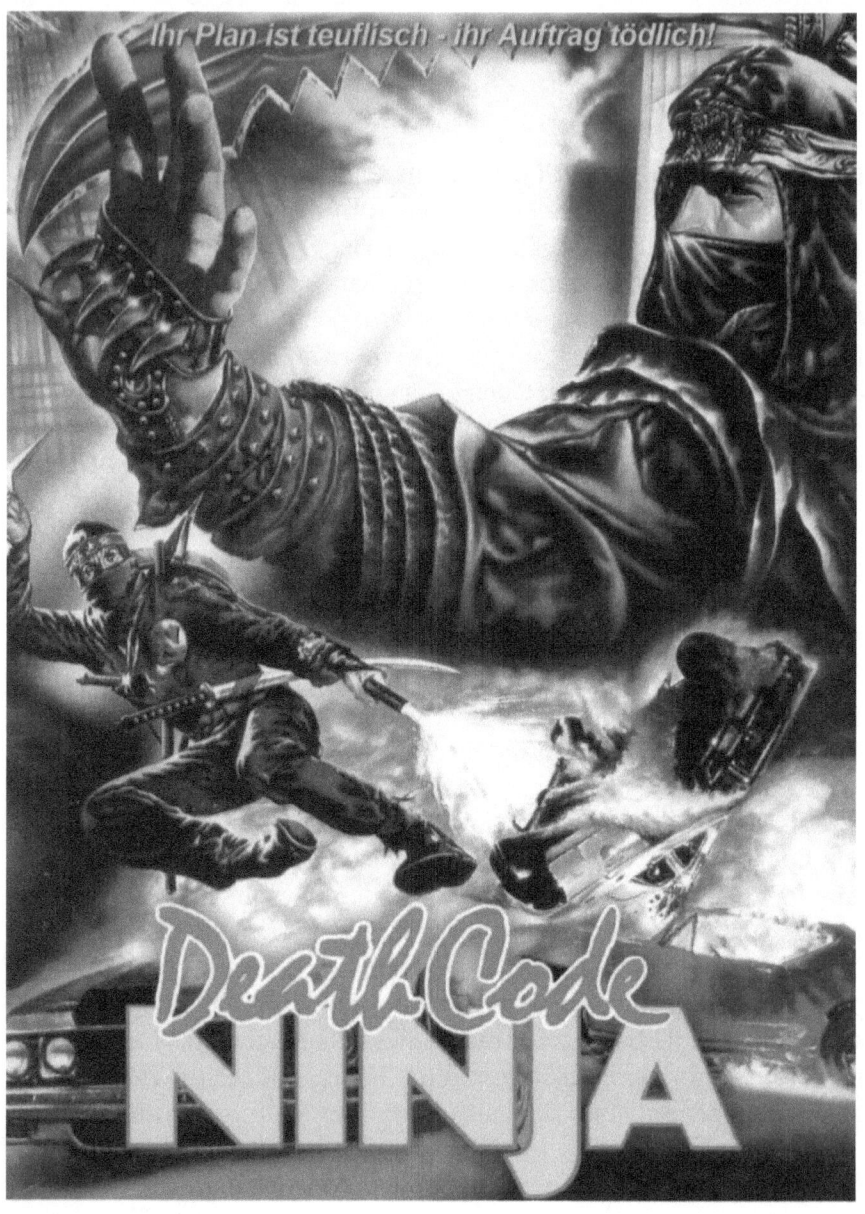

Death Code: Ninja (1987)
Runtime 90 minutes
Directed by Godfrey Ho

During the 80's distributors IFD and Filmark would buy up ultra-cheap action films from Thailand and Taiwan (among other countries) that may have been never finished or couldn't gain distribution outside of their native countries. They would then give the footage to and ask that they film some new footage (usually involving ninjas) to cut into the films. Death Code: Ninja is one of many cut-and-paste films directed by Godfrey Ho.
Death Code: Ninja begins with a dirty deal between nefarious men (one of them played by Ho regular Mike Abbot) involving a briefcase. It isn't long before ninjas appear, and all hell breaks loose. Eventually we get a modestly priced sedan full of ninjas trying to run down a mysterious yellow ninja. From this spectacular opening we are introduced to the "real" movie. This film, likely shot at least 5 years before the ninja footage, involves an affluent family and the kidnapping of their young boy. The kidnappers don't know that the boy is diabetic, and he dies quickly. That's not all the killers are unaware of... turns out the parents are assassins! Seeking revenge, the boy's father attempts to take on the rogue's gallery but gets dispatched himself. Now the matriarch has lost her only child and her husband. All bets are off as she gets her sweet revenge. Mostly random ninja stuff is intercut into the "real" film at any point when it becomes dull. So, what we get is a revenge flick with a sprinkling of ninja action to help boost the fun factor.

The amount of fun that can be derived from these types of films depends heavily upon the "bulk" film used. In this case it's a fun one with lots of action and ridiculous setups, including a bizarre game of dice that results in the "loser" stabbing himself. The ninja action is cheap but also wonderfully over-the-top. The film as a whole doesn't make a lot of sense but it's 90 minutes of action. They aren't meant to "say" anything or be any sort of commentary. Ho directs some satisfying ninja action and cuts out all the boring bits from the "real" movie. This may result in confusion on the part of the viewer, but you just have to go along with the ride and enjoy it for what it is: cheap, silly, fun.

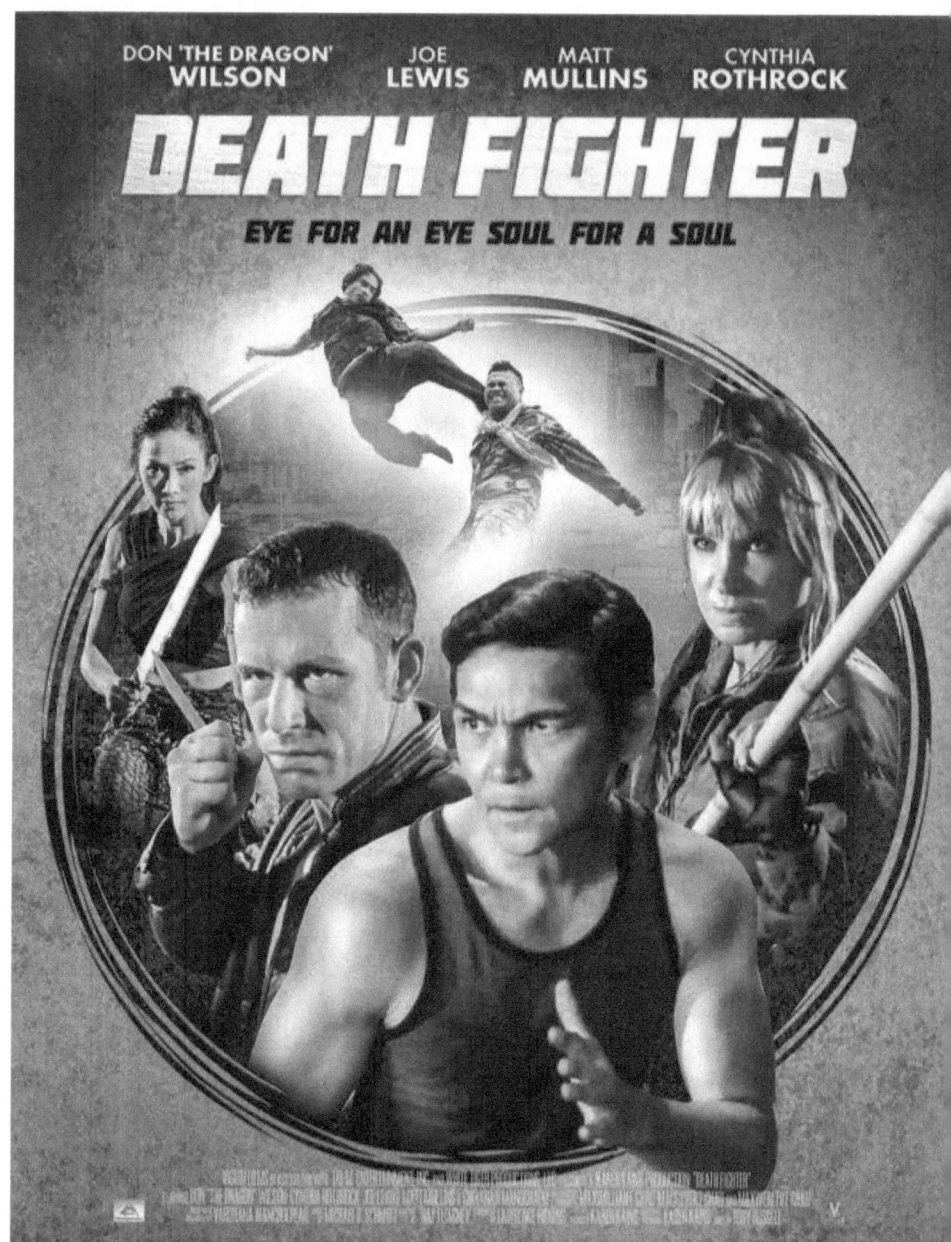

Death Fighter (2017)
Runtime 90 minutes
Directed by Toby Russell

Death Fighter is about Michael Turner, a young cop whose mentor is killed in a shootout in Thailand. The pair had traveled there to hopefully catch an evil Russian crime boss. Just as they were about to finally nab their quarry the pair came under fire and the mentor was killed. Turner, now enraged and hungry for revenge, chases down the evil crime boss. He runs into Bobby Pau (Don "The Dragon" Wilson) who also has an axe to grind against the bad guy. They pair up and hatch a plan to infiltrate his hideout and take him down once and for all. Cynthia Rothrock plays Valerie, the top henchman for the bad guy who is unstoppable and features truly terrible hair.

The plot of the film is one of the most cliché the action genre has to offer. There is honestly nothing new here for action fans. The location is somewhat novel but frankly there have been plenty of jungle action films, and of those, plenty take place in Thailand. If it wasn't for Wilson and Rothrock there would honestly be no particular draw for the film. The budget is low but not micro and the action is decent but nothing particularly fascinating. Even Rothrock and Wilson's fight is a bit underwhelming. The lead actor who plays Turner is a physical specimen but he's pretty baby-faced and dull. Rothrock gets few lines and isn't given much to do in the film until the end. She does feature in the film a fair amount, but she isn't asked to do a whole lot (she's just kinda... there). Wilson on the other hand features prominently in the film and plays the role of the new mentor for Turner. I love Wilson so I enjoyed his performance in the film but again he doesn't fight a whole lot, and when he does the camera work is shaky so it's hard to make out.

Death Fighter is worth watching if you're a big fan of Rothrock and Wilson. It isn't embarrassingly bad nor is it boring, but it's a long way from their former glory. It's a mild time waster and one that won't be remembered in their filmographies.

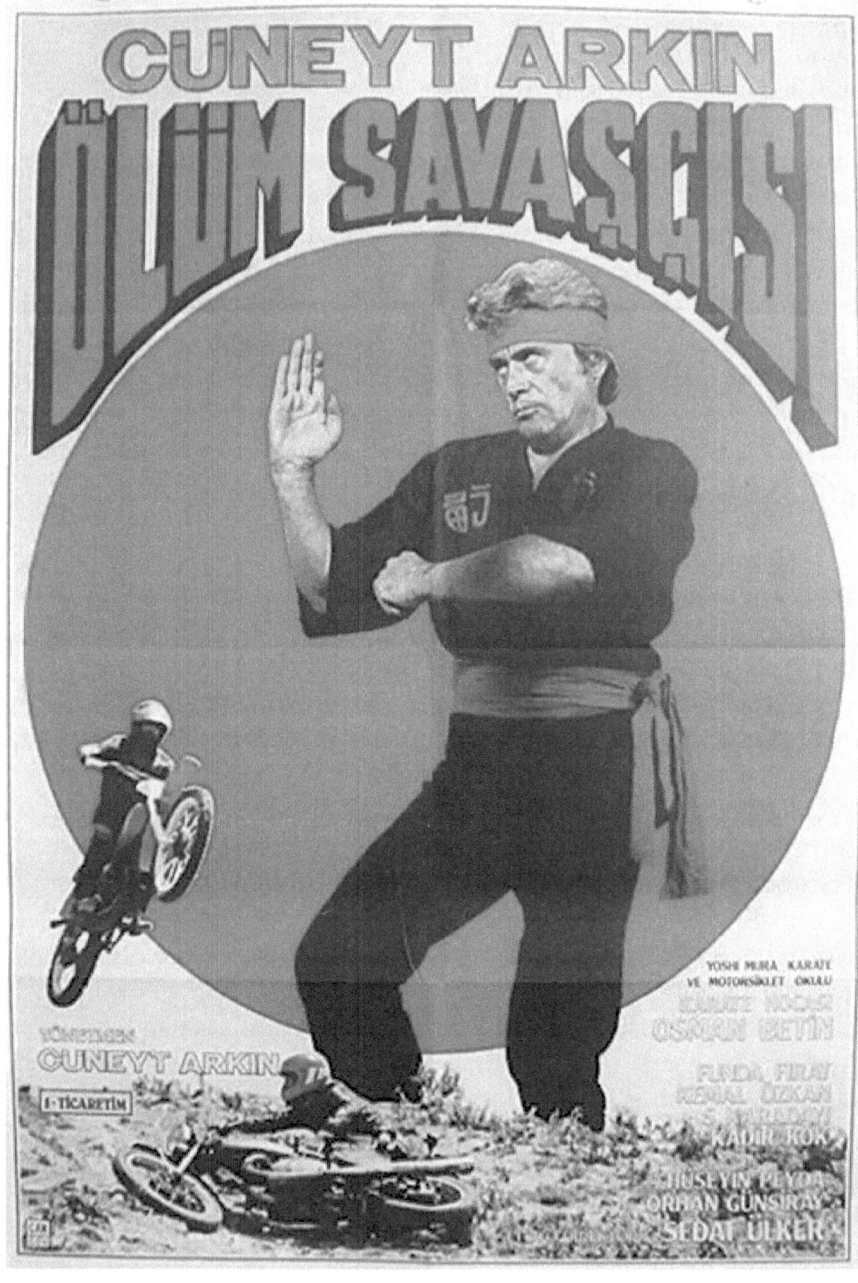

Death Warrior (1984)
Runtime 70 minutes
Directed by Cuneyt Arkin & Cetin Inanc

Death Warrior (which shares the same star and writer as Turkish Star Wars and was co-directed by the director of Turkish Star Wars) is about a secretive and deadly clan of ninjas that are murdering folks in Turkey. These are some seriously bad dudes with the ability to hold their breath indefinitely, use playing cards as weapons, and move large objects with their minds. There's only one man that can possibly stop the Ninjas – Turk Cop played by suave grey-haired 47-year-old Cuneyt Arkin. He's a loose cannon but gets the job done. His superiors have had it with his cavalier attitude and try to stop him from taking on the ninja clan, but nothing will stop Turk Cop from destroying the evil ninjas.

Death Warrior (unlike Turkish Star Wars) has a very simple storyline. It's one we've seen many times from action movies of this era. The film is different in that it has nearly 0% fat and some of the most bombastic action I've ever seen. Turk Cop is a martial arts master (naturally) and destroys everyone he meets. Scenes slam together with no rhyme or reason, the movie moves on with the plot whether you want it to or not... and whether you understand what's going on (you won't'), or not. It has the highly-caffeinated vibe seen in Turkish Star Wars; the type of exuberance usually attributed to 7-year-olds on a sugar high. The film features a couple of bloody scenes, steals footage from Gone in 60 seconds, uses toy cars to shoot crash scenes, steals music from The Thing, and has some weird zombie creatures randomly for no apparent reason. The film borrows footage from other unrecognizable movies as well to create a strange mishmash of cop action, ninja, and horror movie. It's a unique brew that left me highly entertained and exhausted after the film ended.

The high-flying kicks so famously used in Turkish Star Wars are here too, and so is a boatload of machismo. The film hurtles towards its conclusion at breakneck speed, entertaining at 100 mph. There is no nuance, no meaningful character moments, just a whole lot of hastily-assembled action that rarely coalesces into a plot that can be followed by mere mortals. Death Warrior is that cult gem I was hoping for.

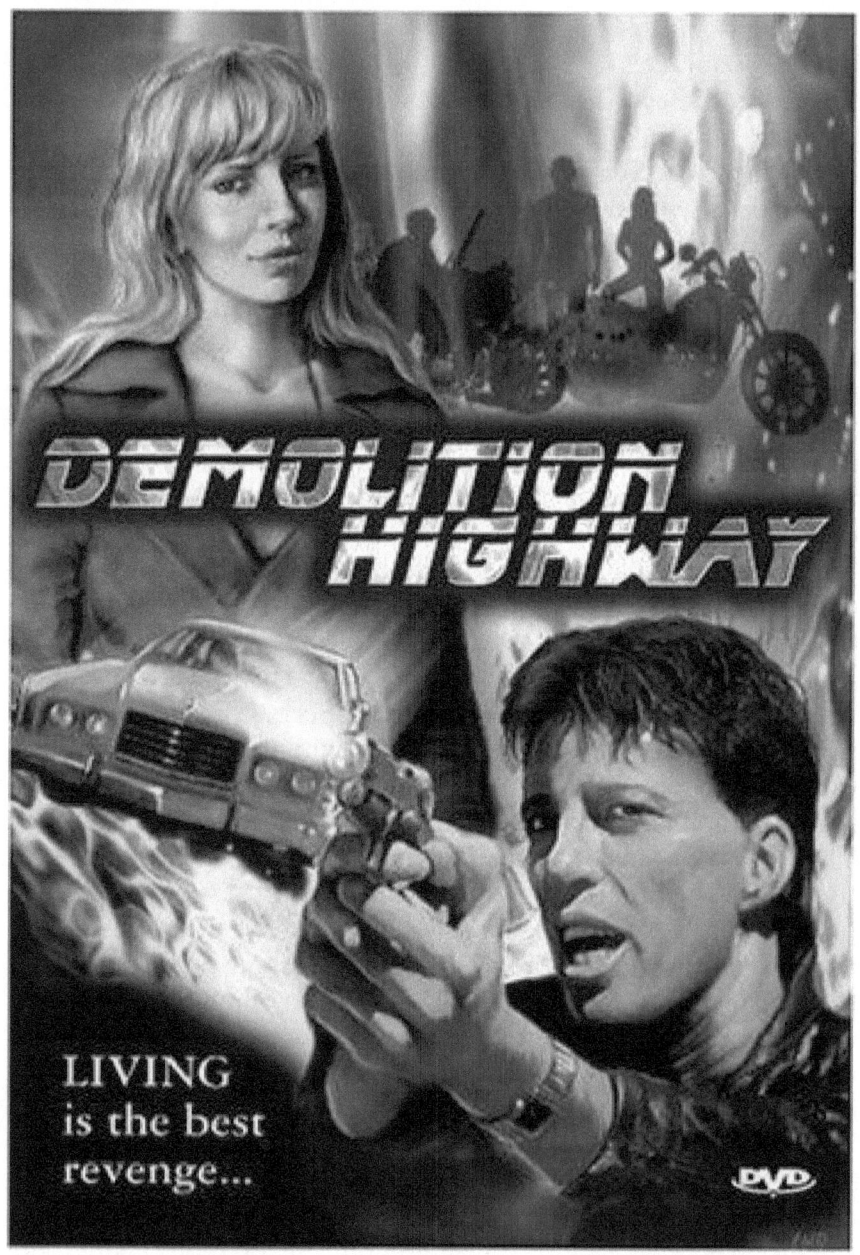

Demolition Highway (1996)
Runtime 84 minutes
Directed by Donald Farmer

Demolition Highway begins with a couple making a getaway with a briefcase full of money that they have purloined on behalf of a criminal organization. That organization sends some goons to chase them down and kill them so none of the loot has to be divided. The mulleted bad guys shoot at our hero's car and cause them to crash. Our hero's girlfriend is murdered, and he almost dies but is instead incarcerated for five years. He doesn't give up any information and has to do the whole stretch. After being released from prison he's met with some of his old goonish associates who congratulate him on his silence. They reward him with another attempt at murdering him! Our hero gets the upper hand and now he's out to get the money he's owed and revenge against the crime boss that put the hit out on him.

Shot on a meager budget intended for straight-to-video release, Demolition Highway stars Joe Estevez as the head bad guy and thankfully he's given a fairly meaty role. Often, he's only given brief bit parts, so I was very happy to see him have the opportunity to chew up the scenery throughout the whole film. Our hero has a very nasal voice which was endlessly entertaining to me for all the wrong reasons. Later in the film we meet a woman that has been kept under lock and key by Estevez and she becomes our hero's partner... figuratively and literally. Throughout most of the film she wears a denim dress which is basically the female equivalent to the Canadian Tuxedo. We also get to see a whole lot of her in a bizarrely vigorous sex scene next to a fireplace (yay?). Our hero gets his gun taken away CONSTANTLY in the film, which begs the question: why does he even try to brandish it? We get sloppy fights, shootouts, a ragtag biker gang, mulleted goons, and a climax that features a conversation shouted from opposite sides of a giant gorge. The film's plot takes many twists and turns as our hero tries to reclaim his money and get his revenge. At times these twists feel completely needless and aren't satisfying thematically, but these strange detours are fun in an Awful Awesome sense. Demolition Highway is a breezy treat with enough action, hammy acting, and bad fashion to make it a fun flick with friends.

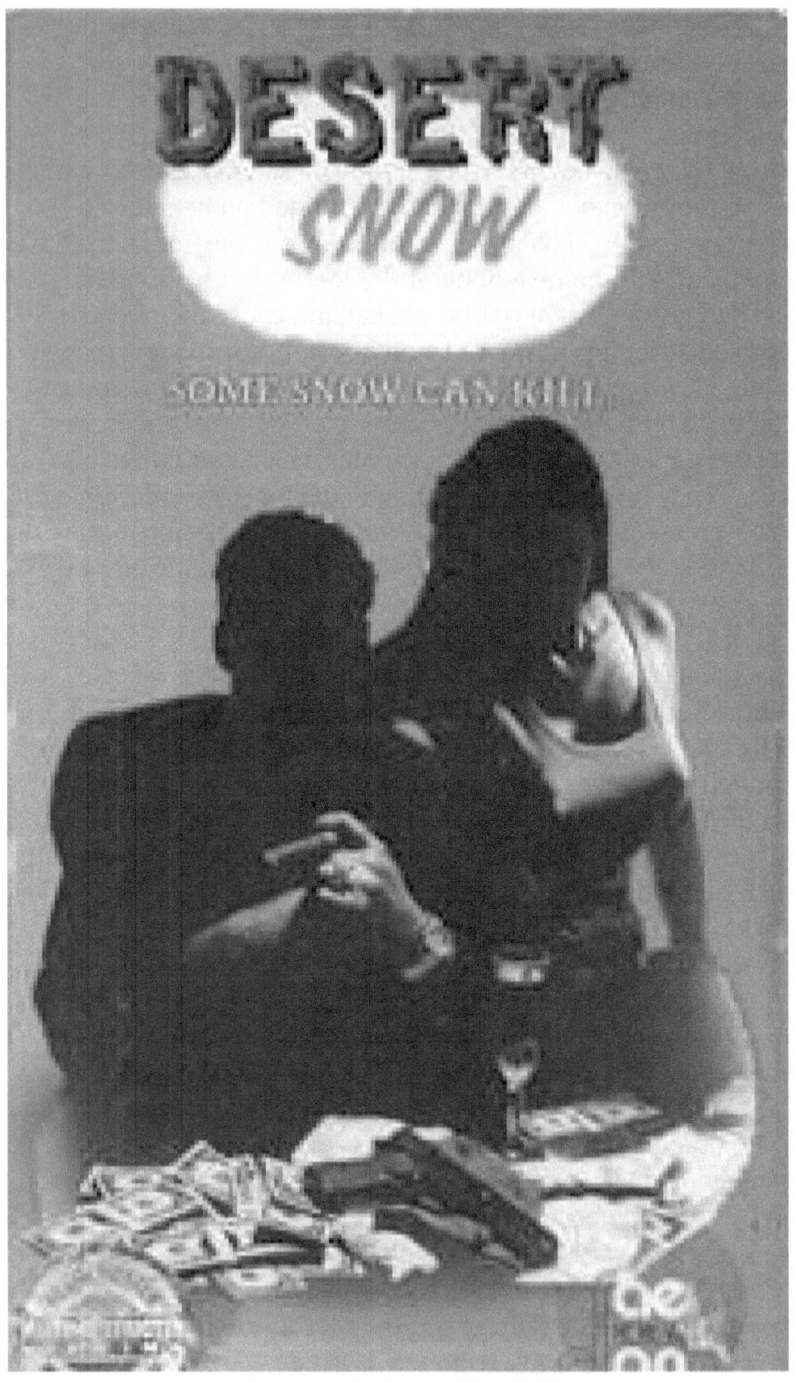

Desert Snow (1989)
Directed by Paul DeGruccio
Runtime 92 minutes

Released on VHS by the infamous Rae Don Video, Desert Snow is a regional action film that tries to deliver on everything a dad could want: shootouts, nudity, an explosion, cocaine, and cowboy hats. Also, lots of casual racism.

Shot in Arizona on a modest budget, Desert Snow begins with a Native American man having some kind of solitary ceremony in the desert. His ceremony is interrupted when he observes a coyote bringing a van full of Mexicans across the border. The coyote and his secreted immigrants are all gunned down by some armed men that come out of nowhere. Their guts are slit open, and balloons of cocaine are extracted. The old Native American gets spotted and of course he's killed too. What the bad dudes don't know, is his grandson, Stone, is a badass and won't stop until the drug dealers are destroyed. He and his mustached white guy partner band together to take out the trash. Randomly a teenage girl and her mother trespass on our heroes' land and refuse to leave... because they want to go camping. After the cocaine is discovered, a subplot involving the teenage girl is initiated when the bad dudes capture her. Now our duo not only have to take out the trash but save the girl too. Being a hero sure is tough.

Desert Snow is rough around the edges. Several scenes are impossible to see due to the low lighting. The action is sloppy, but the squibs are bloody, which is a plus. There are some interesting tidbits that I've only ever seen in this movie, for instance, one man gets punished by having salsa rubbed on his face. Tacos are mentioned in the film frequently, one female character is apparently turned on by anything and everything (including a gun put in her mouth), an entire dialogue scene is filmed through a doll house, and a bag gets filled with horse manure and then the characters drive around with it right next to them. Lots of people are murdered in the film and a whole lot of racist language is used. It's a film that has a fairly standard story but has numerous memorably strange moments in it. I'd give this one a recommend.

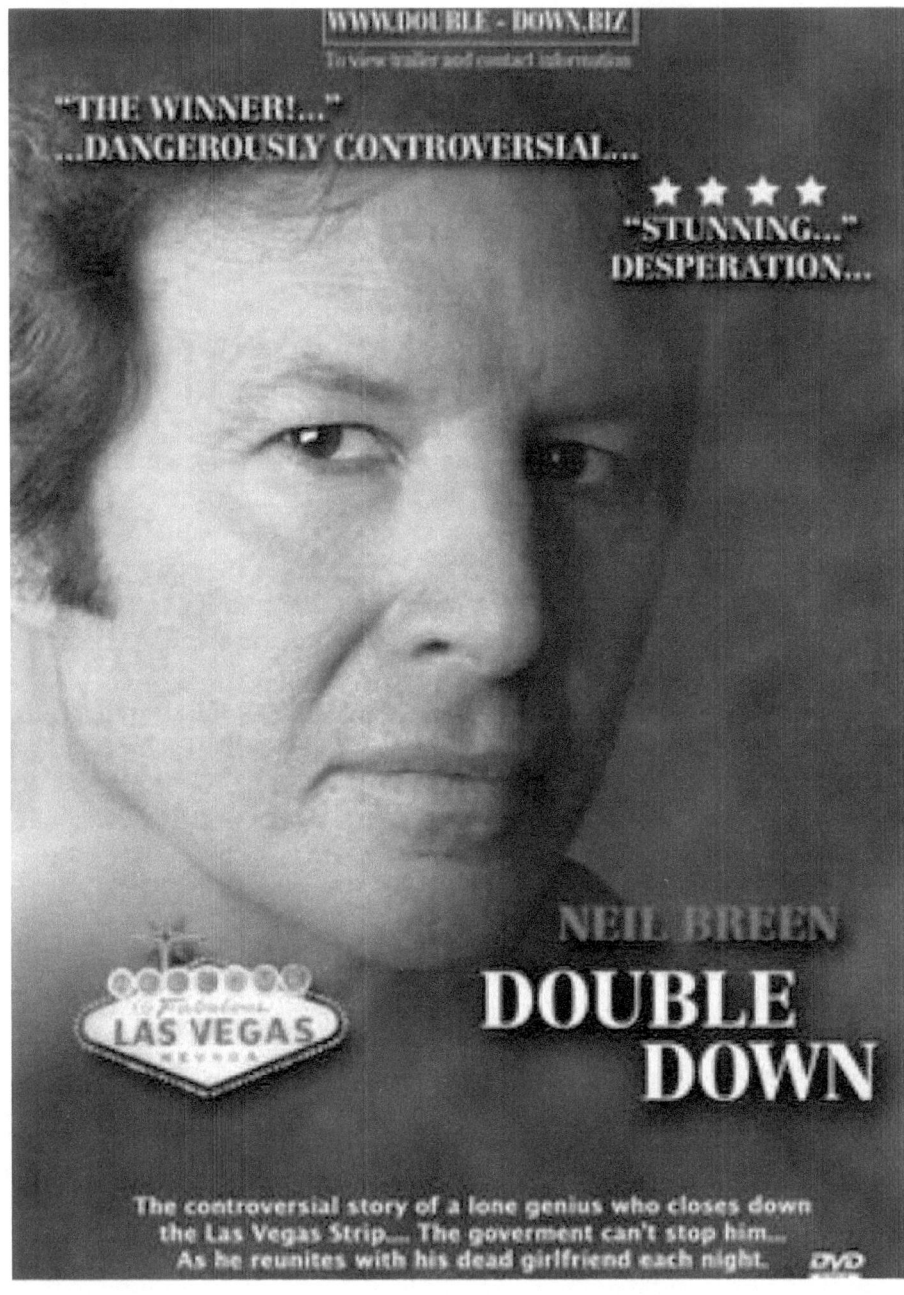

Double Down (2005)
Runtime: 94 min
Directed by Neil Breen

Double Down is a vanity project by writer/director/producer/editor/caterer/star Neil Breen. Neil Breen plays Aaron Brand. Aaron spends his days in the Las Vegas desert hanging out in his sweet 80's Mercedes, eating tuna straight out of the can, and hacking THE WORLD. He starts off claiming that he's a simple man. Then he lists his ridiculous accomplishments. He's a former fighter pilot and he graduated at the top of his class in computer science. Now he's a mercenary who does dirty work for the highest bidder, hacking banks, the stock market, water supply (?) for cities, and apparently dealing in Chemical and Biological poisons. He can hack ANYTHING and mentions it repeatedly. I'd believe it, he's got 5 laptops and 3 cell phones, none of which are ever turned on during the film. His wife (who is clearly young enough to be his daughter) is murdered because of his hacking ways early on in the film. He's a lone wolf that constantly mourns her passing and yet pretty much does exactly what he's been doing all along, although to his credit he questions his own actions for the ENTIRE film.

The first 18 minutes of the film are spent listening to Neil's omnipresent voice-over that lacks emotion but is somehow soothing in its quiet way. Finally, we get a line by another character... and it's only a single line, and then we're back to the voice over until 24 minutes in where we're treated with characters talking about how amazing Neil is. This is quite possibly the vainest vanity project I have seen. Nearly the entire film is footage of him either hacking, sleeping, climbing rocks in the desert, or hanging out with his ghost wife. In the movie he cures cancer. Literally. I'm not joking or exaggerating. I'm not sure he ever has a real conversation with anyone in the film. Typically, in the rare moments that he's sharing a scene with another actor, they say one line followed by twenty for him. It's damn near impossible to follow and I'm fluent in bad movie. From his scenes where he shoots people off-screen whom we never see, to his invisible killer force field around his car, to his claims of winning every medal one can receive in the military, this movie is insane, and I absolutely loved it.

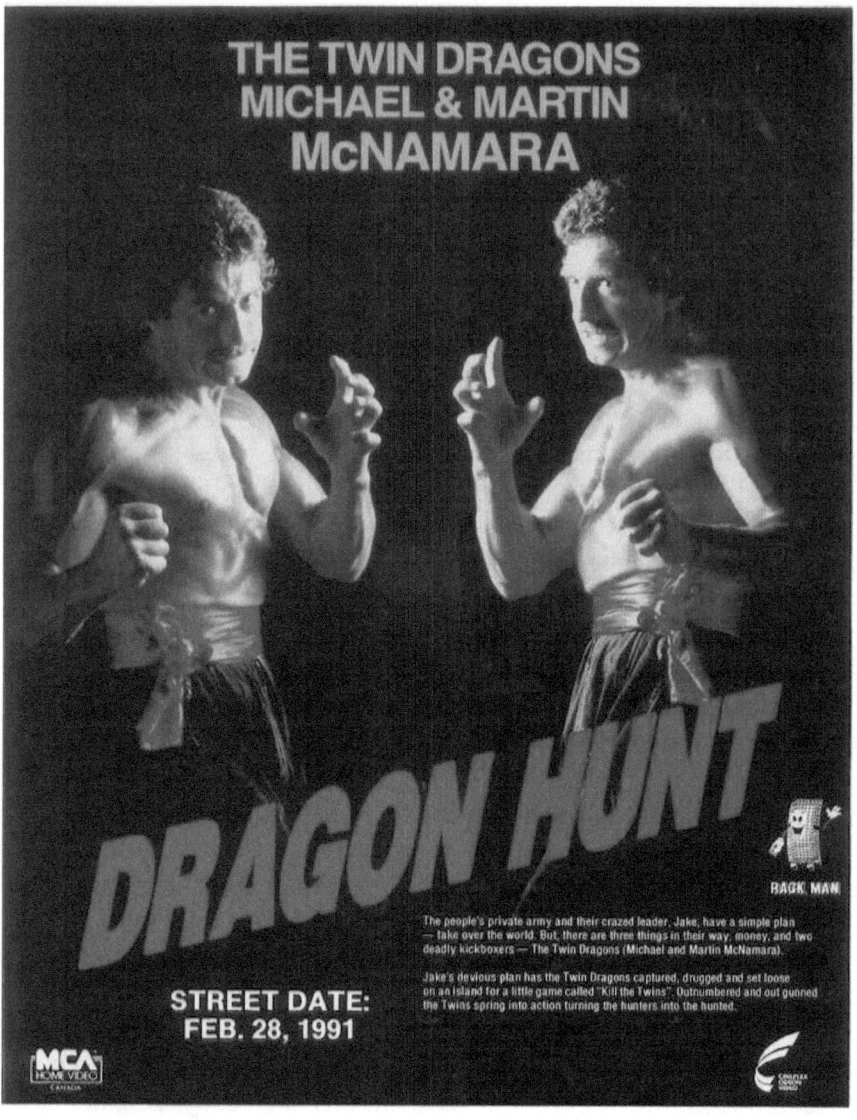

Dragon Hunt (1990)
Runtime 90 minutes
Directed by Charlie Wiener

Dragon Hunt is both a remake AND sequel of sorts to Twin Dragons Encounter (1986).
Out in the back woods of Canada there is a secret army assembling to take over the great white north. They're called the People's Private Army and despite their very communist name these are gun-totin' rebels who apparently have no real political ideology other than wanting to be in charge. Their leader, reprising his role from the first film, Jake wants to get sweet revenge against the brothers for stomping him in the first film and leaving him with a very silly silver fake hand. The hand is just flat. Not a fist or a pointy finger or in a gripping position, it's just flat. The only thing it's good for is slapping people and maybe carrying plates. Jake wants his revenge and he's going to get it after paying some ladies to pretend to like the Twins (I hope they got paid well) who then drug the duo. They awaken to find themselves in cages, captured by Jake. The twins are set loose but now they have become the hunted in a riff on the Most Dangerous Game. They're pursued by Red Skull, The Beastmaster, and.... Carl. Of course, the twins are total badasses, so the tables are turned when the hunters become the hunted!

Unlike the first film there aren't really any draggy bits this time around. The movie is chock full of action and I never felt the runtime. The twins don't have a ton of dialogue, which is probably a good thing, instead they silently skulk around the forest, setting up booby traps to take out the bad guys. Red Skull is a ninja with a red bandana and gold skull on his forehead, The Beastmaster looks like a roadie for Pantera, and Carl looks a lot like former UFC fighter Chuck Liddell. Jake has a Mohawk, a jacket with pins on it, a stubby cigar he never lights, and his infamous silver hand. He also sings cheerful songs in his affected gravelly voice. The plot is fast-paced and there are numerous opportunities for the twins to stroke their egos as they mow down 1-dimensional bad guys. This one hits all the marks: bad fashion, silly dialogue, lots of action, and a soundtrack provided by a musician named Billy Butt.

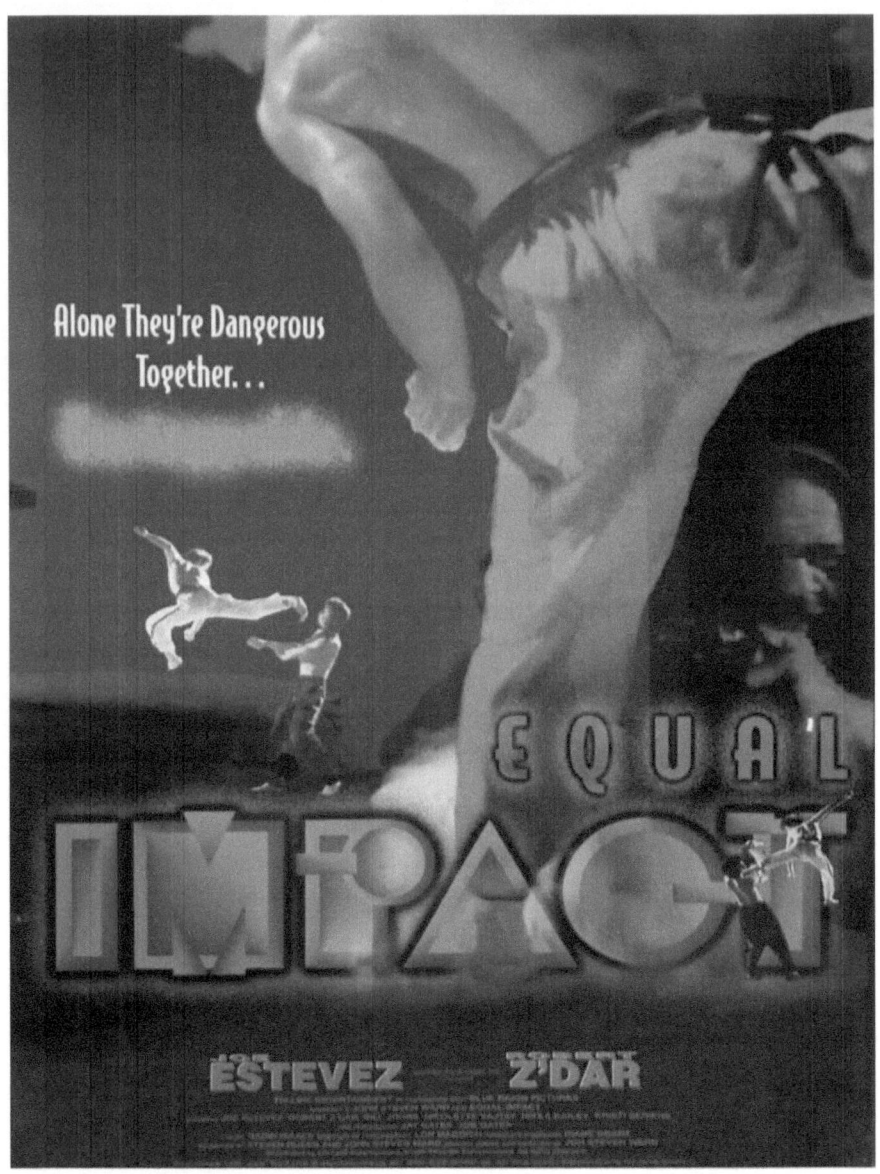

Equal Impact (1995)
Runtime 105 minutes
Directed by Jon Steven Ward

Full disclosure: I'm a sucker for Robert Z'dar and his films; and when you throw in Joe Estevez plus promised martial arts action, then I'm an eager viewer. Equal Impact has all of these things plus it's about twin martial artists and it was made in the 90's? Sign me up fella. Equal impact begins with a slow-motion martial arts tournament. One of the twin martial artists is competing against a sleazy fighter with a mullet. The sleazy guy owns a popular martial art studio, and the twin owns a dumpy place that no one goes to. A winner is called and really the result of the fight has almost no bearing on the rest of the film. And honestly, it's the most martial arts we're going to get until the end of the film. Robert Z'dar is a chain smoking, drink guzzling drug dealer. He's involved with shady drug types, and we don't learn how he fits into the orbit of the twin martial artists until the end of the film. Joe Estevez is a drug kingpin who hires the sleazy mullet guy as muscle for his drug dealing enterprise. The twins witness a crime taking place and they intervene, but it leaves the bad dude dead. The bad dude was working for Joe Estevez counterfeiting money and one of the twins takes the phony money and now they've got the whole nasty crew on their tails... including the sleazy mullet martial artist (seriously bad news). Z'dar continues to smoke, sweat, and drink until he becomes an ally to the twins. Then he smokes, drinks, sweats, and marginally helps.

There's far too little punch fighting here but we do get a glut of dialogue and actors trying to emote. Estevez and Z'dar are great but they aren't given much to do but talk. It's a shame because Z'dar's role is actually fairly meaty, but they don't even give him that many lines because his character is supposed to be quiet and stoic. The budget here is very small and thankfully has one of my favorite tropes: the timeless "empty-box-factory fight scene". The long runtime however hampers the fun significantly as well. As much as I would love to recommend this movie, I can't. It has all the right elements for a trashy good time but there just isn't enough action to justify its very bloated runtime and despite having some of my favorite actors in it, it suffers from a boring plot.

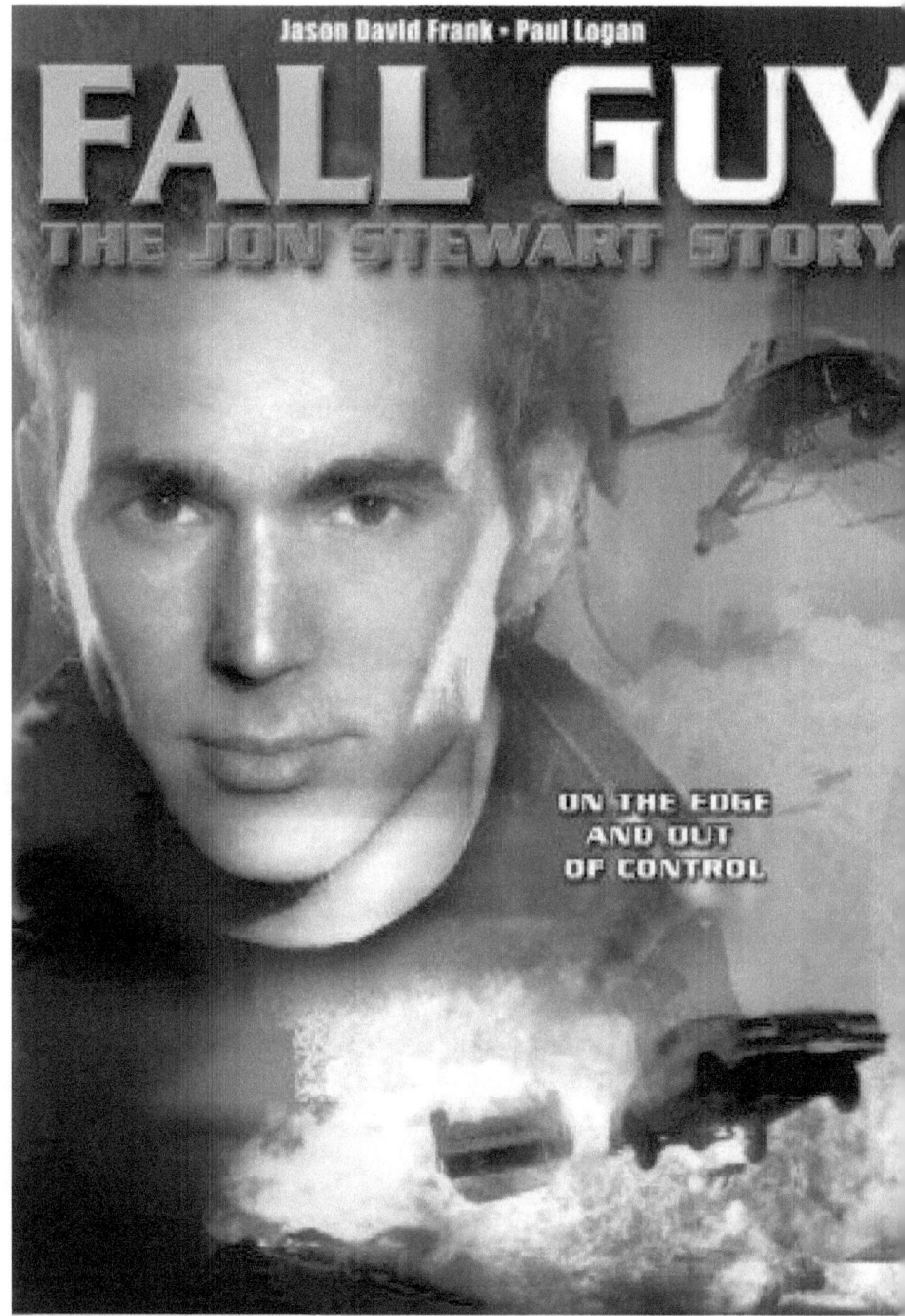

Fall Guy: The John Stewart Story (2007)
Runtime 92 minutes
Directed by John Stewart

Years ago, I was introduced to the film, Action U.S.A. Directed by John Stewart, it had it all: action, explosions, stunts, William Smith, and lots of hilarious dialogue. Fall Guy is written, directed, and produced by Stewart and is an autobiographical movie about his life as a stunt man.

The film stars Jason David Frank (the Green/White Ranger in Power Rangers) as John Stewart, stunt man par excellence. The film begins with him as a child thieving a car to hot rod around at about 15 miles per hour. It's supposed to look action-packed but it's very obvious that the car is driving slowly, being pursued by a couple of mustachioed cops. The film then cuts to John doing a dangerous stunt and getting injured. This is when we learn how badass he is: despite being bedridden he gets his buddies to break him out of the hospital so he can make it to another shoot and another stunt. From here we watch his meteoric rise into the world of stunts and film making based on the unequivocal respect he has earned through years of excellent stunt work. We see his first marriage crumble (likely due to his philandering ways) and his second marriage crumble too. We see reenactments behind the scenes of his favorite stunts and the struggles he went through to make films his way. We see him learn to fly a plane and badmouth the Power Rangers in a very meta moment.

And that's one of the problems with this flick. There is no central conflict. It's just a bunch of cool moments in his life mixed in with some of the tragedies. Surely a movie about a stunt man will have lots of great stunts, right? Wrong. This movie was shot on a shoestring budget these all the cool stunts in the movie are the actual footage from the original film blended (poorly) with *this* film. The acting is poor, the melodrama an inch thick, and the production values cheap. This seems like it would be a contender for pantheon status but really, it's pretty mediocre. Had the movie been a bigger ego stroke, it would have been much more fun. I did have fun with it, and it did make for a decent evening watching it with friends, but it isn't the homerun I was hoping for.

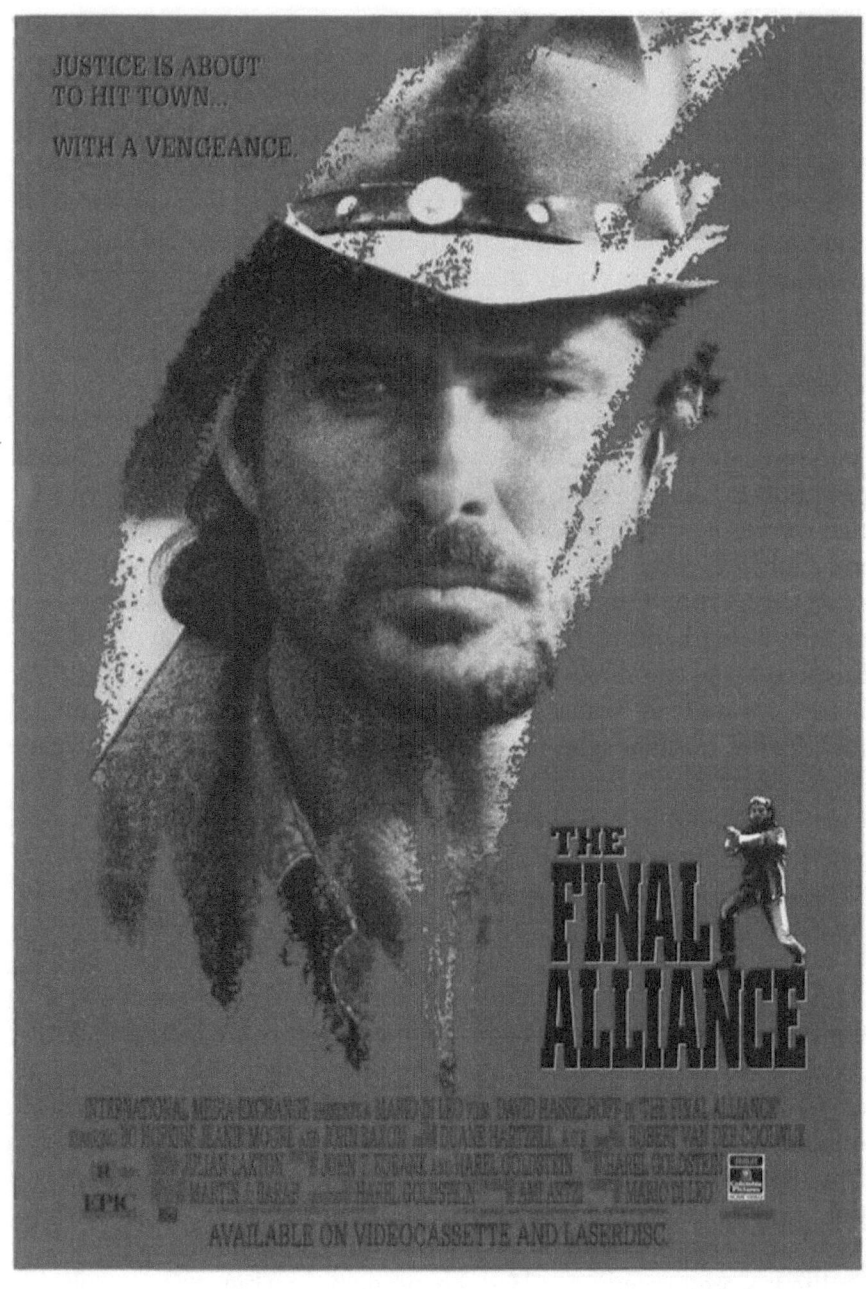

The Final Alliance (1990)
Runtime 90 minutes
Directed by Mario DiLeo

The Final Alliance stars David Hasselhoff as Will Colton, a rugged man with a dark past. He has come to his ancestral home where his whole family was murdered when he was a child. The time has finally come for him to come reclaim his property and get revenge against the savage men who slaughtered his family. He owns a pet puma named Felix (get it?), loves to wear a cowboy hat and double denim, buys a horse, and starts work on his house. Unbeknownst to him his house has become a squat for local biker gang, the Vipers. They're into dealing drugs and guns and it isn't lucrative enough to buy a sweet mansion. Apparently, crime doesn't pay that well. The gang is led by Ghost (played by cult film veteran John Saxon) who for some inexplicable reason is an albino. He's in cahoots with Sheriff Whistler (played by Bo Hopkins) and together they own the town and do whatever they want. That is until Colton comes to town and swears vengeance against the gang for murdering his family. Colton (and his puma) take a stand against the gang and he's a one-man (+puma) wrecking crew.

The Final Alliance gave me everything I hoped for in this cheesy action flick. It gave me Hasselhoff acting uber macho, a puma intimidating bad dudes, lots of biker shenanigans, John Saxon chewing the scenery, and plenty of action. As far as direct-to-video action cheese goes, this one is competently directed but the hamminess of the actors assembled make it a fun ride. This is a perfect movie to watch with friends and have a good time. It's not so low-rent or poorly done to turn off Awful Awesome movie newcomers but it isn't so mediocre as to bore hardened vets. The locations were interesting, although clearly not the U.S. as the movie wanted us to believe. It's obvious the film was shot in a colonial country from the architecture of the buildings and the bad American dubbing on all the local actors.

The Final Alliance isn't a must-see flick but it's a lot of fun. If you enjoy watching the Hoff ham it up, this is a good flick to watch with friends. I had a good time with John Saxon who is always reliable as a bad guy and Bo Hopkins isn't any slouch either.

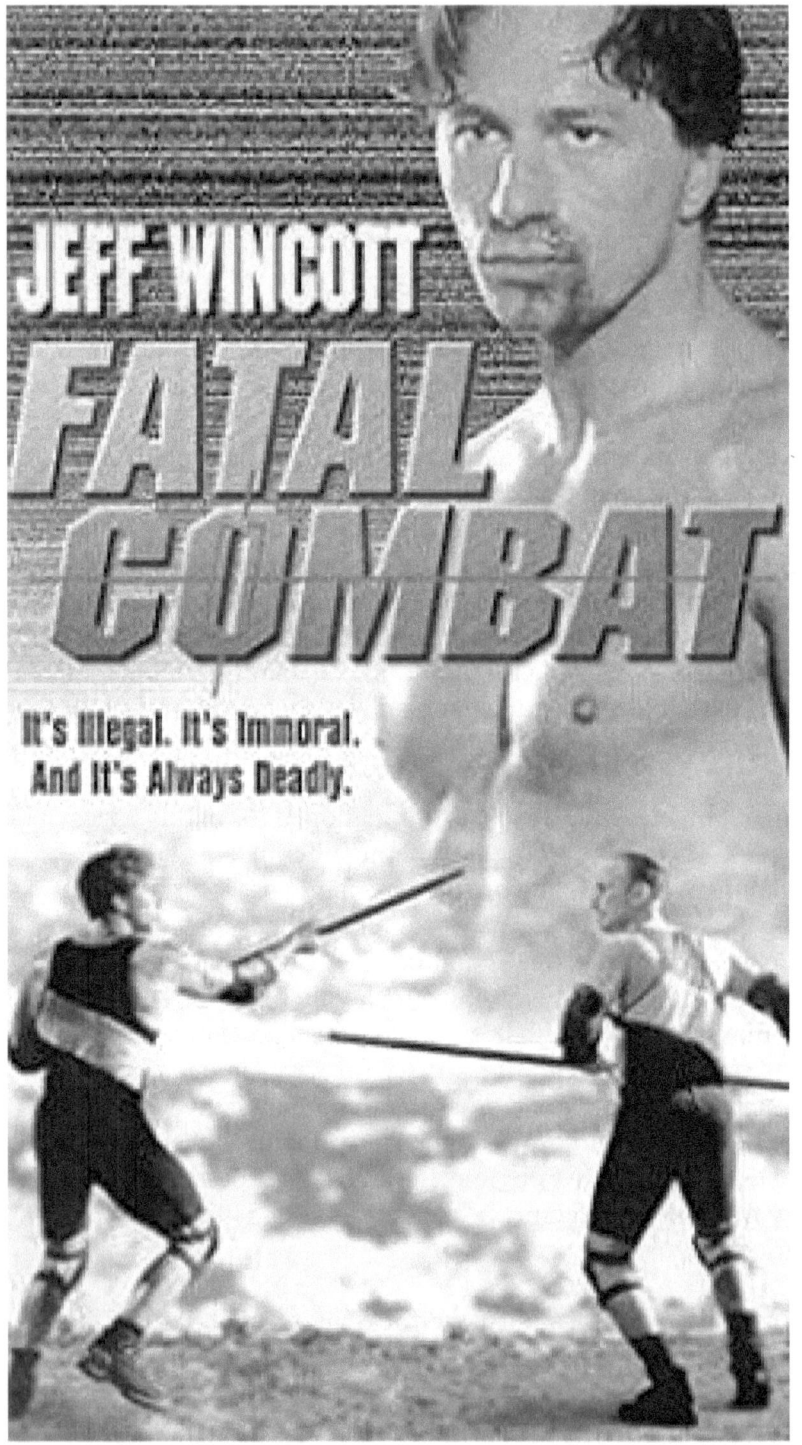

Fatal Combat (1995)
Runtime 93 minutes
Directed by Damian Lee

Fatal Combat is about philosophy professor John Stoneman (Jeff Wincott) who preaches the importance of non-violent conflict resolution. After a doctor's appointment the Stoneman and his wife are attacked in a parking garage which leaves his wife in critical condition and the hoods dead, after Stoneman busts out his 10th degree black belt skills on them. Morally conflicted about his actions, he waits to hear about his wife's condition. News of the attack spreads to our villain, a guy who has a facility set up in the Artic to pit fighters against each other in... Fatal Combat. He broadcasts the event to a select few who pay heavily to watch grown men murder each other. His champion is Darcona (Sven-Ole Thorsen), and our villain needs a new challenger. He kidnaps Stoneman and forces him to fight or die. Stoneman doesn't agree and hatches a plan to take down the organization and break out. Fatal Combat is very cheap. The fights that take place outside are filmed at night to hide the fact that they aren't actually fighting in the snow since it's supposed to be the Arctic. The fighters wear warm clothing and ski goggles to create the façade that they are fighting in snow but it's obvious they aren't. We get to see Sven-Ole Thorsen operate a very small hovercraft a few times during various fights which is pretty dang rad. The technology used to broadcast the fights as well as create unique challenges are very silly which adds to the fun. Wincott tries his best with the material and does an admirable job. Thorsen also gives his best, chewing the scenery with gusto. The villainous head of the organization however is a bit of a bore. His performance is too understated for such a mustache-twirling role and frankly it harms the film. The film's tone is also very dark.

The assault on Wincott's wife is rather unpleasant and Thorsen rapes one of the fellow fighters in a move to make the movie more "relevant" and "real." What it accomplishes is taking a silly film and making it distasteful which kills the fun factor for a while. The movie also lacks enough fights which considering "Combat" is in the title is a hard pill to swallow. While not a complete waste of time, Fatal Combat isn't a film you should run out and see right away.

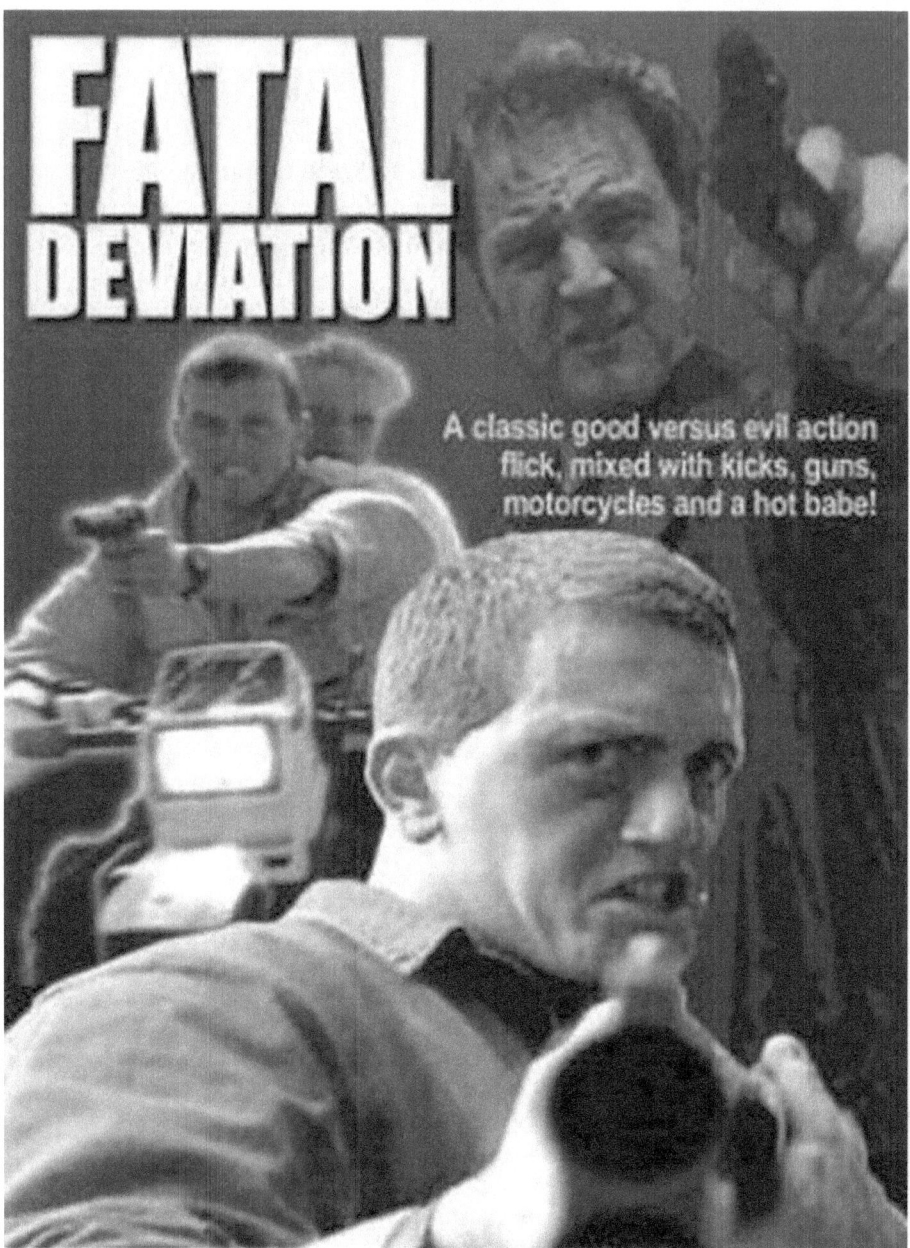

Fatal Deviation (1998)
Runtime 76 minutes
Directed by Shay Casserley & Simon Linscheid

Fatal Deviation hails from Ireland and is reportedly the only martial arts movie ever produced there. The film begins with our hero, Jimmy Bennett, moving back into a small town after being gone for 10 years. Jimmy's dad was murdered by local gangsters and Jimmy has finally returned for revenge. He isn't alone; however, he's brought some impressive "guns" with him. While they don't shoot bullets, they do impress the ladies and work very well at cracking bad guys upside the head. Jimmy is jacked. He's an impressive physical specimen even if he is on the short end of the height spectrum, something bad guys remind him of just before he smacks the taste out of their mouths. Jimmy can't go anywhere in town without getting into a fight, which is bad for him but great for us viewers. He impresses a mysterious monk enough that he's invited to a special fighting tournament that is only held once every 10 years. The local monks, robed in brown, put away their pesky vows of non-violence to host a sweet bare knuckle, no holds barred fight to the finish. While training, Jimmy's girl is kidnapped by the same ne'er-do-wells who killed his father. In order to get her back, he's going to have to win the tournament and then hunt down the men holding her captive and kill everyone.

While it takes a bit to get going, it isn't long before we get to see our hero in action. The fight choreography is pretty sloppy, and his katas are even worse. He looks like a child pretending to do martial arts. But what he CAN do is the splits Jean-Claude Van Damme style... and does so frequently. We get a fantastic chase/shootout on a motorcycle that needs to be seen to be believed. Many of the stunts in the film look perilous, even the simple ones. The short runtime allows the film to breeze by quickly, though the tournament does become a bit tiresome and repetitive. The music in the movie also undercuts the emotion of the scenes. Romance music and training montages do not go together. Fatal Deviation lived up to the hype for me. It is a fun action flick that has stilted acting, sketchy stunts, lots of fights, nonsensical plot developments, and truly terrible music.

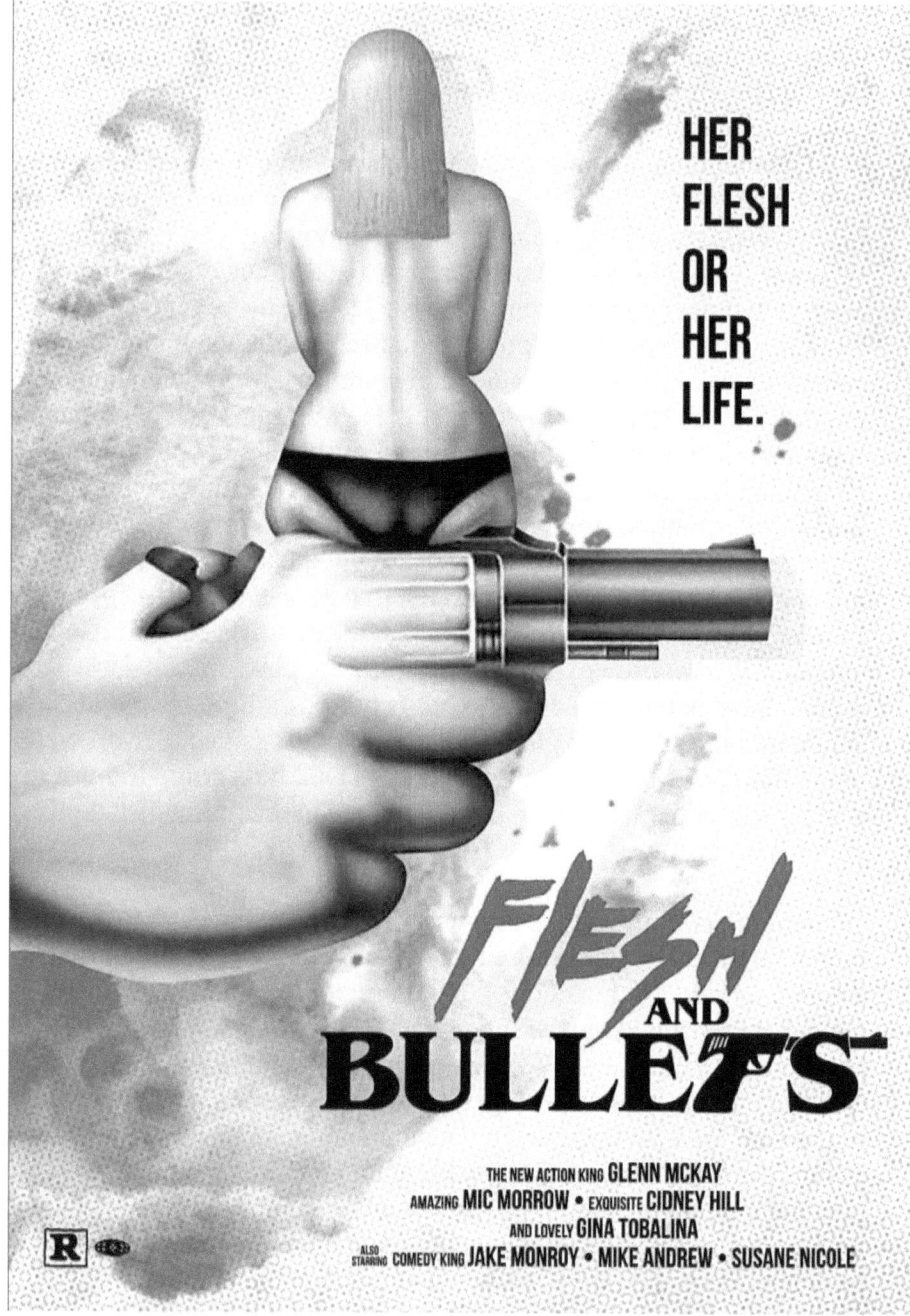

Flesh and Bullets (1985)
Runtime 85 minutes
Directed by Carlos Tobalina

My love for actor Robert Z'dar's cinematic output is very evident by his multiple appearances in this book. Flesh and Bullets is the Z'debut of Z'dar.
Flesh and Bullets is about a couple of dudes with mustaches, expensive taste, and a hunger for the company of ladies (even the kind that require payment), but they've got one problem: their ex-wives. On a chance meeting at a bar, they drink, reveal deep personal secrets, and make a pact: they will kill each other's wives, so they won't have to pay alimony anymore. Misguided, misogynist, and mustachioed pact made, they both hunt their prize but discover that the lady assigned to kill is one wonderful dame. Both men fall in love with the other's ex!

In case you're wondering, no, Z'dar does not play either lead He-Man Woman Hater, instead he plays an abusive ex-boyfriend who comes to stomp the new boyfriend/secret killer but instead gets humiliated when he brings fists to a gun fight. He looks great in the film, very muscular and his infamous jaw looks much smaller in the film. But enough Z'digressions.
Flesh and Bullets feels like an adult film made without the sex. The acting is as wooden as a rocking chair, the shots wide and workmanlike, the budget meager. The style of the characters is very porno-esque too. The whole running time I was waiting for some graphic sleaze, but aside from some mild nudity this movie has no adult content. Much of the film is spent hanging out with the characters as they go on picnics and learn to love the offspring, and ex of their blood-pact mate (basically becoming stepdads). There isn't a whole lot of tension since the movie is so crudely made and acted, but that adds to the fun of the movie. The film does, however, lack action. It's mostly a lot of talking, which is very funny at times but overall, I wasn't bowled over by Flesh and Bullets. It isn't a film I would suggest all lovers of Awful Awesome films run out and see, though it will appeal to some for sure. I got a big kick out of seeing Z'dar (obviously), so for me it was worth watching to see him alone. The restoration of the film is quite good, I doubt it's ever looked better.

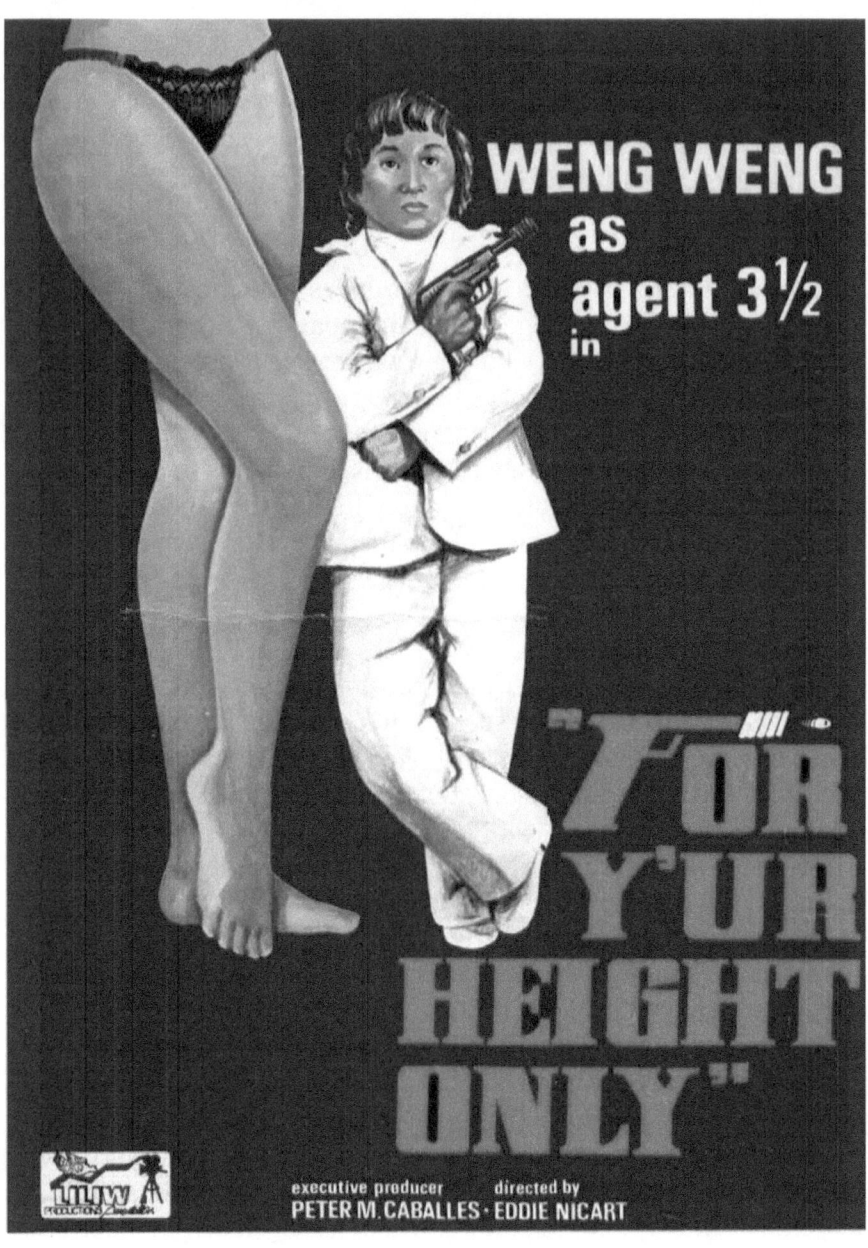

For Y'ur Height Only (1981)
Runtime 87 minutes
Directed by Eddie Nicart

Weng Weng is only 2'9" tall, making him the smallest leading actor in a movie. Equally proportioned, he looks like a child but make no mistake, he's a fully grown man. During the late 70's and early 80's he made a handful of action films in the Philippines. The rest is history. Weng Weng stars as Secret Agent 00 (something he tells EVERYONE so it's not really a secret, is it?). His mission this time out is to stop a drug ring and rescue a fat white dude who was kidnapped. He has to fight his way through oceans of woefully unprepared goons along with the help of several pretty ladies who, like Agent 00, know how to kick some major ass. That's pretty much the entire movie, there's very little to it really (see what I did there?). Every scene is there simply to setup an action scene of Weng Weng destroying testicles with his tiny fists and feet of fury or shooting bad guys by the bushel with his tiny pistol.

For Y'ur Height Only delivers the goods. It's action-packed from the very beginning. The film wastes little time on anything that doesn't involve Weng Weng jumping from great heights, beating up bad guys, or shooting lots of people. He uses secret weapons supplied to him via his boss who also cuts an impressive fashion. Weng Weng himself always wears slick leisure suits with giant lapels. He's always stylin' when out in the street looking for nards to mash. Nearly all the goons he fights are literally caught sitting down on the job, how else would Weng Weng reach? He's also very good at mackin' on the ladies. Weng Weng does some impressive stunts throughout the film as well. Of course, no stunt double could be used because no one but a child is the same size as Weng Weng, so he does them all! Say what you want about his height, but he must have had some serious cojones to do some of the stuff featured in this film.
For Y'ur Height Only is a cheap rip off of James Bond films starring a very tiny man dishing out some serious pain and carnage. You'll be cheering for Weng Weng and not sneering because the film is so much fun and Weng Weng is a blast to watch in action. I loved it. This is a pantheon film.

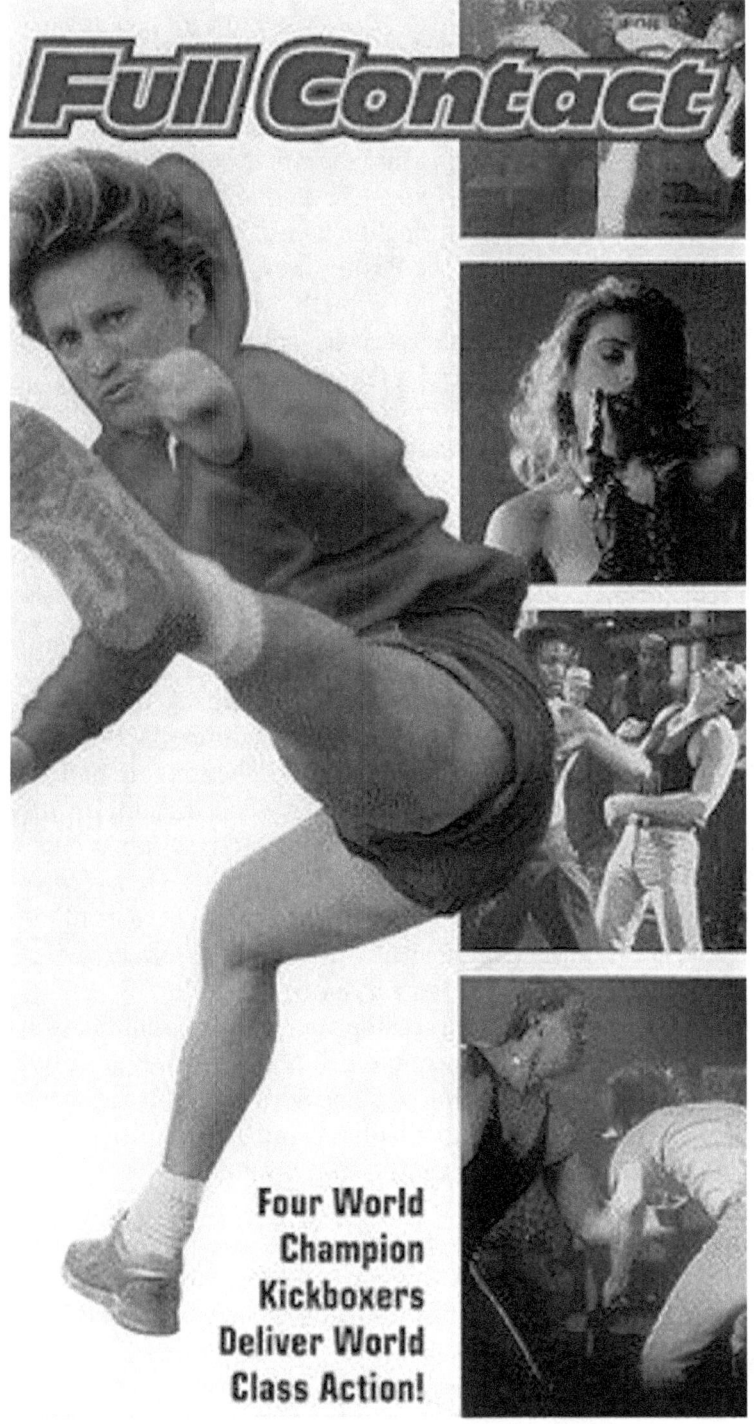

Full Contact (1993)
Runtime 95 minutes
Directed by Rick Jacobson

Full Contact stars Jerry Trimble as a double-denim-clad Mid-Westerner who has traveled to Los Angeles to meet up with his older brother. His brother lives in what has to be the most run-down area in the entirety of Los Angeles. What Jerry doesn't know is that his brother has been making ends meet by fighting in full contact matches against other down-and-out schlubs. The fights take place in dingy warehouses and bets as low as $5 are placed. After leading such a glamorous life, Jerry's brother turns up dead, murdered after his most recent match. Jerry then decides to infiltrate the underground fights by becoming a fighter himself in order to discover the truth about his brother. A denizen of the dump decides to be his trainer and together they fight to win!

Produced by New Horizons, Full Contact is the EXACT SAME MOVIE as Dragon Fire AND Blackbelt AND Bloodfist 2050. I don't mean that Full Contact is derivative. Sure, it's common for movies to copycat each other. I mean that the plot is the same, the story beats, even the character's names are the same. One script was written and then it was turned into two movies: Dragon Fire which is a post-apocalyptic sci-fi martial arts movie, and Full Contact which is just a martial arts movie, but the location is such a shithole it just looks post-apocalyptic. It's uncanny. Never have I seen this before. The movies were made 1 year apart. All three films are based on the same story written by the same writer, produced by the same company. But that's not all, Full Contact and Dragon Fire share the same director, but Blackbelt also had Jacobson as a second unit director too! It's amazing how far New Horizons stretched a buck: they didn't even bother writing original scripts. The films even share actors.

If you love tournament movies like I do, you'll enjoy this. Dragon Fire is a much more entertaining film, which makes sense because it was the third time the script was made into a film. Full Contact's locations are as low-down and grimy as I've ever seen, and Jerry Trimble does an admirable job. There's nothing new to the story and it doesn't take any unexpected turns, but it delivers the meat-and-potatoes action that one would expect.

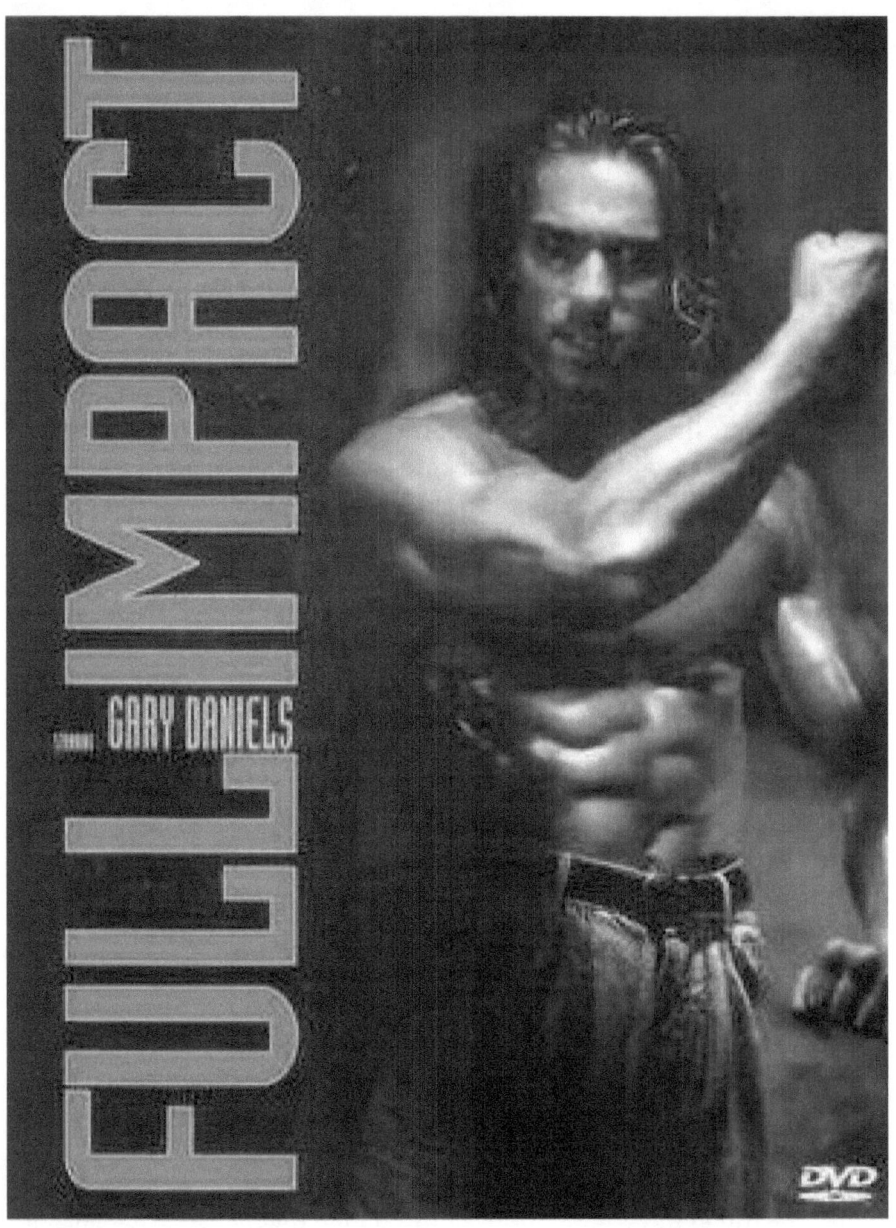

Full Impact (1993)
Runtime 82 minutes
Directed by David Huey

Gary Daniels stars as Jared Taskin. He's a former cop-turned-bounty hunter with beautiful curly blonde locks. Seriously, Daniels has long hair in a lot of his earlier films, but I've never seen one where his hair was so fabulously silly. At one point a bad guy calls him goldilocks and honestly there's no way he should get mad: it's an accurate name. Taskin's daughter was murdered in his home by a masked gunman and since then he hasn't been the same. He still enjoys wearing tight high-waisted pants and tank tops wherever he goes but the joy in his eyes is gone. Instead, he spends his time collecting bounties, much to the chagrin of his former associates. That's just a way to pay rent though... his REAL mission is to find the man who killed his daughter and bring him to vigilante justice. He gets involved with investigating a string of crimes involving sexy ladies, massage oil, and murder. Could this killer be the same man who tried to kill his wife and murdered his daughter? Taskin is on the case and he's only a few roundhouse kicks away from uncovering the truth.

From the creators of films like Future War and Pocket Ninjas, Full Impact begins with a montage of Gary Daniels kicking and punching in some high-waisted khaki pants sans shirt, with his bouncy hair flowing, acting dangerously, but looking very silly. The film crashes into each scene with no discernable connective tissue between them. There were times when I thought the next scene was a flashback and only realized it wasn't halfway through. Fights break out of nowhere in the movie and Daniels dispatches all the challengers with his rippling muscles and fancy hair. The movie doesn't skimp on the sleaze either. The audience is treated to random scenes of topless women being seduced before being dispatched off-screen. These scenes are sprinkled throughout the film without any real rhyme or reason, they're just simply there to keep the audience engaged in the movie. The film is filled with poor acting, badly choreographed fights, a really weak (and hilarious) car wreck, silly fashion, and lots of laughs. I had a blast with this flick. It's that special kind of bad that doesn't come around very often: it's both poorly made and action-packed. Highly recommended.

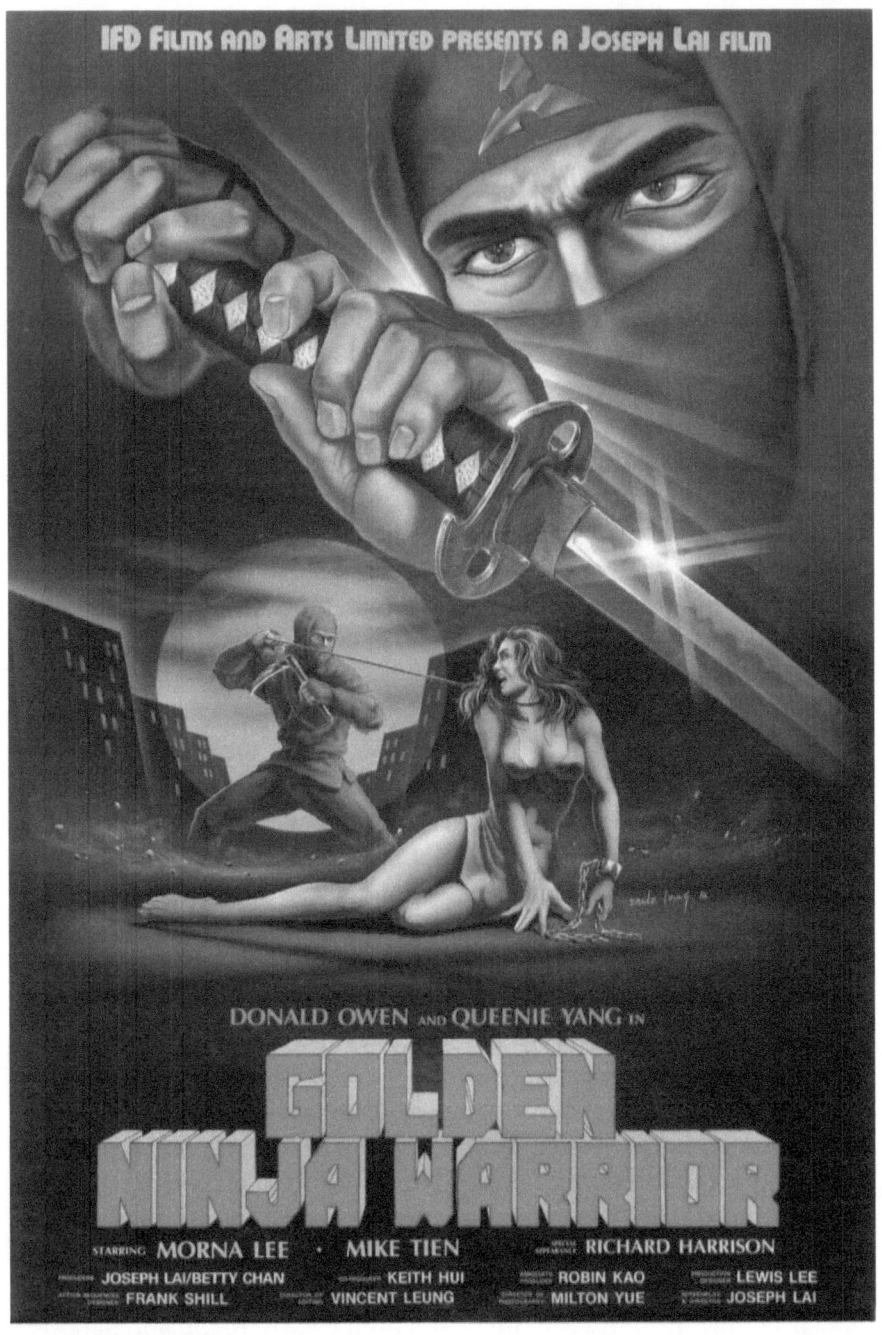

Golden Ninja Warrior (1986)
Runtime 90 minutes
Directed by Joseph Lai

IFD Films would buy up boatloads of low-budget trash films from Thailand, Korea, or Taiwan and then shoot additional scenes, often involving ninjas, and shoehorn them in, passing off the film as a totally new product. Golden Ninja Warrior is one such cut and paste flick and it's a sleazy hoot.
The film begins with random footage of Richard Harrison fighting another ninja set to narration about a golden ninja statue. It's a powerful statue and only the best ninja clan can possess it. Of course, ninjas being ninjas they fight over its possession constantly (gotta prove "most powerful" somehow, eh?). So, sprinkled throughout the film are ninja fights that may are may not have something to do with the golden ninja statue. There's another plot involving a kick-ass female ninja who wants to take out a crime boss and end his filthy ways. She teams up with other sympathetic anti-crime-boss people and together they try to take him down. Ninjas pop up in the middle of fight scenes and make the movie much better.

Fights break out unexpectedly around every corner and the fighting on display is equal parts awesome and over-the –top, making for a fun movie watching experience. What doesn't make the film so fun are the scenes involving the abuse of women. Heck, this one begins with a half-naked woman being whipped. Not my bag, dear reader. That type of stuff is too nasty for my gentle sensibilities. It's good to know they're there should you want to show this to your friends. Caution is the word. There is also a fair amount of graphic sex scenes in the movie as well so it could make for awkward viewing with the wrong crowd (grandma might want to sit this one out). For this type of film, Golden Ninja Warrior is one of the better films out there and a good place to start with "crazy ninja cut and paste" flicks. These are a category of film that even the most knowledgeable cult film fan often avoids. They're cheap, hard to follow, and the genre is a minefield of boring ones. But if you're an adventurous movie watcher with an iron constitution for Awful Awesome cinema, Golden Ninja Warrior will give you what you're after.

CYNTHIA ROTHROCK
GUARDIAN ANGEL

A BODYGUARD WITH HER OWN KIND OF JUSTICE...

Guardian Angel (1994)
Runtime 95 minutes
Directed by Richard W. Munchkin

Guardian Angel begins with two gangs converging in the middle of a public park. They were likely dressed by someone who has never seen actual ne'er-do-wells. They are costumed with brand new shiny outfits and a lot of bandannas. One gang is there to purchase counterfeit money while the other gang is there to supply it. What they don't know is that detective McKay (Rothrock) is watching them, waiting to bring them ALL to sweet justice. The gangs get into an argument, and it looks like the park is going to be turned into a bloodbath so McKay rushes to the scene and fires her gun in the air to scare them? I'm not sure what she was thinking but her tactic has the opposite effect: the gangs shoot the hell out of each other and McKay chases one who is running away and pumps him for info. She finds out that the kingpin is having a party and the sum total of her plan is to crash it, posing as a lady with loose morals. She gets made for a cop and chased out of the party almost immediately. Despondent, McKay leaves the force, buys a cheap Winnebago and a very understanding wiener dog and begins working as a bodyguard. She gets approached by a rich playboy that fears for his life. McKay begrudgingly takes the job and inadvertently begins her hunt for the Kingpin and the counterfeit plates.

The plot serves to set up as many fight scenes, shootouts, and chase sequences as could plausibly be injected without the film being devoid of plot altogether (a pretty solid approach). Rothrock is on camera from start to finish and gets in so many fights, I lost count. Oddly though she isn't given snappy dialogue, so the villains always get the last word. I guess she gets the last laugh with her fists. The plot moves along at breakneck speed, hurtling towards the conclusion we all saw a mile away but couldn't wait to watch. For fans of Rothrock (and for fans of PM Entertainment in general), this one is a must-watch. With action around every corner, really bad 90's fashion, bad acting, hammy clichés, and Rothrock scorpion kicking her way through hordes of bad guys, I had a blast with this flick, and I highly recommend it.

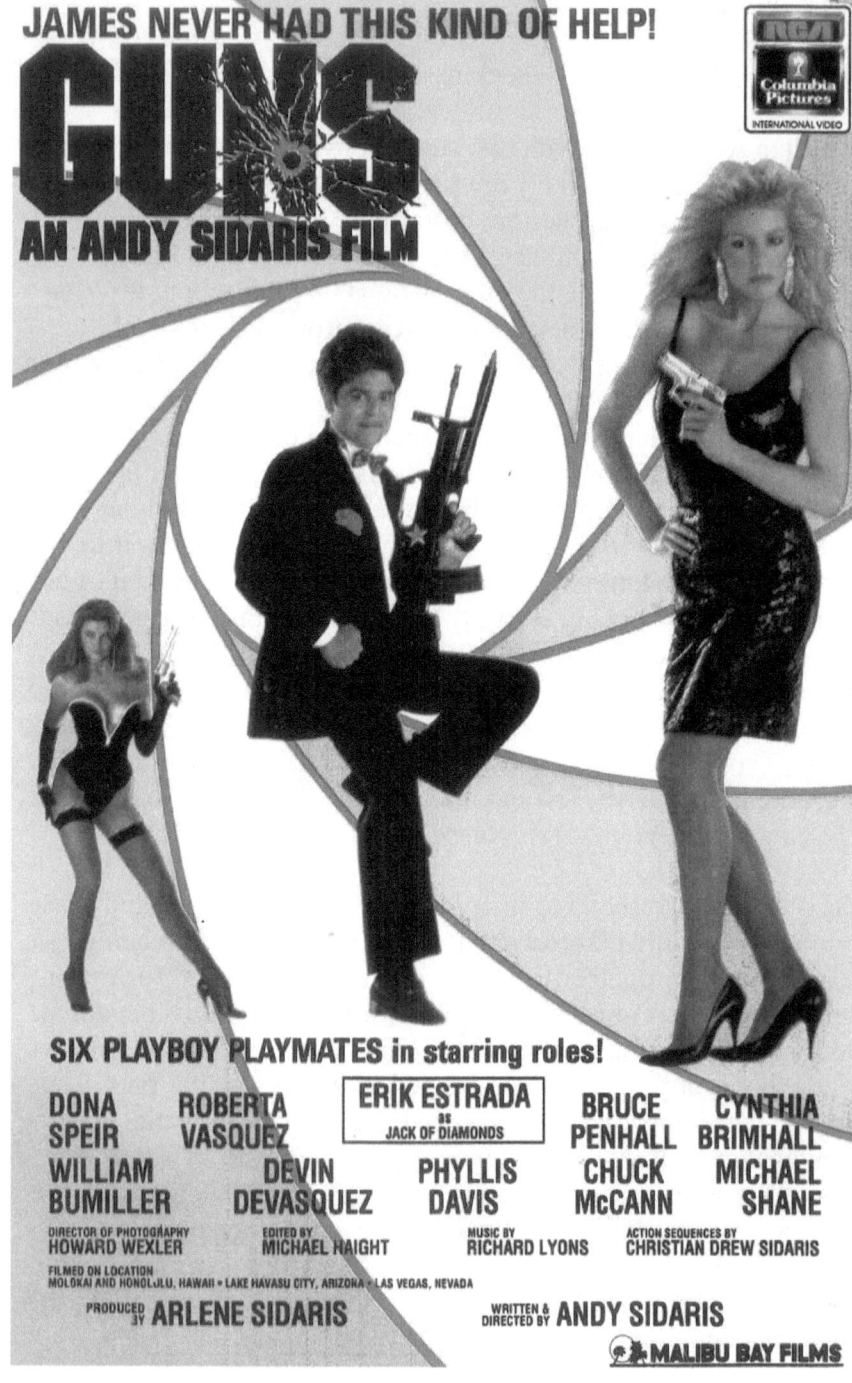

Guns (1990)
Runtime 96 minutes
Directed by Andy Sidaris

From the director of Hard Ticket to Hawaii (1987) (as seen in Action, Vol 1), Guns stars Erik Estrada as Juan Degas. He's a sleazy gun dealer who wants to sell top of the line Chinese guns to mustache-twirling bad guys in Hawaii. He didn't count on one thing though: the ladies of L.E.T.H.A.L. (a special squad of beautiful women who work for the government as operatives when needed). After a woman is murdered in broad daylight by a couple of cross-dressing goons, the ladies investigate. That investigation turns them onto Juan in a roundabout way. Juan wants all of the girls dead as well as their man-hunk co-agents. Juan kidnaps the mother of one of the agents and brings her back to Las Vegas. Big mistake. Now it's personal and all bets are off!

Guns is just as silly as it sounds. Thankfully it's much more action-packed than the previous installment in the series. We see rockets launched from improbable guns, an exploding plane, an exploding helicopter, exploding cars (and an exploding rubber boat), more shootouts, lovemaking on a motorcycle, and Danny Trejo inexplicably playing an Asian character named Tong. There's nothing new here that you haven't seen in the previous films, but it also never drags. There's plenty of action and far less sleaze than in Malibu Express and Hard Ticket to Hawaii. Erik Estrada is fun to watch, and he's well cast as the villain. Guns is clearly not the best in the series, but it's far from the worst. If you're a fan of Sidaris, you know what to expect. This one delivers on all fronts without being bogged down with needless expository dialogue or uninteresting subplots.

I was all but ready to throw in the towel with the Sidaris films after being underwhelmed by the previous couple of entries. I'm glad I didn't. I had a good time with Guns. While it isn't the best of this films it scratches the itch and gives the viewer what they want.

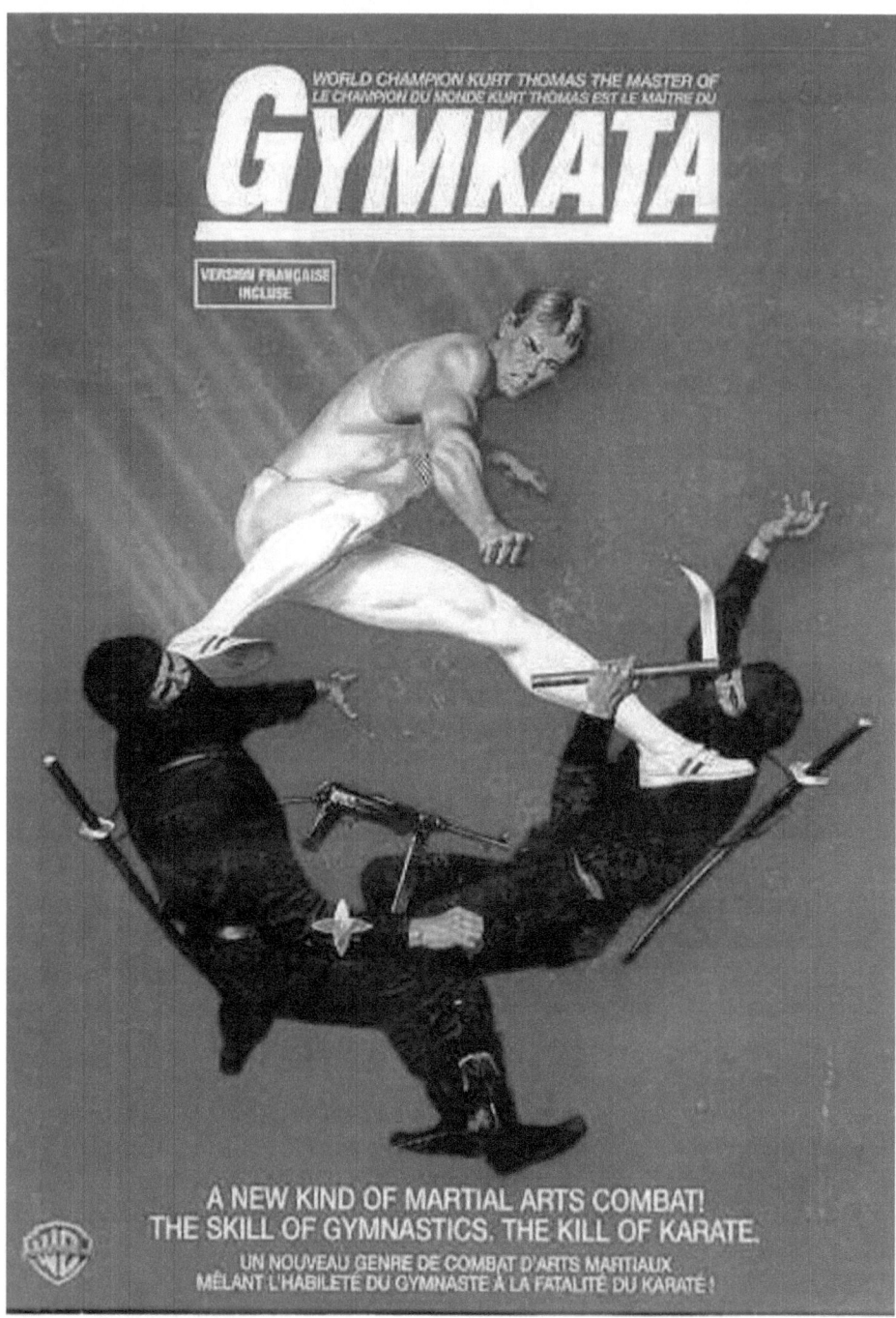

Gymkata (1985)
Runtime 93 minutes
Directed by Robert Clouse

The film makers behind Gymkata had the audacity to blend Karate (which was at an all-time height in popularity partially due to Director Robert Clouse's Enter the Dragon) with gymnastics, which also surged in popularity due to the Olympics televising the event. And so was born Gym-Kata (gymnastics + Karate kata). The producers of Gymkata hired gymnast Kurt Thomas to play gymnast/secret agent Jonathan Cabot. Jonathan's father was doing some super-secret spy stuff in a very small (and totally made up) mountain country of Parmistan. He was competing in a race/murder hunt and got hunted. The race part consists of treacherous terrain with a variety of obstacles like a giant rope climb, crossing a canyon by shimmying across a rope... all while avoiding the "hunt" part, Eastern European Ninjas who are actively hunting them every step of the way! Jonathan is then tasked to train in order to compete in the race/murder hunt to find out what happened to his father and bring back intel about the country. Jonathan's job is to compete in the race/murder hunt, get close to the King and try to win/convince the King to be cool with the U.S of A (sounds easy enough).

Gymkata features an extended training montage filled with training that has nothing to do with the event Jonathan is expected to compete in. For instance, walking up a flight of stairs on his hands while doing a handstand. That never comes into play at all during his competition. But it's impressive, so what the heck. Our hero has a sweet spikey-haired mullet ala MacGyver, and he wears a red sweater that looks like he stole it off a kid in elementary school. The film also stars Richard Norton, who plays a villain allergic to wearing a shirt. The plot hums along nicely and never gets dull or devolves into melodrama. Our hero gets many opportunities to show off his gymnastics skills by using strategically placed bars for him to swing on or a stone pommel horse in the middle of a courtyard for no apparent reason. The trouble is he's a goody-two-shoes and despite the plethora of sharp weapons everywhere he only punches/kicks/gymnastics his foes, which frankly does get old by the end of the movie. There's a genuine sense of adventure and innocence that permeates the film, so it's hard to dislike it.

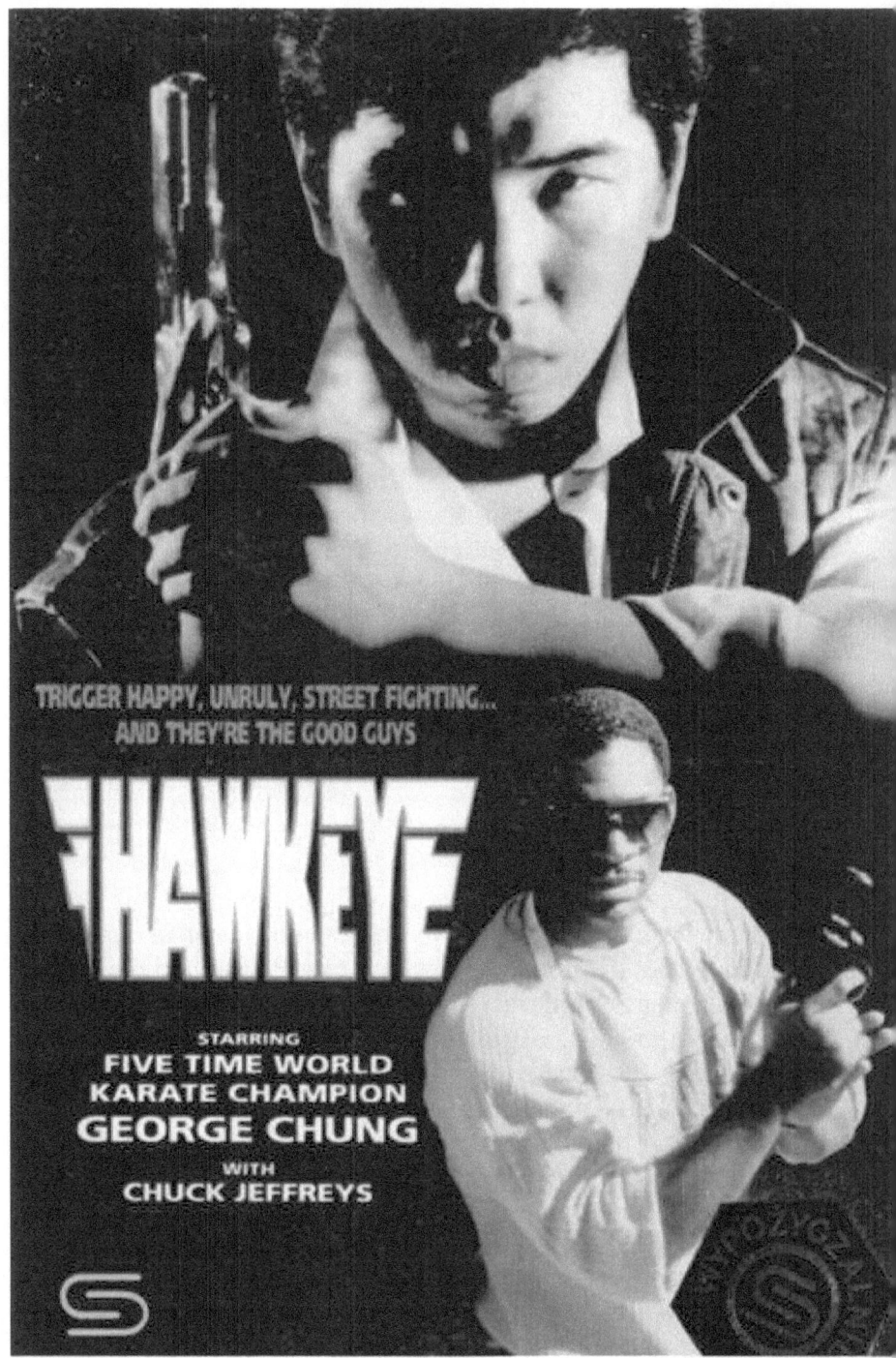

Hawkeye (1988)
Runtime 90 minutes
Directed by Leo Fong

Astute readers of this book will recognize the director, it's none other than Leo Fong, the lead actor in Awful Awesome favorite Low Blow (1986). He's directed twelve films so far, though ironically Low Blow was not one of them. The film's leading man George Chung also wrote Hawkeye and another Awful Awesome favorite, Kindergarten Ninja (1994)! The connections don't end there though. Co-star Chuck Jeffreys (who imitates Eddie Murphy here to chilling precision) also starred in another favorite Awful Awesome film, Bloodmoon (1997), starring opposite Gary Daniels.
Hawkeye is the nickname of Alexander Hawkamoto (Chung), he's a Texas cop slumming it in Las Vegas due to a dark past. He's a loose cannon but he gets the job done. After EVERY SINGLE hostage is killed during a bank robbery because of Hawkeye's cowboy ways, he's assigned a new partner, Charles Wilson (Jeffreys). Unlike Hawkeye, Wilson is a top cop with a clean record. Together they investigate the murder of a fellow cop and friend of Hawkeye that leads them straight into the world of drugs, the Mafia, AND Yakuza. Hawkeye is completely divorced from his heritage, which plays as a running joke throughout the film as is the term "pack shit" which is an apparently Texan colloquial term for hanging out with the fellas. You can already imagine the "jokes."

Given the pedigree of Hawkeye I was expecting something mind-blowingly awesome. I'll admit I watched the film twice, the first time without my bad movie buds and I did enjoy it plenty. However, when I showed it to them it didn't play as well as I had expected. Sure, we had a good time, it's a silly film. But the slower bits were much more pronounced in a group setting with some particularly painful scenes of dialogue. That said, the movie has enough unexpected character moments, bad fashion, cheesy music, and action to carry it to the end without causing drowsiness. While not the pantheon example of Awful Awesome excellence I was hoping for, it is a fun flick and one with plenty going for it to recommend for Awful Awesome veterans. If you are a well-traveled connoisseur of crap, Hawkeye delivers enough personality and stupidity to leave you satisfied.

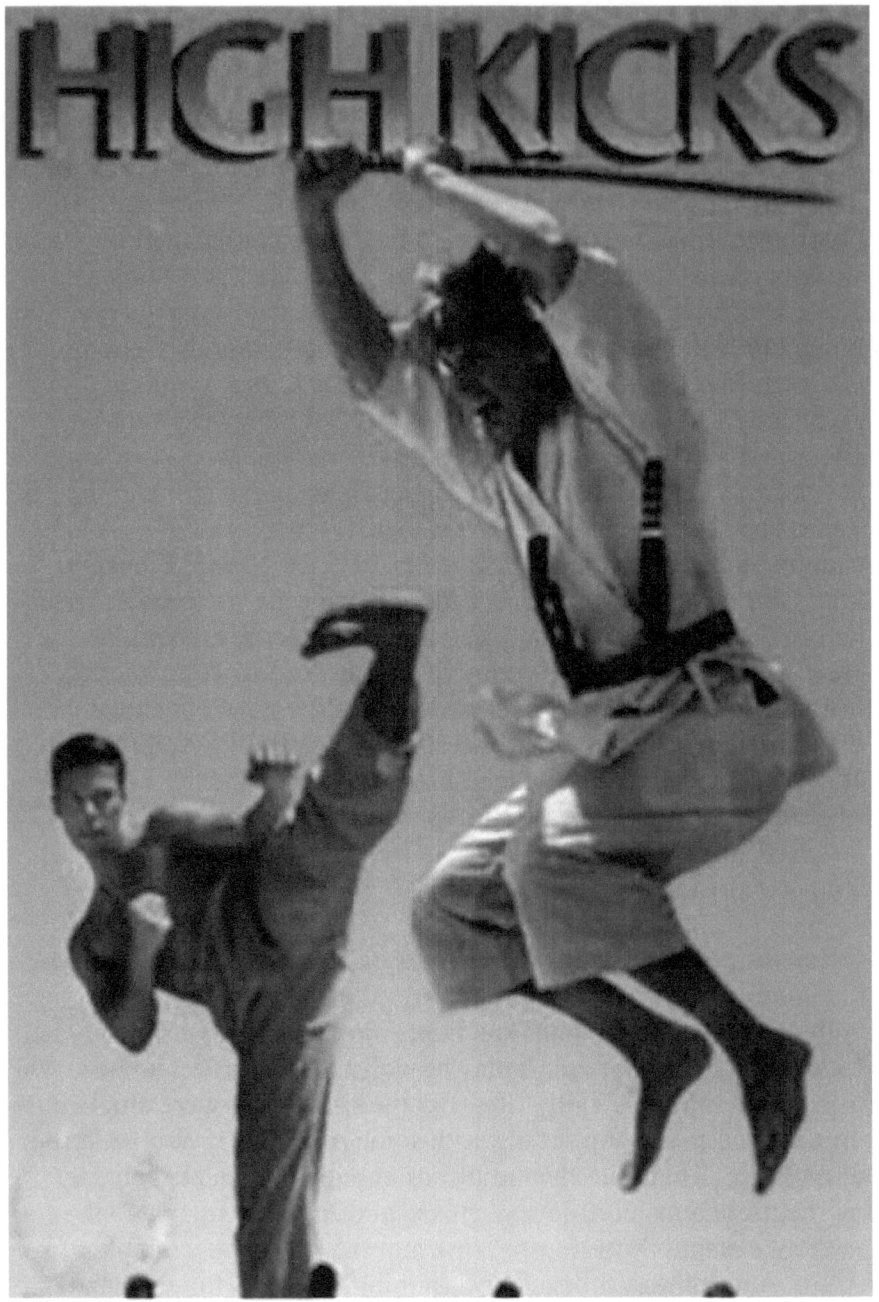

High Kicks (1993)
Runtime 82 minutes
Directed by Ruta K. Aras

High Kicks, shot on video, begins with an extended credit sequence of sailboats, people enjoying the sunny California beaches, and more sailboats over a bed of Casio synth music. After which, we're treated to a montage of boobs and butts thrusting, sweating, and shaking at an aerobics studio. Finally, we meet one of our main characters, Sam. He's got a sweet mullet and he's rocking double denims (a refined gentleman indeed). He wanders into the aerobics studio (named "High Kicks!") and there he meets Sandy who owns the place. She's in need of a handyman and it just so happens that Sam is handy. After scoring the job, Sam leaves just as some local thugs enter. The gang is made up of not so much an ethnically diverse bunch as they are living, breathing stereotypes. They've got a cholo (whose performance made me cringe) an Asian guy who knows martial arts, a big black guy, and a swarthy Latin guy. Led by T.C., a fat white guy who inexplicably wears a hat that says RUDY on it, the gang decide to rob Sandy and rape her (not cool dude). Caution here for more sensitive audiences, consider previewing this scene before you show it to friends. Sam shows up and offers to teach Sandy the martial arts. Turns out he's a world champion-level Karate master. Who knew? Together they train along with some of his buddies who show up just because he asked. After a smattering of training, they track down the rapists (somehow...) and beat them all up one by one, teaming up on the individual bad guy. You know, just like how good guys always do it (two on one!). High Kicks is just the kind of direct-to-video weirdness that I love to find. The lead actress has no rhythm and clearly isn't a martial artist either. The budding romance between Sam and Sandy contains 0% chemistry and a lot of huffing on Sandy's part and a lot of befuddlements on the part of Sam. The bad guys are cookie-cutter, and their portrayal is borderline racist. The music is obnoxious and so is the writing. I loved every second of it.

 There are enough strange directorial decisions and overall enthusiasm to carry the viewer through to the show-stopping freeze-frame ending. I only wish the film didn't have the rape/revenge element to it. That lowered the fun factor for me but the rest of the movie is an absolute blast to watch.

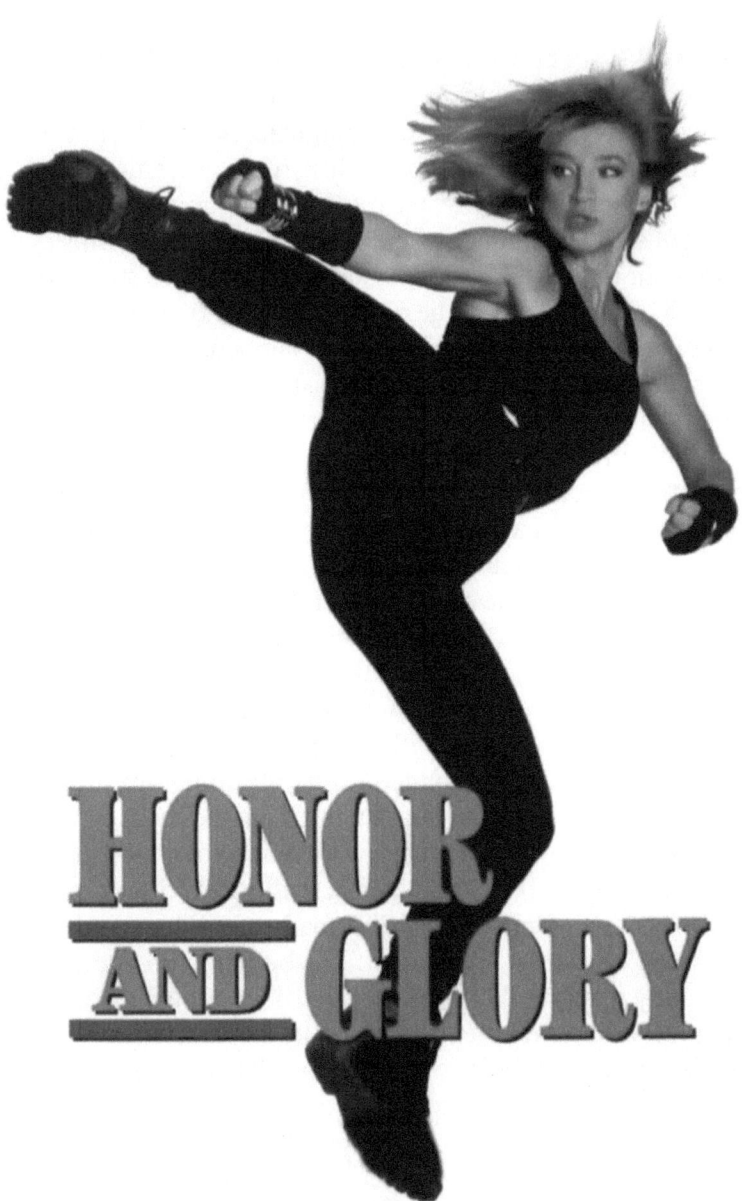

Honor and Glory (1993)
Runtime 84 minutes
Directed by Godfrey Ho

Honor and Glory stars Cynthia Rothrock as FBI agent Tracey working in Hong Kong. She asked to come back to the states by the Feds, and upon her return she reconnects with her sister. Her sister Joyce (played by Donna Miller, Undefeatable (1993)) is a local news reporter who also knows Karate (doesn't everyone in these movies?). She's on the trail of dirt bag banker Jason Slade (played by Jason Miller, who was ALSO in Undefeatable). He's got big muscles, greasy hair and a complete disregard for the law. His new bodyguard Jake (Chuck Jeffreys, Hawkeye (1988)) is starting to suspect his new boss is the dirt bag Joyce warned him about. Slade wants to buy a nuclear device and sell it to some shady Arabs, so it's up to Joyce and Jake to take on Slade. Rothrock pops up here and there, but the movie is really about Jake and Joyce. Also, there's a needless subplot about the father of Joyce & Tracey and how Joyce doesn't like him but he's desperate to reconnect with her.

If you go in expecting a Rothrock fight extravaganza, you will be bummed. She's in the movie, but she's hardly the star despite the fact that she's on the poster of the movie (marketing knew what they were doing there). If you're expecting a Godfrey Ho cheese-fest that barely makes sense, then you will have a great time. True, it isn't as over-the-top and silly as Undefeatable, but really, what movie is? It was great to see so many familiar faces in this flick and it does feature some seriously great fight scenes in-between all the hammy nonsense about Tracey and Joyce's dad. The film also features Robin Shou briefly, who some may recognize from Mortal Kombat (1995), he played Liu Kang. The movie features bad music, bad acting, way over-the-top bad guy moments, Rothrock in a green leather biker jacket, and a final fight in a warehouse full of explosives. Honor and Glory is total cheese, and I had a good time with it. It would make a great double bill with Undefeatable. In many ways it feels like an alternate version of Undefeatable as the locations are all so similar. Similar enough that I kept thinking I had seen this movie before. It's likely they were filmed simultaneously or at the very least back-to-back. It gave me a weird sense of déjà vu. In between all the silliness that is.

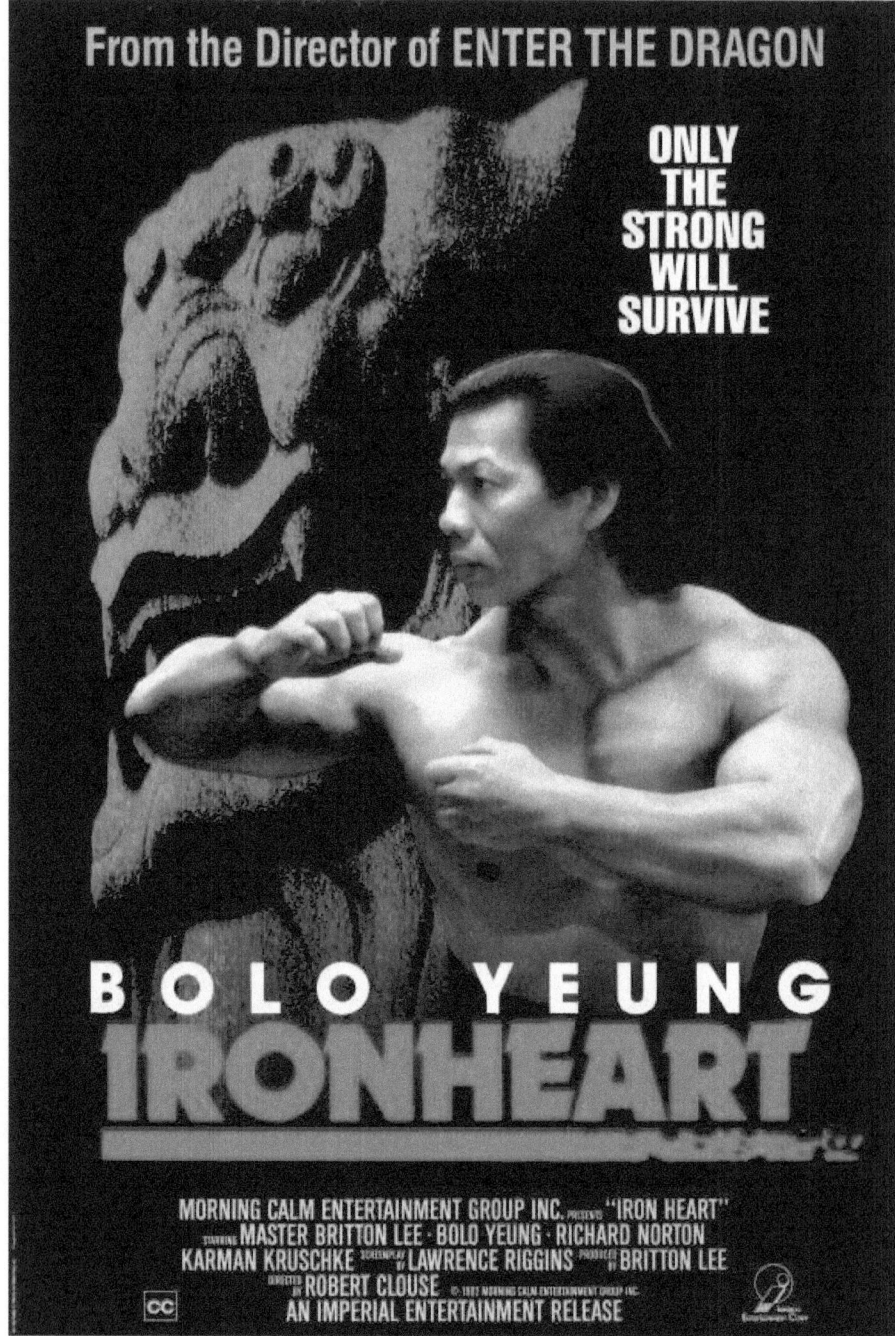

Ironheart (1992)
Directed by Robert Clouse
Runtime 92 minutes

Ironheart opens with an undercover cop trying to infiltrate a human trafficking ring that operates out of a sleazy night club run by Richard Norton. He gets killed in the process so his former partner, who drives a sweet Porsche, travels several hundred miles to the Pacific Northwest to find out what happened. He knows martial arts, of course, and uses a Porsche to do his investigating. What could go wrong? He quickly realizes that dancing plays a prominent role in this crime and so investigates the local club. There he runs afoul of crime boss Richard Norton and his underling, Bolo Yeoung. He meets a dance instructor that who knows a woman that was abducted and also knew the dead partner, so they team up to investigate and get to the bottom of the murder and the disappearances of young dance-loving women.

Sadly, Bolo is not the star of Ironheart despite the cover art. Instead, our hero is Britton K. Lee who only starred in this one movie. While his martial arts skills are impressive, his acting is not. He has almost no charisma, but thankfully the film is not ruined by him. It still features no less than SIX extended scenes of dancing, a grimy club that has chain-link fence, Bolo making a cute cocktail for Richard Norton, a soundtrack FILLED with some rip-off Bobby Brown singer, car explosions, a gang of toughs that take on our hero multiple times and fail each time, did I mention the SWEET ASS PORSCHE? A VW bug gets blown up needlessly after featuring in a very slow chase scene. The fashion is also worth noting because so many people on the dance floor wear parachute pants shamelessly, it's almost inspiring. We also get some vogue-ing. Sadly, Richard Norton never fights in the movie, but his death scene is pretty shocking and fantastic.

Ironheart has the vibe of a vanity project because of how badass our hero is and how all the ladies want to be with him. The plot makes little sense, but it doesn't really need to. Bolo is under-used, but to be fair he always is. The movie delivers plenty of action, dancing, bad fashion, cheesy music, and badly-written dialogue and will certainly be a hit with you and your friends.

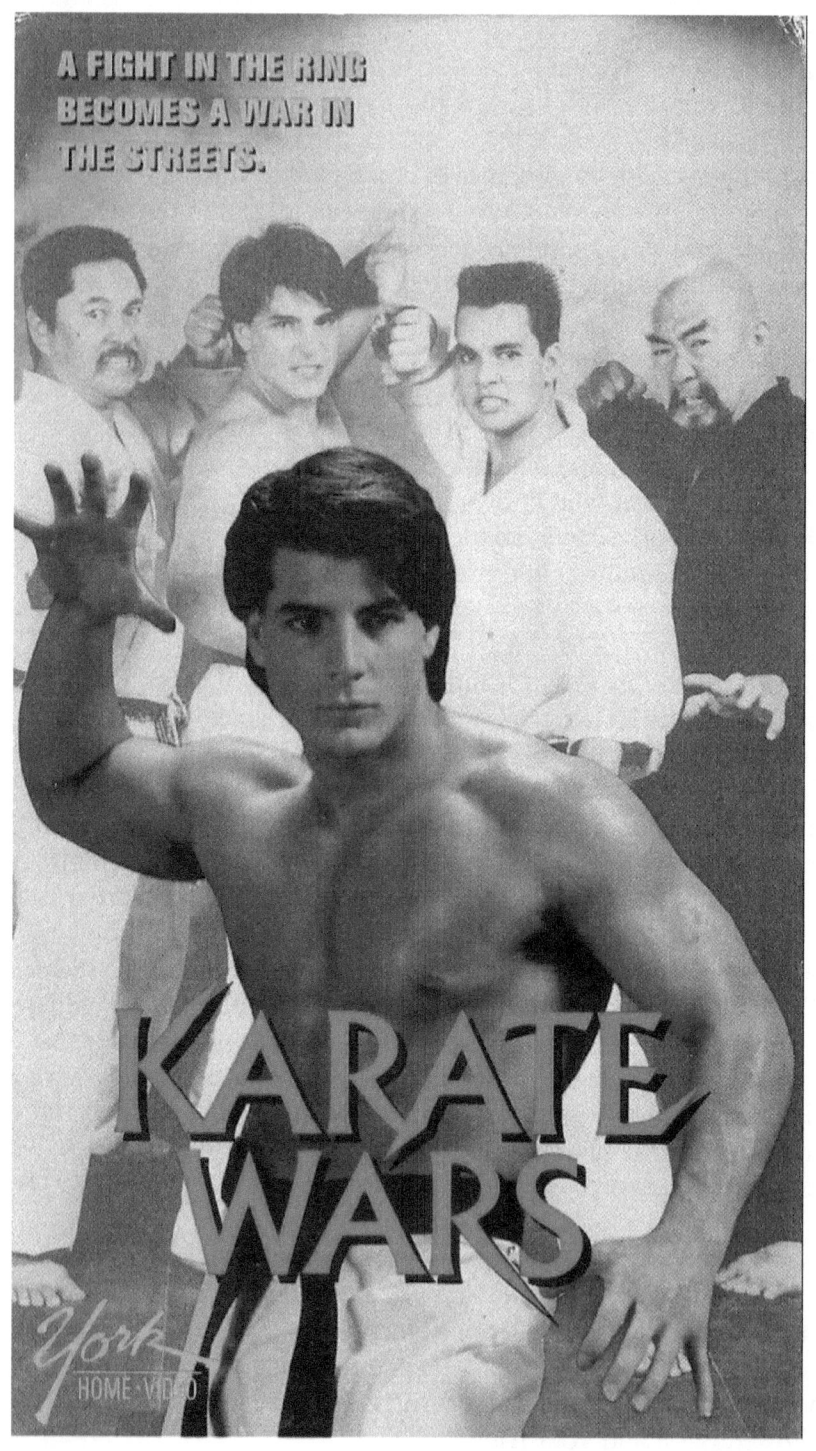

Karate Wars (1991)
Runtime 87 minutes
Directed by David Huey

As a producer running Cine Excel, David Huey released Awful Awesome royalty like Future War (1997) and Pocket Ninjas (1997) and as a director made films like Full Impact (1993) and Capital Punishment (1991). Karate Wars is a film that he directed, produced, and wrote, so with a pedigree like that I had very high expectations. Karate Wars is about a Karate tournament called…Karate Wars (didn't see that one coming, eh?). One year at this tournament a master of Karate, Oyama, fought and actually killed a dude in the ring (this dude's hardcore). Ever since, he's never been the same. He drinks a lot and teaches Karate at a local high school. His former star pupil gets in trouble and is "punished" by being forced to take Oyama's Karate class. The two butt heads. His pupil, Jason, is mad at Oyama for being such a drunken loser and Oyama is mad at Jason because he quit years before. A rivalry between Oyama's students and the evil Nakaso (Gerald Okamura) ensues after some scuffles. Jason is back into Karate and now he wants to show Nakaso that he and Oyama are true Karate warriors by accepting a challenge to enter Karate Wars once again.

As I expected, Karate Wars is super threadbare. Every location feels burned out and dirty, characters dress in dumpy old clothes and everyone drives beaters. Oyama is a broad stereotype, clearly trying to ape Mr. Miyagi from The Karate Kid. Jason is a handsome muscular beefcake that spends much of the movie with a chip on his shoulder. There are many attempts at humor throughout the film that only elicited groans from me. The movie is primarily focused on the relationship between Jason and Oyama and unfortunately not on sweet fight scenes. This drags the film down tremendously because as an audience member, I don't really care. Gerald Okamura is a welcome diversion, but he doesn't get enough screen time to save the movie from itself. The finale of the film features some brutal bloody fighting but it was too little too late. The focus on the melodrama between the two male leads was attempting to mimic The Karate Kid but the writing isn't there and frankly, neither is the acting. It wasn't a complete waste of time, but it isn't worth recommending either.

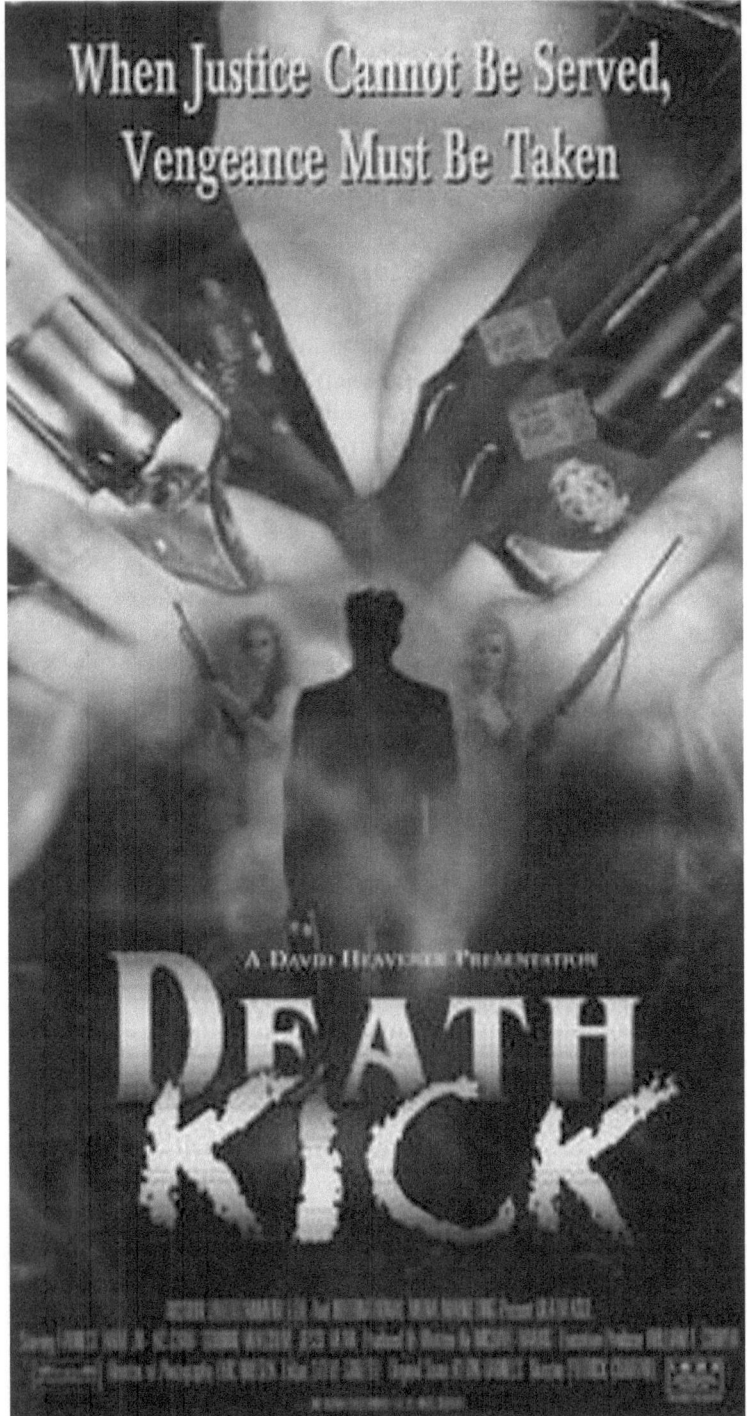

Kick to Death: Death Kick (1998)
Runtime 86 minutes
Directed by William Patrick Crabtree

Kick to Death: Death Kick is about a group of angry individuals who are plotting a nefarious kidnapping and murder in the back of a dirty tile store (off to a pretty greasy start). The group feels that their lawyer did them wrong and they want sweet revenge. They plan to kidnap him and then pay people to beat him up one at a time. Apparently, they don't want to sully their own hands but rather want to hire professional fighters to attack him, Mortal Kombat style. They kidnap the lawyer and subject him to beatings, but there was one thing they didn't count on: this lawyer can fight. Sort of.
A professional fighter gets top billing in the movie but he's only in it for about 5 minutes and has one line of dialogue. Our actual hero is an older fella who clearly does not know how to fight in real life. He's just a dad-type guy, complete with neatly trimmed mustache who throws haymakers throughout the whole movie and somehow defeats all of the professional fighters with his sloppy and telegraphed moves. Every female character (sans two fighters) wants to have sex with our hero and shows their boobs to him. It's really weird and awkward. What's even more strange is how formulaic it is. They come on to him, show him their boobs, and then unleash their fighter on him just when he thinks he's going to get laid. In one scene there's even a close up of mammaries while they jiggle and thrust. It's super strange. The fighting is very sloppy and never convincing. The acting is actually pretty solid for a super low-budget flick like this, in particular the villains have a lot of fun chewing the scenery. The music consists of a bevy of hot licks which never match the mood of the scene, which only adds to the fun. Beware though: this movie is filled with dull monologues. Even at under 90 minutes it can be a bit of a slog because of the reams of overwritten dialogue the characters have to get through before the action (such as it is) gets started.

I enjoyed it more than my friends because of how bizarrely the plot plays out, and how the writer/actor/producer just wanted to get as many pairs as possible of boobs in his face during the making of his movie. It's trashy, sleazy, strange, and unique, and for that I'd say it's worth a watch.

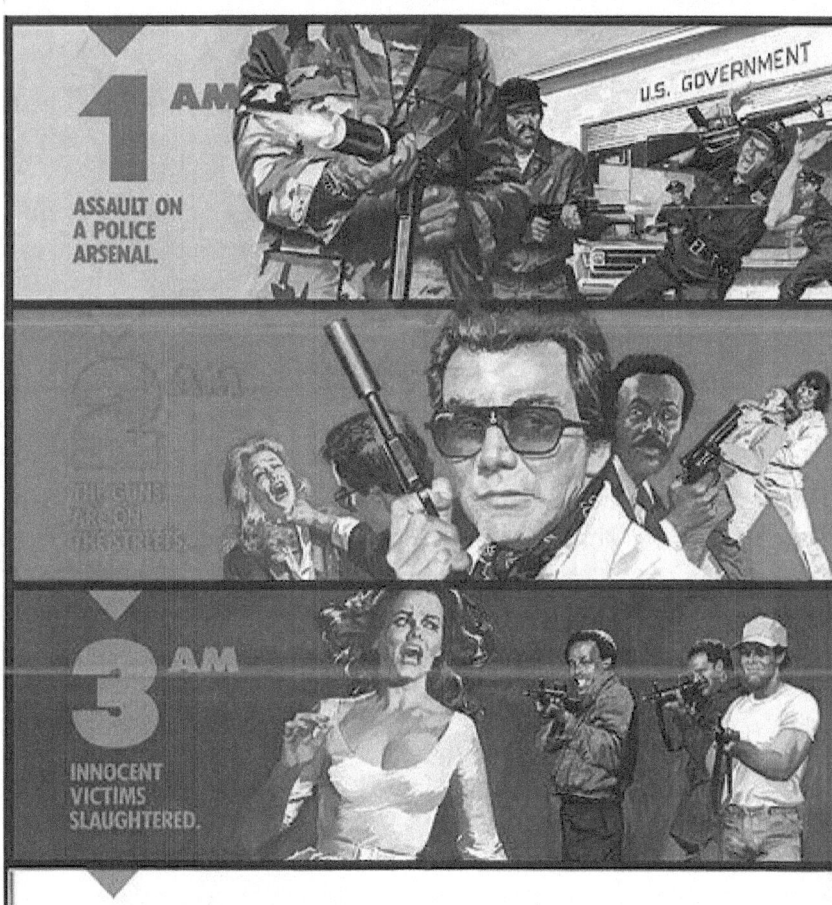

Killpoint (1984)
Runtime 90 minutes
Directed by Frank Harris

After having lots of fun watching director Frank Harris' film Low Blow (1986), starring Leo Fong, I was hungry for more! Low Blow managed to be nonsensical, inept, but infused with lots of action so the film never became dull. Leo Fong was about as charismatic as a block of wood, but it only added to the fun.

Killpoint begins with a violent raid on a military base and the robbery of several machine guns. A guard is blown through a glass window, it's pretty nuts and silly. This sets the hyperviolent tone for the rest of the movie. Soon those pilfered machine guns make their way to the streets and into the hands of violent criminals. Lt. Long (Fong) is given the case to track down the arms dealers before the criminals take over. His search leads him to Nighthawk and Joe Marks (Cameron Mitchell), a man who refuses to stand, take off his sunglasses, or stop playing with his black teacup poodle. He also has no patience for ladies and kills any that annoy him. Lt. Long decides to go into deep cover as a buyer looking for some big guns in order to trap Marks and bring him to sweet justice. His pursuit leads him to shady bars, a very low-rent (and real) strip club, and inexplicably a Karate tournament until a final showdown between the cops and the bad guys.

It's hard for me to say whether or not Killpoint is more fun than Low Blow. Both feature Cameron Mitchell in bizarre roles well-suited for his abilities, both feature Leo Fong, though Killpoint has him sporting an awful Prince Valiant haircut that never gets old, and both have some over-the-top action... but Killpoint likely has more action. The film never has a chance to get dull because Harris wisely pumped the film full of what everyone came for: violence. In fact, some of the violence comes out of nowhere, with characters unexpectedly dying left and right. There were many scenes that had my friends and I rolling with laughter, and we found that the film was very easy to comment on. Low Blow's reputation as an Awful Awesome flick has grown considerably. Fans would do well to check out this earlier, and possibly better, effort from Frank Harris and Leo Fong.

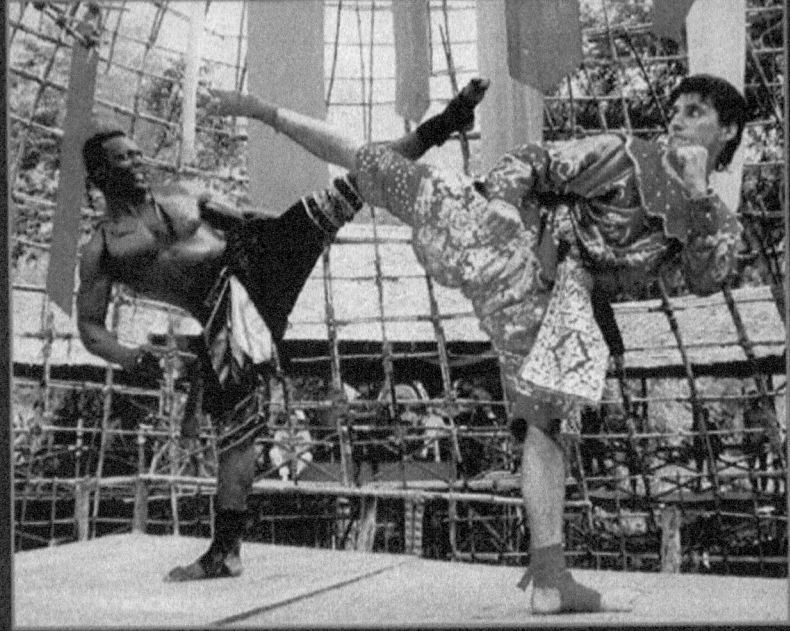

The King of the Kickboxers (1990)
Runtime 99 minutes
Directed by Lucas Lowe

Loren Avedon plays Jake Donahue, who as a child witnessed the murder of his kickboxing champion older brother at the hands of Khan (Billy Blanks) in Thailand. He returns to the states and grows up to become a martial artist as well, but instead of competing he uses his skills to bust bad guys as an undercover cop (hell yeah!). He's a loose cannon but he gets the job done. When he's offered the opportunity to go to Thailand to try to infiltrate a film production company that hires American fighters to star in their films, he jumps on the opportunity. The illegal part of the story is that the movies are just bait to convince the fighters to show up to the set where they unleash Khan to kill them for real. Jake's job is to be a brash loudmouth to attract the attention of the snuff film makers, so he'll be invited to an "audition." He accomplishes the mission, but he is no way prepared to survive Khan and avenge his brother. He must first go to the country and train with a master who almost defeated the unstoppable Khan once. The film continues as you might expect with lots of training culminating in a final fight with Khan.
The King of the Kickboxers lives up to the hype. It really is a lot of fun. Fights are injected routinely throughout the film's runtime in order to keep the audience entertained. Avedon plays a cocky American jerk very well and inexplicably Billy Blanks sounds like a caveman when he talks (I'm not complaining). Thankfully the film's love interest sub-plot is barely there and literally only serves to shoehorn some nudity and sex into the movie (it's almost obligatory). The training sequences are memorable, ridiculous, and a lot of fun. The fights are furious, fast, and brutal and the kills are shockingly graphic.

The King of the Kickboxers is legitimately solid rather than threadbare and low-rent. It does feature some period-era fashion faux pas and general silliness associated with the time and place the film was made, but it isn't poorly made. This would appeal to fans of Canon films craziness like Revenge of the Ninja (1983).

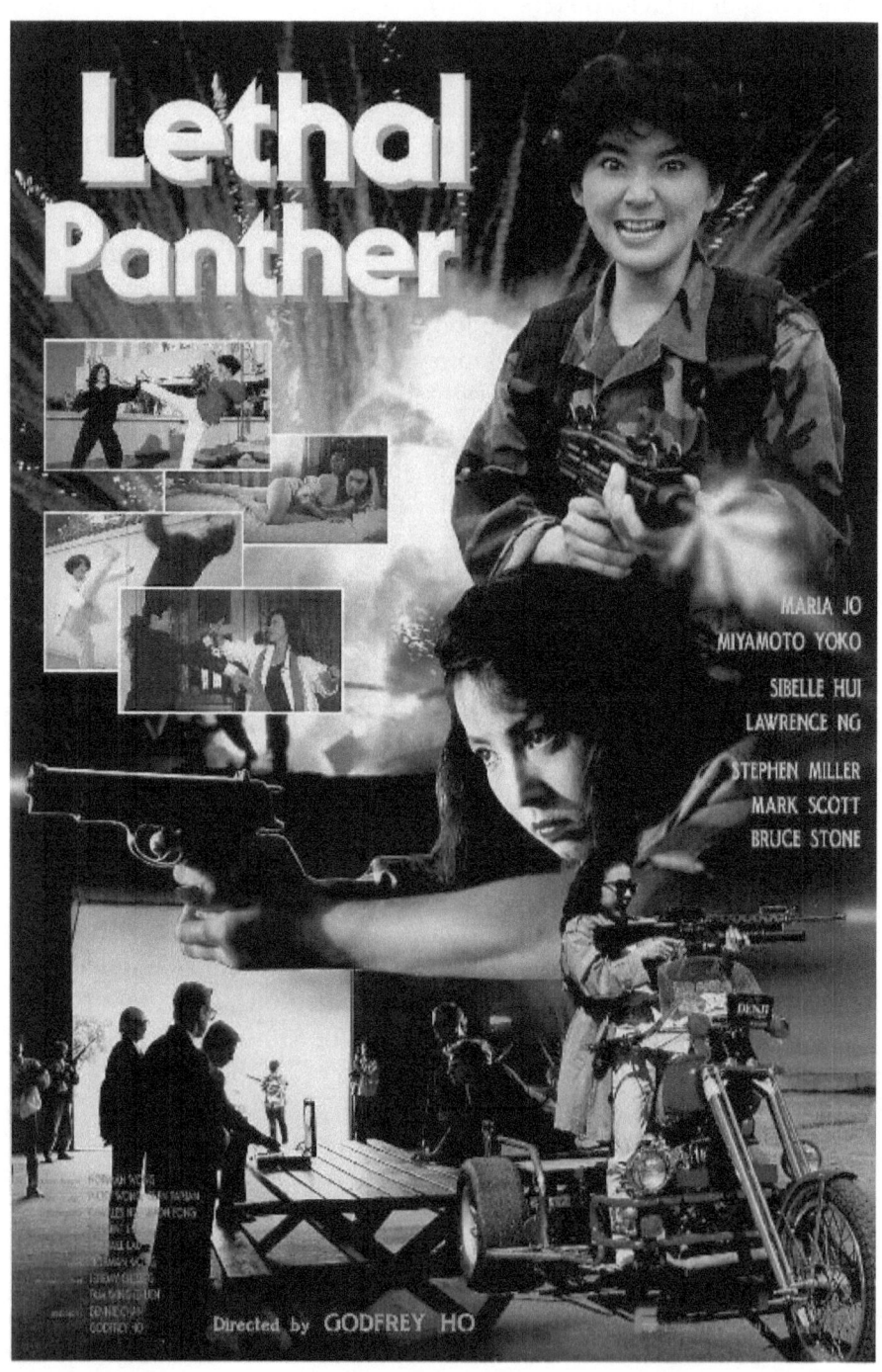

Lethal Panther (1991)
Runtime 90 minutes
Directed by Godfrey Ho

Lethal Panther begins with an illicit deal involving counterfeit $100 bills. The deal is busted by a very plucky female C.I.A. agent with some serious martial arts skills. The film then cuts to a female assassin carrying out her grim assignment. The movie follows her for a while until one of her assignments is interrupted by yet another female assassin. The two square off frequently throughout the film and the plucky C.I.A. agent pops up to talk about trying to bust them. Eventually they all end up pals in a house owned by a prostitute. There they have their final stand, the three of them versus some bad dudes and the boyfriend of one of the girls who is also an assassin.

Lethal Panther is a blast to watch. This is Godfrey Ho's attempt to crib John Woo's heroic bloodshed films and though he comes nowhere near those films in terms of storytelling or a sense of "cool", he got one thing right: the bloodshed. Everyone dies spectacularly in this film with big bloody squibs and dramatic slow motion. The movie keeps throwing new characters into the mix, but they're there just to get shot by someone else. I couldn't make heads or tails of the film as a whole, though individual scenes made sense. Those individual scenes didn't seem to work together to form a cohesive story. At times the film felt like a parody of Woo but it's far too straight-faced for that to be true. It's an honest attempt at copying his style that falls flat on its face.

Unfortunately, there are sexual assaults in the film as well as physical abuse on female cast members so if you're sensitive to that kind of material (and who could blame you?) I would suggest caution with this flick. I found myself just fast forwarding through the rough material in the movie since it feels out of place and brings down the fun factor considerably. If you can get past (or just fast forward through) the nasty bits in the movie, Lethal Panther is an action-packed, confusing, and super cheesy flick. If you're looking for some bonkers Hong Kong action with a heavy dose of inept storytelling, Lethal Panther is your jam.

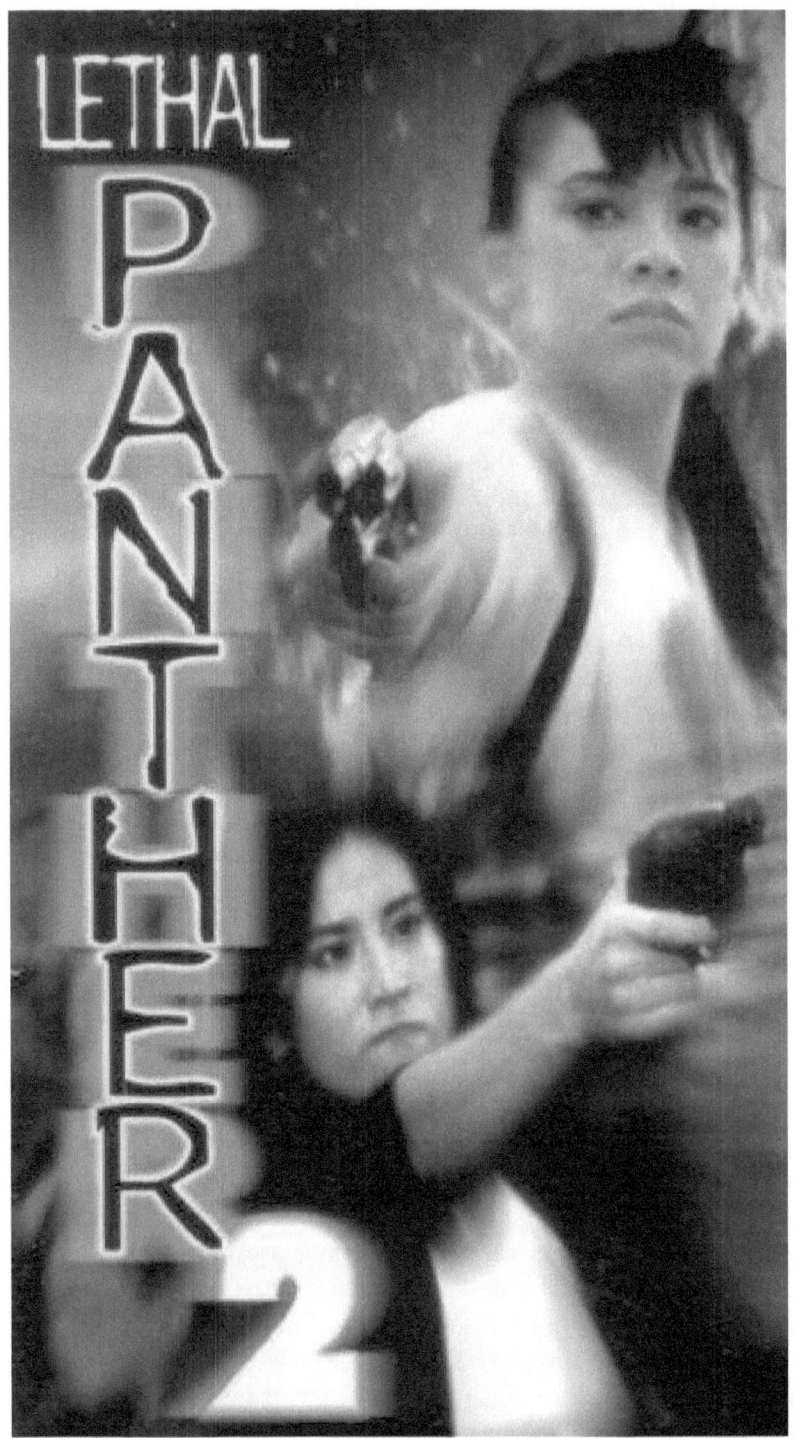

Lethal Panther 2 (1993)
Runtime 84 minutes
Directed by Cindy Chow

Lethal Panther 2 begins with a fantastic shootout involving goons vs. cops. They all have machine guns and there's thousands of rounds fired in the first few minutes. We are also treated to some hand-to-hand combat and some silly wire-fu. I have no idea why they are shooting at each other and really, we never find out. The film pivots to the main story of the film after this very fun action sequence. We meet a tough as nails cop who doesn't play by the rules. He's a loose cannon but he gets the job done. And by job, I mean shooting bad guys. His family was murdered by criminals (ala Punisher) and so now he uses his badge to kill as many as he can. His partner's wife is murdered, and the pair decide to take out the bad guy trash. During their shootout they meet a young woman who is being pursued by another bad dude and they decide to protect her. As it turns out a well-connected criminal organization based in Japan now has it in for our hero after he kills some of their men. The only way to defeat the gang is to take them out, all of them!

As you can imagine Lethal Panther 2 is chock-full of action sequences. This film was made during the heroic bloodshed era of Hong Kong cinema and the film makers had to go to extremes in order to keep up. We get lots of shootouts, car chases, crashes, impressive stunts involving mysteriously-suspended black wires that allow the heroes to slide down while firing machine guns. Seriously, it happens at least three times in the movie. Thankfully the dialogue is kept to a minimum in favor of injecting more overwhelming action. The short runtime of the film helps to keep things moving as well. The scant dialogue scenes are there to loosely string together the violence. Speaking of the violence, it's slopping, over-the-top, graphic, and at times very funny. I would recommend Lethal Panther 2 to fans of the cinema of Arizal, though of course no one tops Arizal at his most over-the-top-insane. Lethal Panther 2, however is in the same ballpark. Or maybe it's in the minor leagues. I'm not sure about baseball metaphors. If you like ultra-violence on the cheap and don't mind a somewhat confusing plot (this isn't a Godfrey Ho movie, so it's mostly coherent), check out Lethal Panther 2.

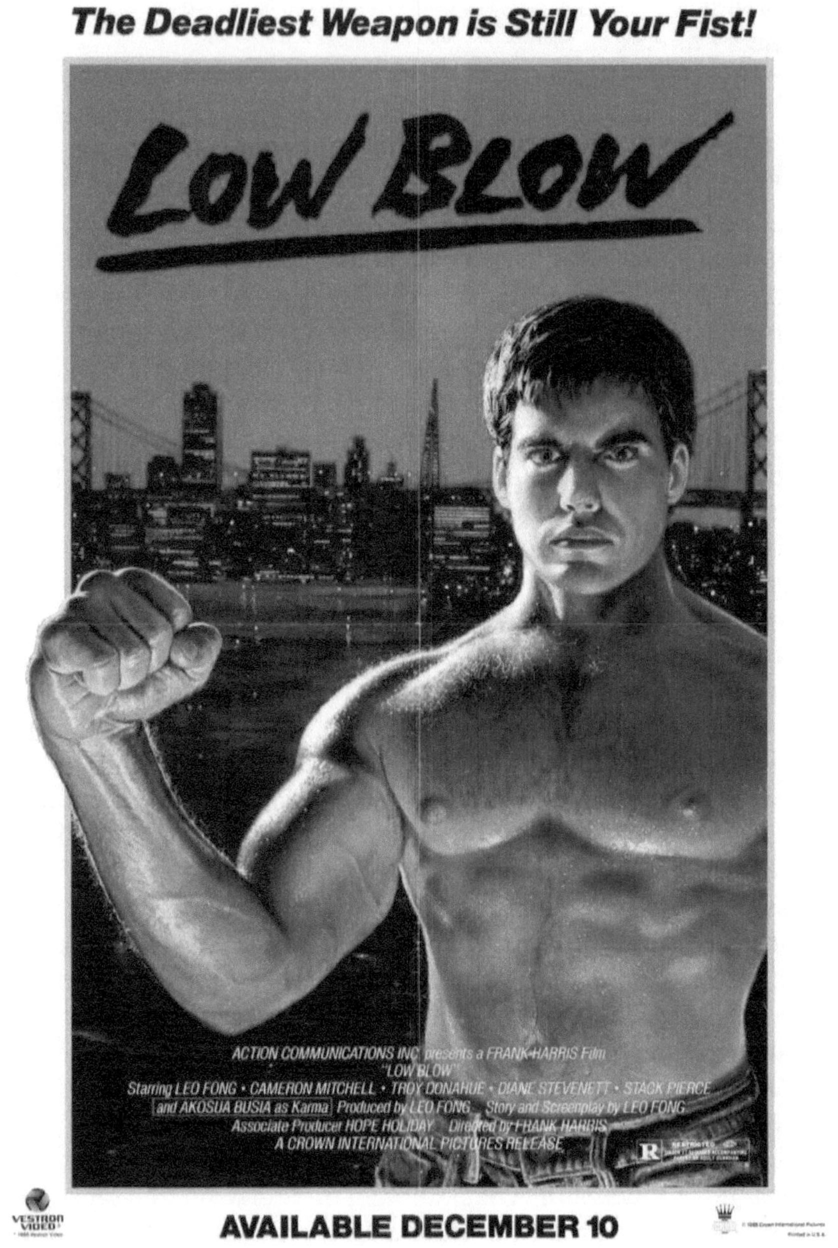

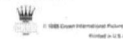

Low Blow (1986)
Runtime 83 minutes
Directed by Frank Harris

Low Blow stars Leo Fong as John Chan (sometimes Jack, sometimes Joe). He's a slovenly private eye with a hatred for his car. He smashes and crashes the thing every chance he gets. The fact that the car is a hunk of junk is a running gag in the movie and one that I can appreciate having been the owner of several lemons in my life. He's always ready to smash heads and does so frequently. He's hired by a rich guy (Troy Donahue) to track down his daughter who has joined a cult (how typical). The cult is headed by Yarakunda (Cameron Mitchell), and the cult members have to relinquish all their worldly goods and live a very dilapidated farm (kinda like a discount Manson). They spend their days hoeing dirt and listening to Yarakunda ramble while sitting in a ratty recliner. Chan decides the best way to get the daughter back is by gathering a rag-tag group of tough guys to raid the compound and take her back by force (hell yeah!). He recruits his force by digging a big pit and holds a fighting competition with no rules. The winners get to accompany Chan in his totally illegal attack (that's a helluva motivation... I guess?). Chan even advertises this highly illegal fighting competition in the local newspaper and somehow the police take no action. Incredible.

Low Blow is a lot of fun. The action is nearly non-stop and so is the overwhelming soundtrack. The entire movie is scored with bombastic keyboards, electric drums, and a seemingly non-stop guitar solo. This movie has more hot licks than a cinnamon lollipop factory. Leo Fong is indeed without charisma, but he isn't without charm. His delivery is so quiet and so nonchalant that it's hard to dislike him. It's like he's mentally shrugging his shoulders and saying meh, throughout the entire movie. Except when he's fighting, then he's all business and can sell the fights well. Cameron Mitchell spends the whole movie wearing black sunglasses and a black hoodie like he was the Unabomber, and he sits the entire movie. This bizarre and largely incoherent performance was also a pleasure to watch. Billy Blanks pops up in his first film role playing one of the cult member enforcers as well. Low Blow has lots of action, an overwhelming soundtrack, cheesy performances, a short runtime, and a simple plot. This one is highly recommended.

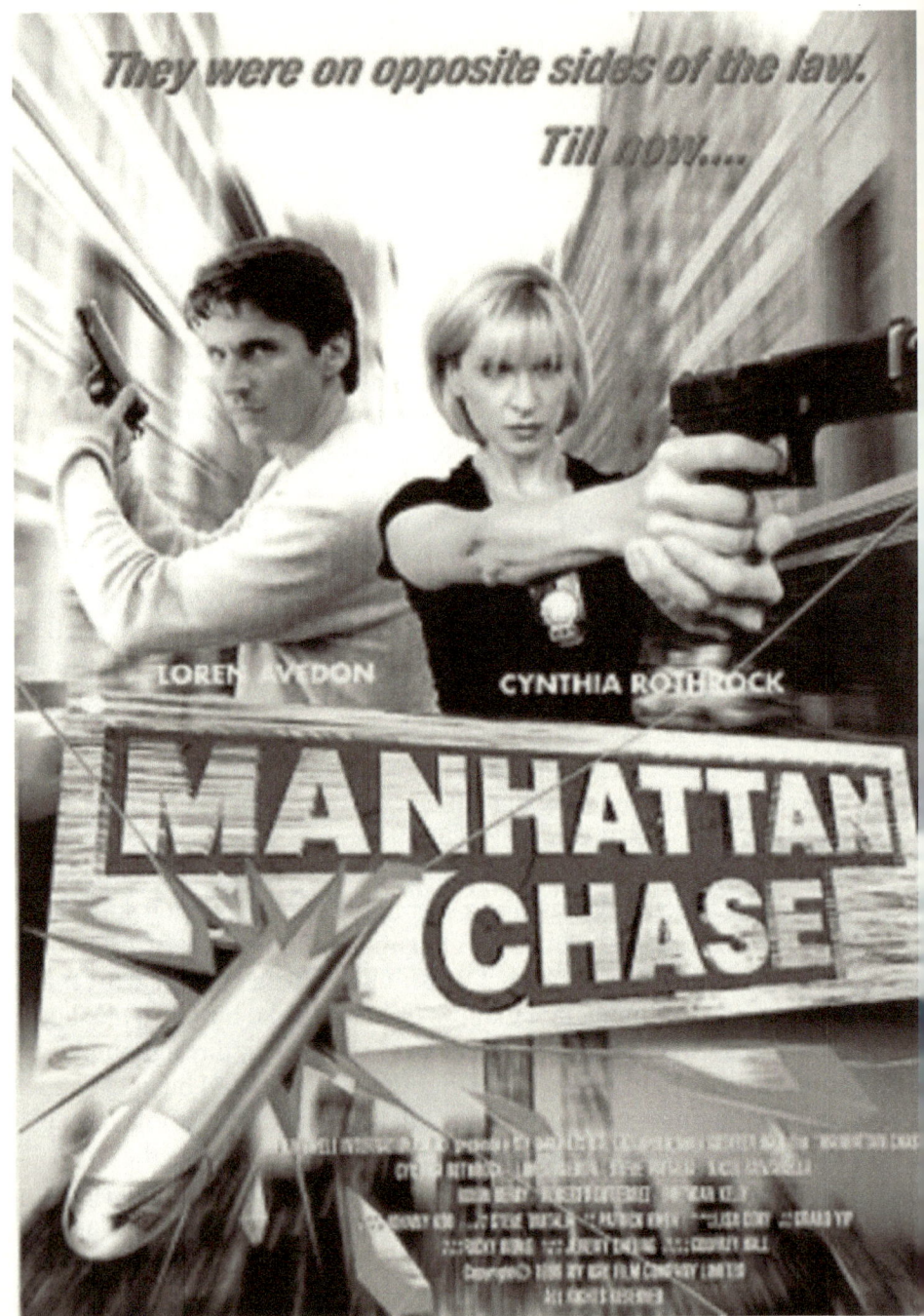

Manhattan Chase (2000)
Runtime 90 minutes
Directed by Godfrey Ho

Cynthia Rothrock plays a badass police detective (doesn't she always?) who enjoys beating up bad guys and cleaning up her city. Her sister is in town in the hopes of reconnecting with her ex-husband (Loren Avedon) who just got out of prison. The two of them have a son who has been living with Avedon's sister while he was in the cooler. Avedon runs into a girl in trouble who needs help. She stole some drugs from her stepdad who is connected to a major drug cartel. Her whole family was murdered because of the missing drugs and now she's on the run (wow, THAT escalated quickly). Avedon has to keep his nose clean, but he helps her anyway. He has to protect his son while getting to know him again, help the girl in trouble, all without his wife's sister (Rothrock) finding out. It's a complicated plot but thankfully Ho shoehorns in lots of opportunities for fights, many of which have no bearing on the plot. Manhattan Chase looks like it was filmed in the 80's. In fact, I assumed it was, or at least an early 90's flick. Ho directed films for decades, so it makes sense that he stuck to what he knew when it came to the technical end of thinks utilizing cameras and film stock, he was familiar with. The story itself is very similar in tone and action to films made a decade earlier too. There is a heaping helping of melodrama in this film however but don't worry, it's mostly poorly-written and so it garners as much fun as the fight scenes do. The action in the film is pretty solid, with some great fight scenes throughout the entire movie and some dudes pulling martial arts moves that clearly had never done them before. The movie also features some sleaze, most notably an extended sex scene with one of the bad dudes. It feels like it goes on forever and feels very awkward. Also, the actress involved likely has a malpractice case against her plastic surgeon: her implants look live nerf balls under her skin (eeeeewwwwww). I won't say that Manhattan Chase is a perfect film, but there's enough cheese on display to make it a fun watch with friends. I will warn you though, the beginning is rough and ugly. The violence isn't particularly fun and could sour a fun movie night quickly. After you get over that hump however the rest of the movie more than makes up for it.

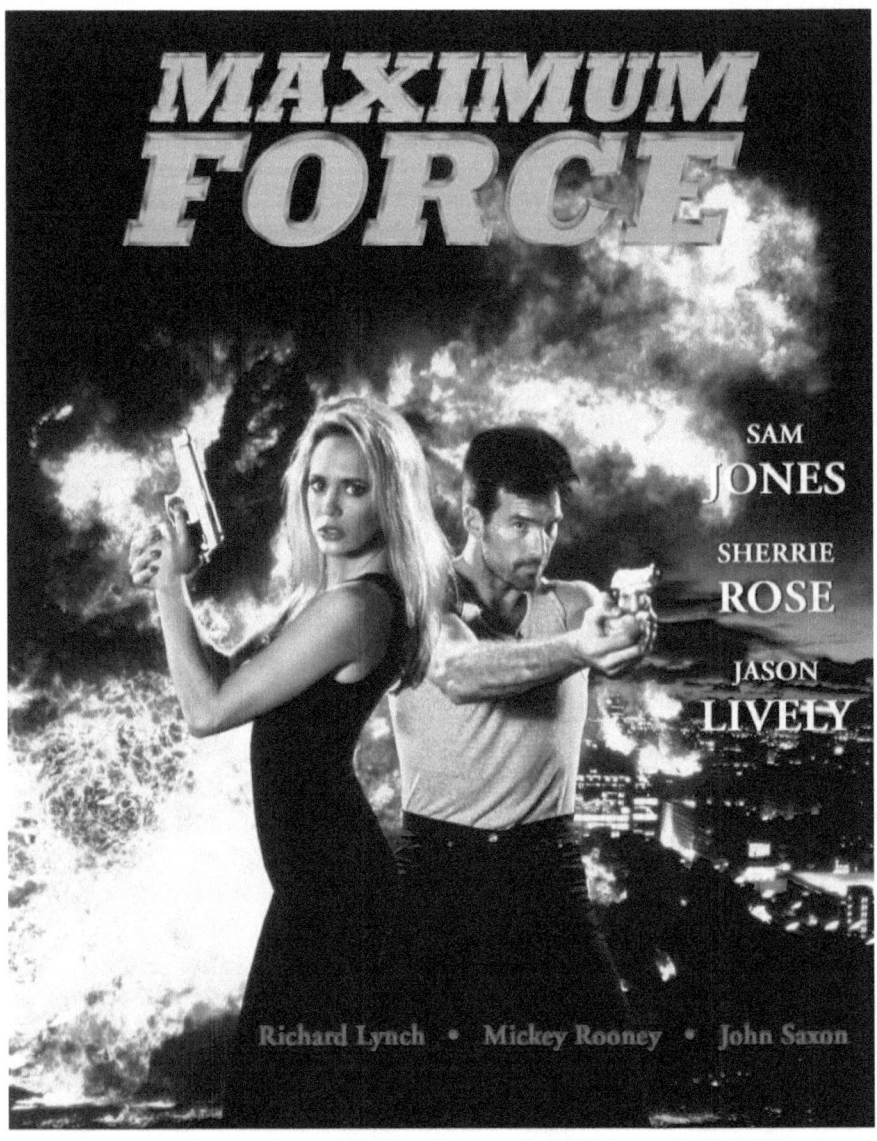

Maximum Force (1992)
Runtime: 90 minutes
Directed by Joseph Merhi

Maximum Force is about a city under siege, crime is organized and ubiquitous. The man who united the gangsters and organized all crime is Tanabe, played by Richard Lynch (with a vaguely German accent despite Tanabe being a Japanese name). Enter our heroes, three misfits from the police department that don't play well with others (except MAYBE each other?). They're all loose cannons, but they get the job done. They're recruited by Captain Fuller (John Saxon) to hang out in a dusty warehouse and train together to take Tanabe out in a clandestine operation. The misfits, played by Sam Jones, Sherrie Rose, and Jason Lively, work on their individual skills in the nasty warehouse. Jones, smokes cigarettes and punches things, Sherrie does yoga, and Lively plays with toys. Perfect. Together they hustle the streets looking for a hole in Tanabe's armor so they can bring him to justice. This being a PM movie that involves fighting, shooting, and a few explosions.

I'm sorry to say that Maximum Force is a lesser PM Entertainment movie. Sure, it's got lots of recognizable actors but aside from Sam Jones, they don't do anything but talk. A lot. In fact, this movie is far too talky. I expect a PM movie to be wall to wall action and this one is not. This was made when they were still trying to make "good" movies instead of awesome ones. The lighting is dramatic and monochrome with big splashes of red, blue and green everywhere. Nearly all the shots are underlit and shadowy, which looks pretty cool but a classic noir this movie isn't. The characters are dull with the exception of Jones. He's basically playing the Punisher with his black hair, stubble, and love of violence. He also smokes like a coal train, which becomes a joke quickly because of how over-the-top it is. We do get some great explosions but for a PM movie, it's pretty slim. There are some shootouts and fights but again, they are mostly bookended in this flick which is a bummer. Maximum Force has all the elements of a good PM Entertainment movie except the vital one: the action. If you want to watch a fun action flick from them, dig into their releases from the following year. They've got a bevy of great flicks to watch with friends but honestly, this isn't one of them.

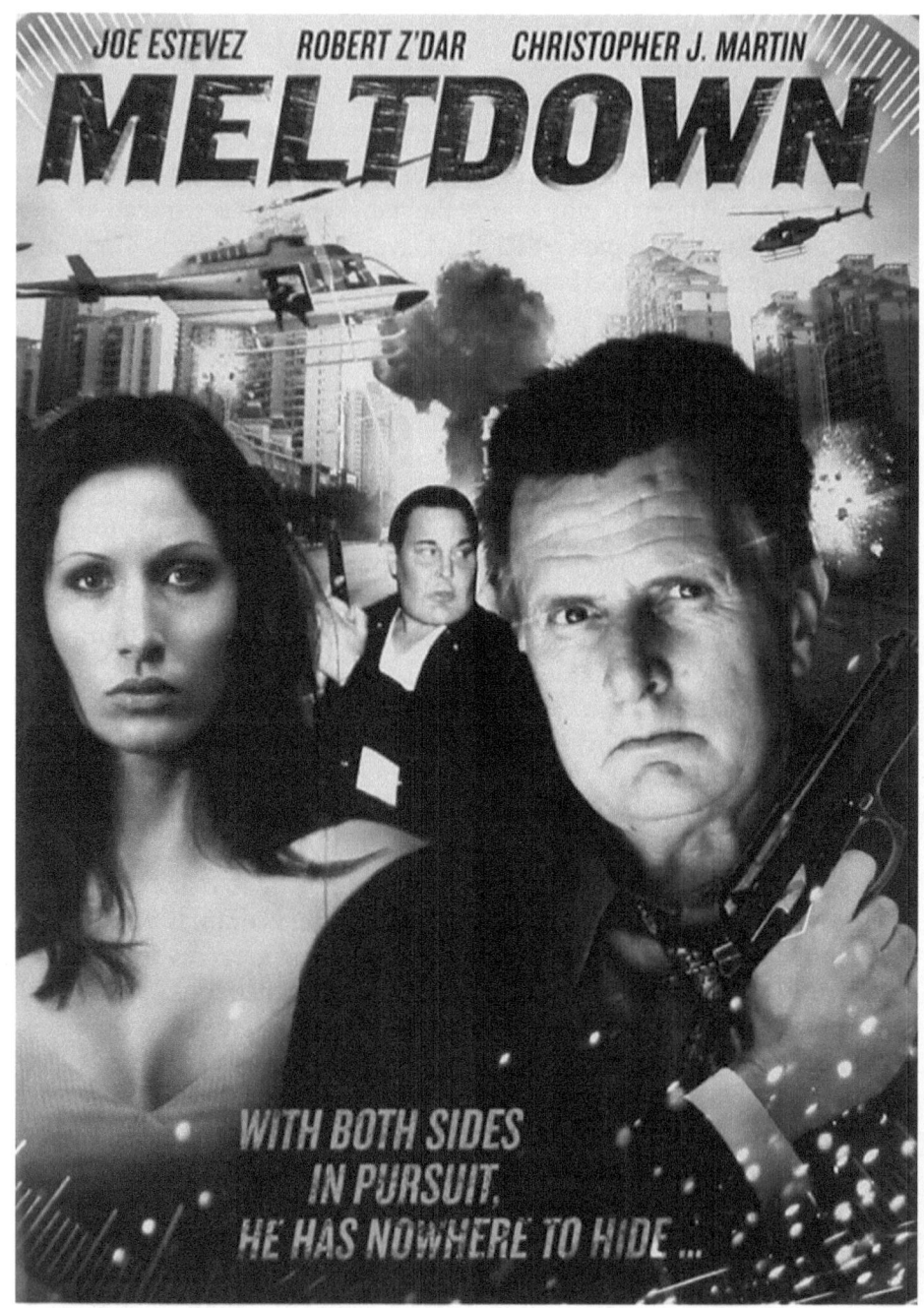

Meltdown (2009)
Runtime: 90 minutes
Directed by Christopher Jon Martin

Meltdown is about an FBI agent (Christopher Martin) who is tasked with infiltrating a dangerous criminal gang and gaining valuable intel in order to bring them all the way down. Robert Z'dar plays the gang's leader and Joe Estevez is a bureaucratic FBI agent who spends much of the movie strutting and exclaiming. Our hero FBI agent has bleached blonde hair cut into a facsimile of a Prince Valiant hairdon't and loves to wear trashy body-builder shirts (made by Hot Bodz. Look them up, their website is hilarious). During his first criminal activity with the gang, the agent murders an innocent citizen, but no disciplinary action is taken because the FBI is apparently cool with it. He meets a sexy agent, and the two-start dating. The gang finds out and realizes our hero is a mole and now he's on the run from the gang, but the feds won't back him up because they don't like him much either. Meltdown is exactly what I was hoping it would be: a glittery body-building t-shirt filled with fun. Robert Z'dar is just as fun as any of his other classic performances as he bellows and whispers his lines and puts his special stank on the dialogue. At one point he sings and plays a piano while two bored women sit on the top of the piano. He chomps cigars and kills people right and left. There's an FBI head honcho that loves wearing red sportscoats (who wears a red one other than the devil and pimps?) and he seems to be trying to out-act Estevez throughout the whole film. This leads to some tremendously hyperbolic performances that are also very fun. Our hero is so goofy-looking, his clothes so ridiculous, and his "fighting" so weak that I'm genuinely bummed that this is his sole credit as actor/producer/director/writer/composer. Seriously, he changes clothes more often than a pop diva. Throughout the film characters have ENORMOUS squib packs under their shirts and as they explode, we can often see the duct tape that was used to hold it in place. Priceless.

 The film continuously feels like it's just about to end but it doesn't. That sense of an over-extended plot is usually the death knell for films, high and low budget alike, but here I couldn't wait to see what ridiculous situation, line of dialogue, or cheap action we were going to get next. I loved Meltdown.

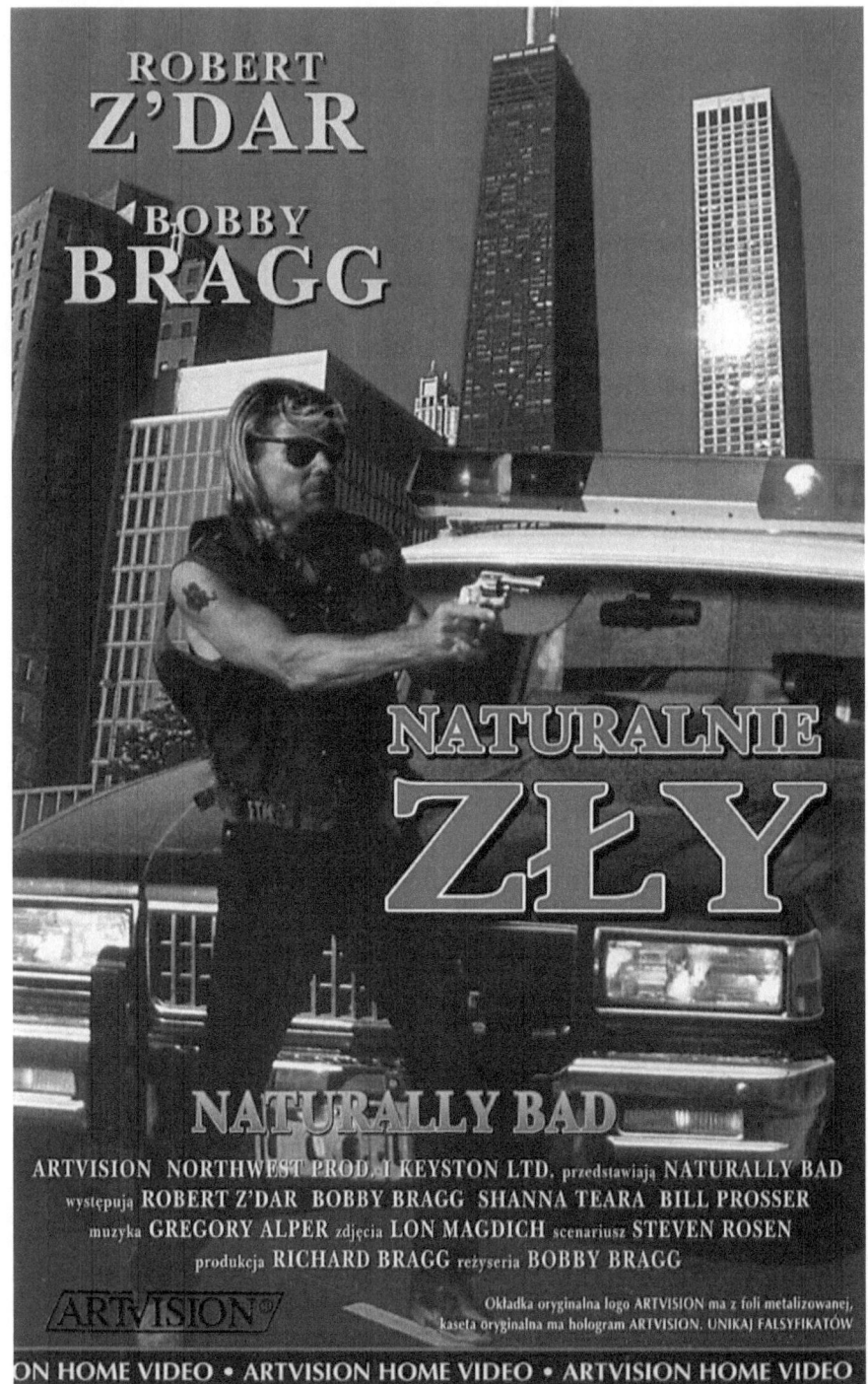

Naturally Bad (1995)
Runtime 82 minutes
Directed by Bob Bragg

Naturally Bad is about a very bad gang that hangs out in the hills near a small town. They're ruthless, dirty, and waiting around for a shipment of drugs to distribute. The drug boss (Robert Z'dar) swears they'll get their merch soon and all they have to do is sit tight. The leader of the gang Billy Slayer (Bob Bragg, director/writer of the film) is a nasty piece of work and hates waiting. He's abusive to his girl, and to his subordinates and we're supposed to hate his guts (mission accomplished I guess). Enter Saundra, a botanist who scores a research project based on the same mountain in which our bad dudes reside. Of course, she runs afoul of the bad guys, who attempt to rape her. She's able to escape to a local dive bar, where she calls her beefcake brother for help. Unfortunately, the gang finds and kidnaps her, so it's up to the brother to come save her from the ruthless miscreants (and kick the requisite amount of ass, of course). First off, let me say that Z'dar's turn in the film is both memorable and all too short. We meet him on a yacht partying with some sleazy ladies. He's snorting cocaine off of their exposed nudity and he looks sweaty and bloated. His performance is full tilt Z'dar and I loved it. But he's only in the movie for about five minutes, and the rest of the time we're hanging out with Billy Slayer and his band of goons.

The vengeance aspect of the film doesn't happen until the very end, which makes the movie's pace a little slow. We get lots of random fights and some shootouts as well as some very weak car chases and crashes, but the film never feels like it's going anywhere. It's shot in the woods with lots of smelly looking men getting in fights, but the film severely lacks focus and momentum. I was baffled by what was going on throughout much of the movie which did make it fun to watch. There's plenty of hammy acting moments, sloppy action, and of course Z'dar. I won't say this one is a must-see but if you have a chance, you'll have a good time with your friends.

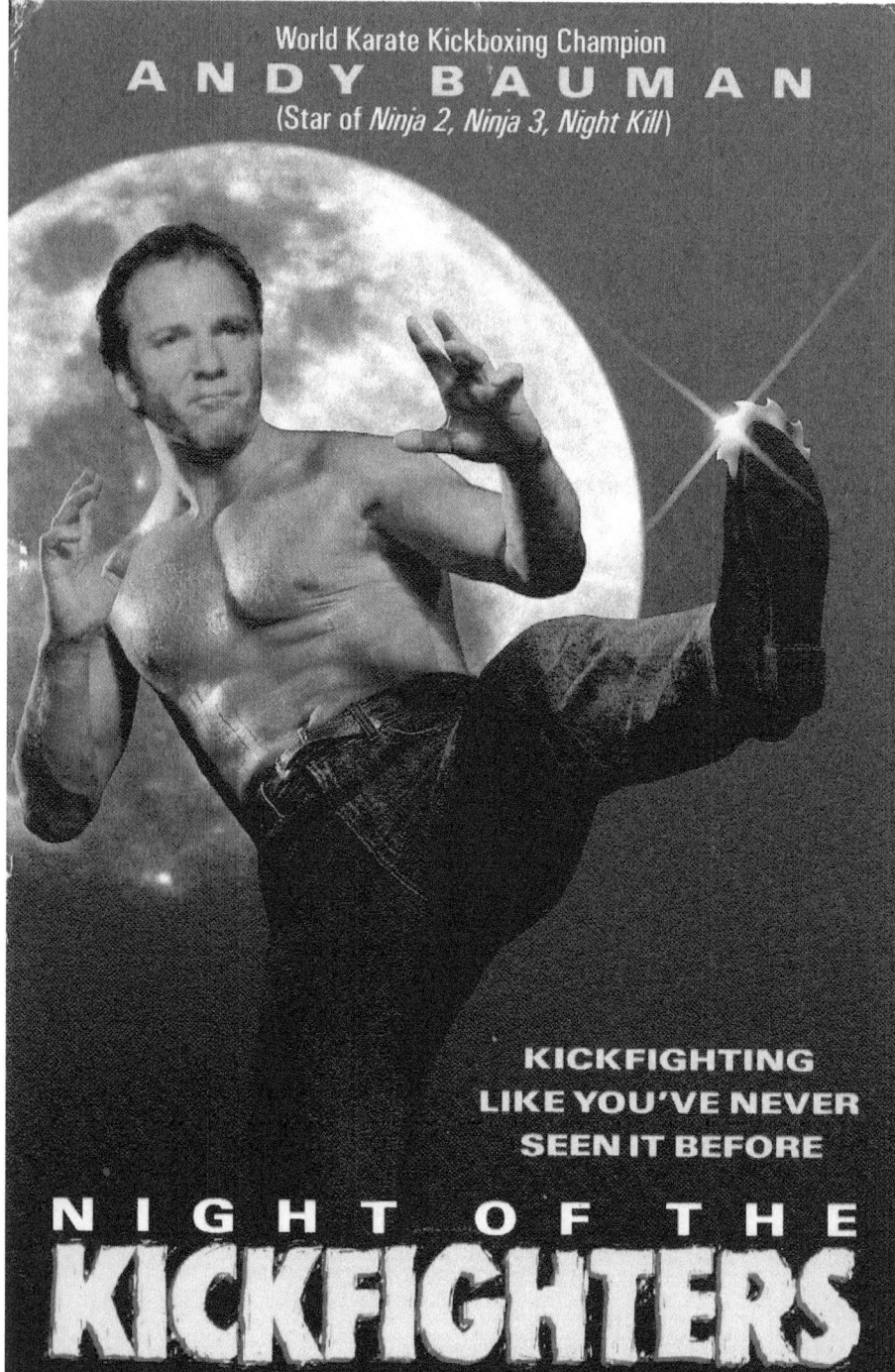

Night of the Kickfighters (1988)
Runtime 88 minutes
Directed by Buddy Reyes

Night of the Kickfighters is about Brett Cady (Andy Bauman), a James Bond-esque man of intrigue and ass-kickery. He's hired to track down and reclaim the kidnapped daughter of Carl McMann (Adam West). McMann has invented a holographic intelligent laser that can blow up anything but "knows" to not shoot "good guys". The gun scans the eyes of potential enemies and if the eyes check out as an ally, the laser beam stops mid-air. It can also scan people from behind, presumably from checking out their taut butts (I'm just guessing here). His invention is super powerful (not to mention improbable) and stands to make him very rich. A group of terrorists has kidnapped his daughter hoping to get their hands on the laser gun. Brett Cady assembles his dream team of operatives, including a hacker and a mechanic/Q-type character who loves heavy metal, to infiltrate the terrorists and bring the girl home.

The box art states that Andy Bauman starred in Ninja 2 and Ninja 3, neither of which seem to be real movies. In light of this, the claim that he's a Kickboxing world champion seems dubious as well. Later in the film we are treated to Brett doing stretches sans shirt on not just a bear rug but a *polar bear* rug (wow, just wow). When assembling his team he interrupts his find-and-peck hacker in mid-coitus with a very macho and very bummed-looking dude. Subsequent fights are equally sloppy as are the segues between scenes. Frankly there isn't a whole lot of action in Night of the Kickfighters... but I didn't mind, there was enough bad line reading, poor editing, silly dialogue, and a general vibe that no one knew quite what they were doing that makes this one a fun ride. It has a silly laser gun, a wooden lead with questionable martial arts skills, mindless goons, explosions, sloppy car chases, and a totally anachronistic ending that had me laughing and clapping. When it comes to low-rent action cheese, Night of the Kickfighters is a treat for those with a taste for it. If you enjoy films by David Prior, PM Entertainment, or just general low-budget direct-to-video garbage, Night of the Kickfighters will have you asking: why the hell is it called Night of the Kickfighters if it takes place over several days?

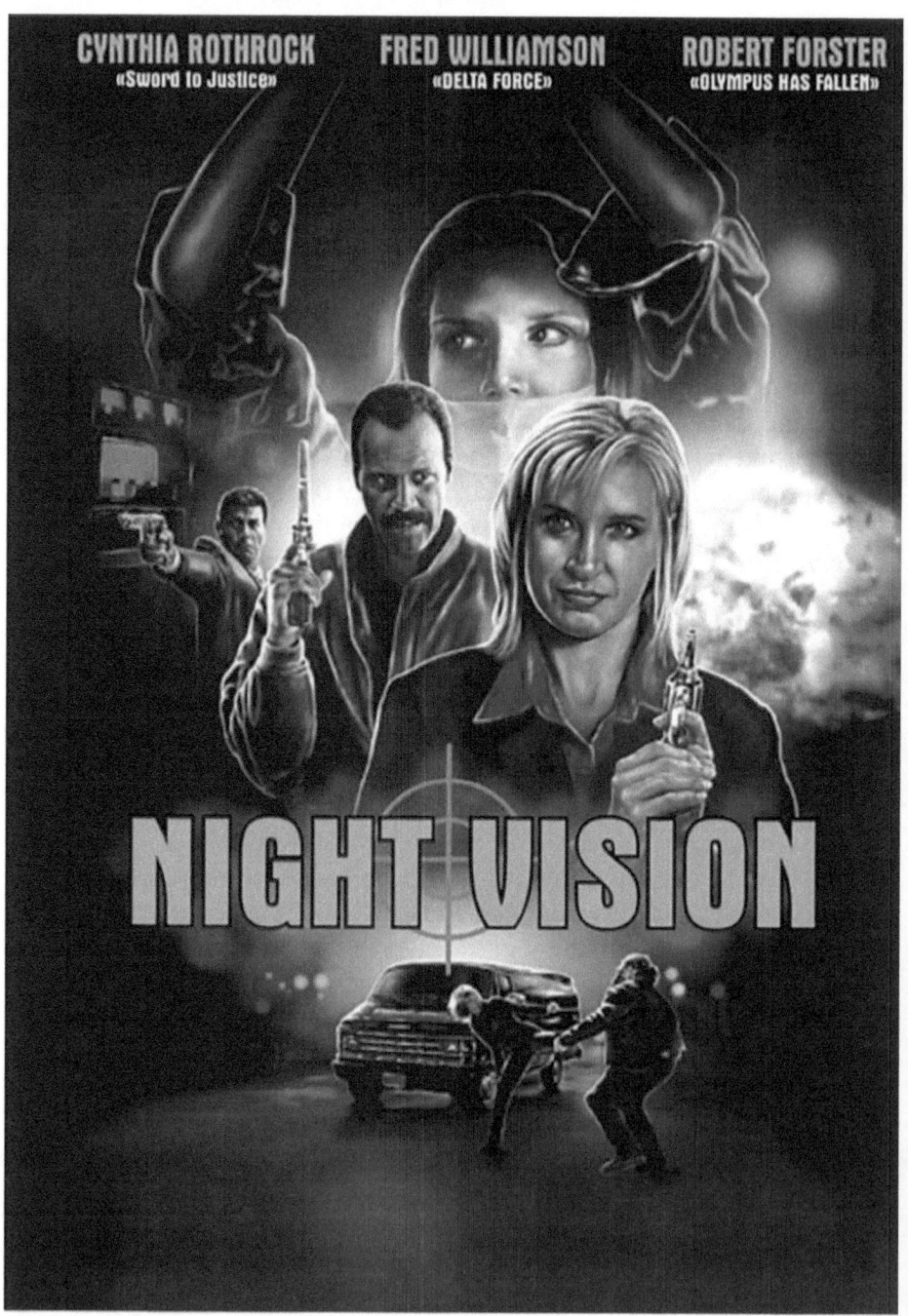

Night Vision (1997)
Runtime 93 minutes
Directed by Gil Bettman

Night Vision stars Fred "The Hammer" Williamson as a burnt-out old cop who used to be a star detective but now, he's a motorcycle patrolman that lives in a rundown halfway house due to his alcoholism. While out on patrol he runs afoul of a black van that contains a serial killer and his female victim. He pursues the van, not knowing its contents but knowing it's up to trouble and gets in a gun fight. He has a pistol and the dude in the van has a GRENADE LAUNCHER. Fred is launched off the freeway into some trees but somehow survives. The kidnapped woman however was killed with Fred's bullet. Oops. We then meet Fred's new partner, another cop that has gotten into trouble for excessive force, played by Cynthia Rothrock. What a great idea! Put two cops known for shooting everyone, together! That'll teach 'em. Together they're on the track of the serial killer. A cat and mouse game ensues that includes Fred walking around his apartment in his underwear frequently, sexually harassing Rothrock, and numerous dumpy locations. Robert Forester also shows up as their boss, and he's always a welcome addition to a film. Much like Williamson's film South Beach (1993) (also covered in this volume), Night Vision isn't action-packed, but it is a lot of fun. It feels like the dialogue was written by a Martian and the plot progression pulled out of a hat. Rothrock gets to show off her martial arts skills but not nearly enough. The film is all about Fred and how he's still super awesome despite his bad knees and chronic alcoholism. He still knows how to get the job done even if he's super sloppy and totally fascist about it. Unlike other action films featured in this book which are tons of fun because of the action, the star of the show here is the poorly written script. It's equal parts macho and unbelievable with a heavy dollop of lecherousness. The female victims are all filmed surreptitiously while doing the nasty with someone they aren't supposed to, so the film has a gross voyeuristic element too. Nudity is involved, including a very fat dude in a bubble bath who then tries to sleep with a woman in a bed made out of a hot pink classic Cadillac. It's bizarre, unique, and gross all in one and that's a distillation of this ridiculous Awful Awesome gem.

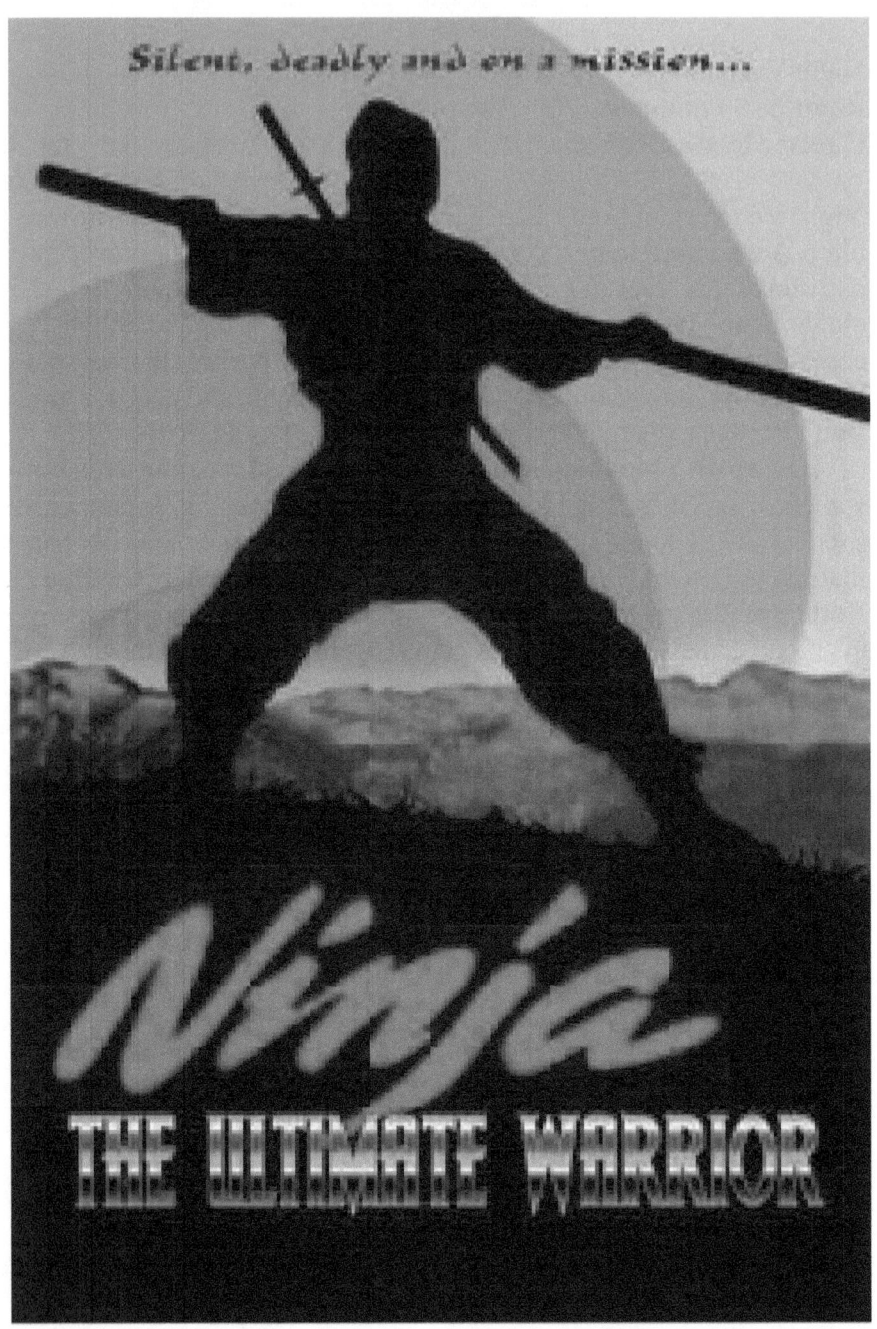

Ninja The Ultimate Warrior (1985)
Runtime 90 minutes
Directed by Parvin Tramel

Filmed in a small town in Missouri and shot on video, originally titled Justice Ninja Style, the film begins with a brief explanation of what a ninja is, and we meet our mysterious titular ninja. He's leaving the sacred ninja grounds in the woods to go on quest. Meanwhile in small-town Missouri we find a police officer who is the poster boy for that thin blue line of abuse. Everywhere he goes he acts like a jerk and tries to get women to sleep with him to get out of tickets. Real charmer this one. He happens upon a woman with a flat tire and he and his partner investigate. The woman knows the cop and she doesn't like him at all. The cop tries to convince her to go out on a date with him, but she refuses. When being polite doesn't work, she also refuses his physical advances with a knee to the nards. He gets angry and hits her with his billy club, killing her. Panicked he sees a local young man walking on the road and invites him over. This guy knows Karate and the dirty cop convinces him to show off his skills with the billy club. Fingerprints on the murder weapon the cop then arrests the innocent guy, but not before he gets some Karate to the noggin. Innocent guy is thrown in the clink with no hope of ever being free again. The setup is rock solid-ish. That is until a ninja starts a fire across the street as a distraction and then climbs up the outside wall of the jail like a gecko and sneakily busts our innocent hero out of jail. Now our framed Karate expert has to find a way to prove his innocence without pulling the ninja card, because no one will believe him.

The fight scenes are pretty laughable but at the same time there's so much earnestness on display here I spent more time cheering than jeering. This film is the cinematic equivalent to the little engine that could, and I found myself thoroughly entertained and excited while observing the many shortcomings of the film. The ninja aspect is shoehorned into the film and really has no business being in the movie, but the gimmick got me to watch, so I guess it worked. I was never bored and always entertained, and although it doesn't reach the bonkers heights of the best of Awful Awesome cinema, it's still well-worth seeking out.

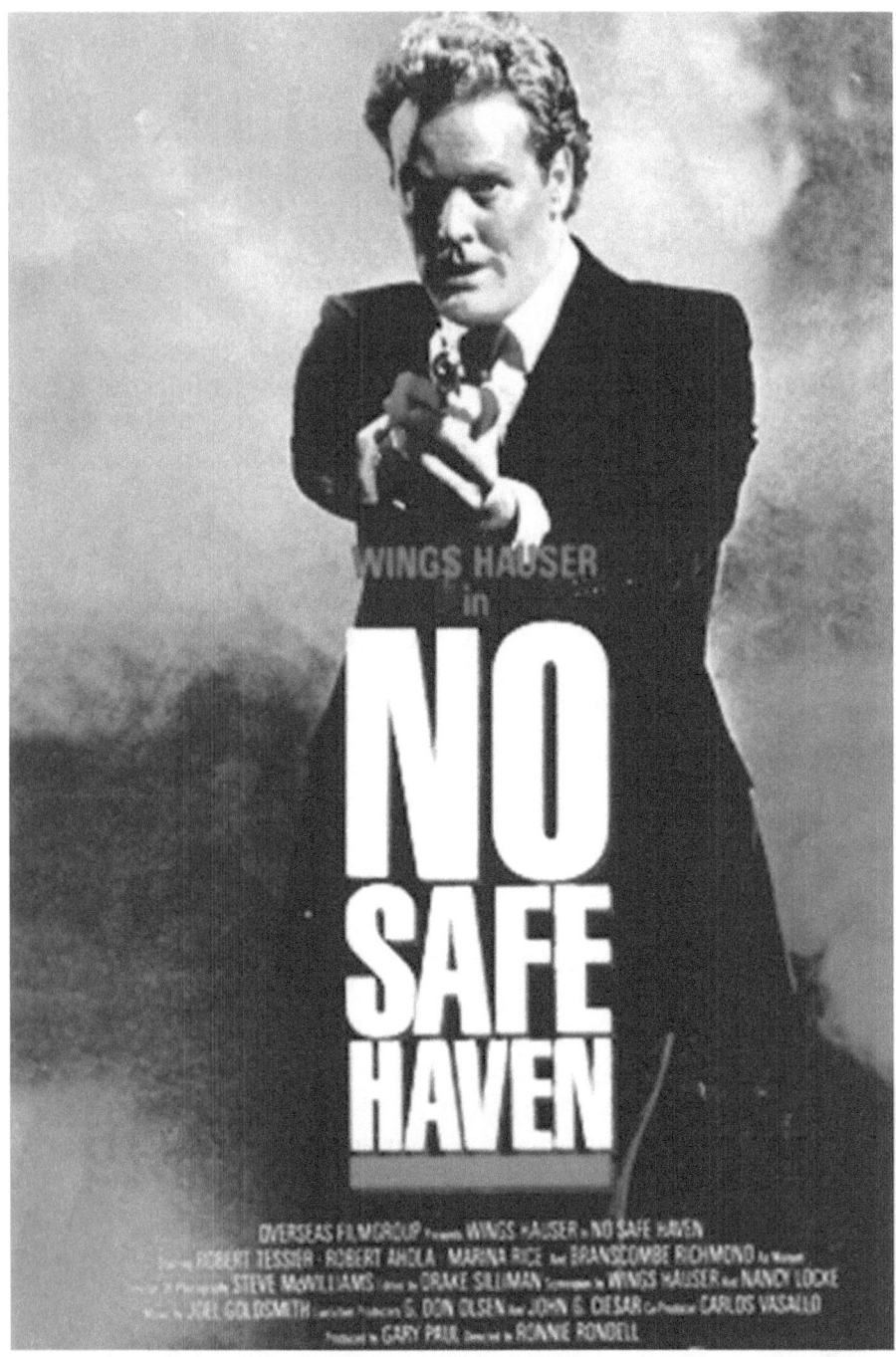

No Safe Haven (1987)
Runtime 95 minutes
Directed by Ronnie Rondell Jr.

No Safe Haven stars Wings Hauser as the brother of a famous NFL player. His brother is up to his neck in dirty dudes however because he's on the take with organized crime. They place a bet, and he does his best to sway the game in their favor. They also deal drugs which is how he got into this mess to begin with. He's a cokehead but he's had enough, he's finally reached rock-bottom. He intentionally injures himself so he can't play, which means the game can no longer be fixed. The bad dudes lose three million dollars because of his forced injury, and they aren't going to take it sitting down. They come to his house and kill his bespectacled mother AND his kid brother before they do him. Wings is living in Honduras, spying for the CIA when he finds out about his family being slayed by the bad guys. Furious, he charges back to the U.S. of A. to kick some major A. And by that, I mean ass, not America.

No Safe Haven begins with an incredible car chase involving a machine gun and a cement truck that reminded me of the best of PM Entertainment. It's totally electrifying. Branscome Richmond also stars in this, and he does his best to tote the machine gun and scream as much as possible throughout the whole film. He's a total joy. Wings is somewhat subdued (by his standards), but he goes off the rails a few times too, much to our joy. Later in the film bald-headed goon Robert Tessier shows up and helps supply Wings with guns and his very own muscle. Wings takes out the bad guys one by one in explosive scenes, one of which even involves a full-body burn. The trouble is the movie also has lots of needless flab. Wings picks up a sleazy dame at some point during his vengeance spree for a comical roll in the hay. Later he meets a classy lady, and he beds her too. He also buys her groceries and makes her breakfast. That has nothing to do with vengeance against the savage guys that killed his family, but I guess a guy has to eat and have sex too. Unfortunately for us, it can't be vengeance time all the time. No Safe Haven is a mixed bag. It features some great scream acting, awesome action scenes, but also lots of needless dialogue and general flab. If you love Wings Hauser, Branscome Richmond, or Robert Tessier, give it a go. If you have no idea who I'm talking about, tread with some caution.

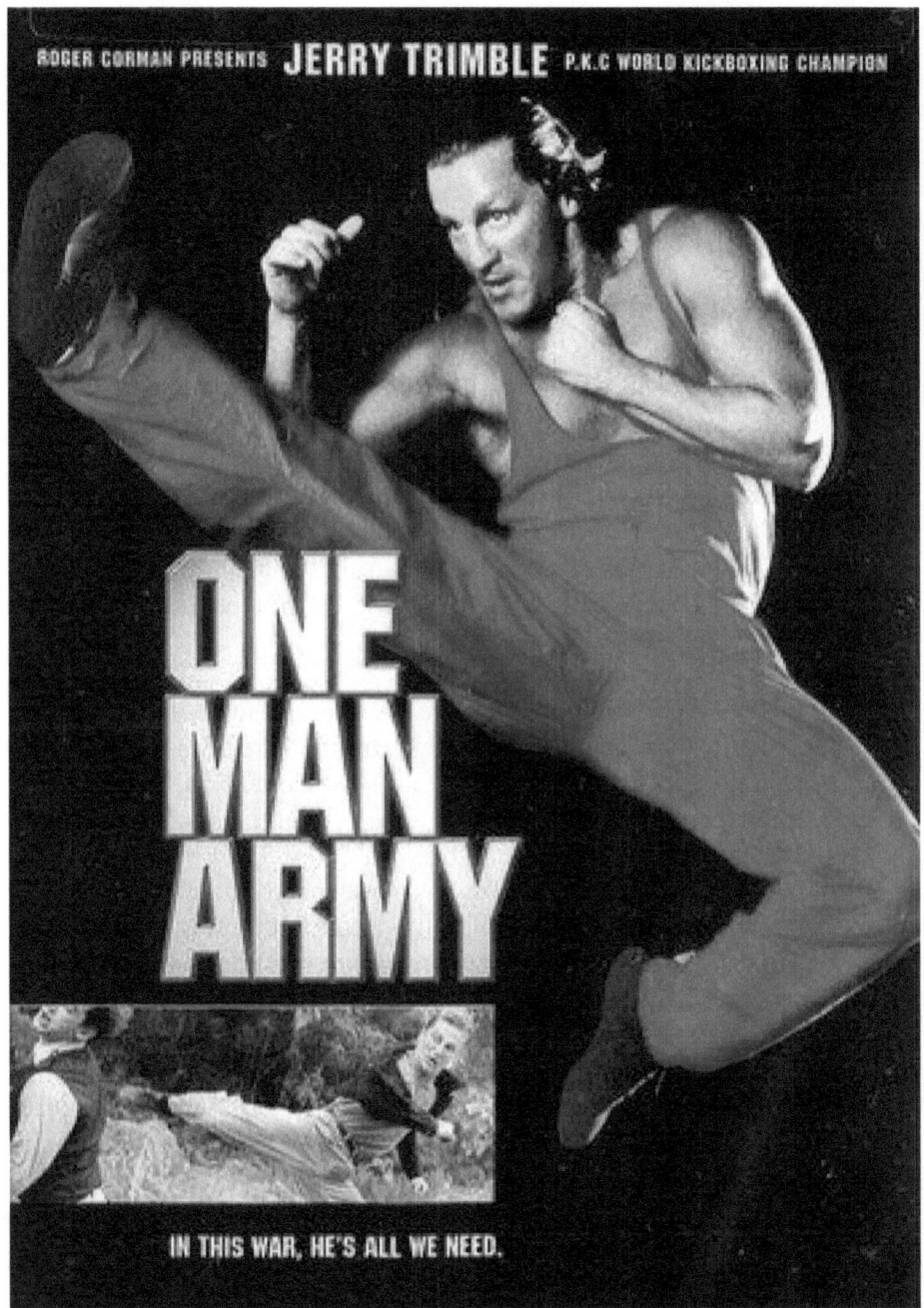

One Man Army (1994)
Runtime 79 minutes
Directed by Cirio H. Santiago

Jerry Trimble plays Jerry Pelt (which sounds like a porn name), in his youth he was a hell-raiser and booze-fighter but now he's cleaned up his act and has his own martial arts studio somewhere near Glendale, California. He gets word that his grandfather has passed away suddenly, and he should come home for the funeral. Pelt drops everything and hops in his VW bug and races (at least as much as it *can* race) towards his childhood home. On the way he gets hassled by some knuckleheads, they wreck his car and so he beats them up and steals their truck... but it's no use. He misses the funeral. Upon entering a bar, he sees flagrant prostitution and hidden behind closed doors, a gambling hall where the crowd takes bets on fights. Jerry learns that all of this is allowed by the local sheriff, Boze (Rick Dean). He gets paid to look the other way by a local kingpin that runs drugs, hookers, and gambling. Jerry decides to run for sheriff to clean up the town and now he's got to fight Boze and his deputies as well as goons hired by the kingpin.

The great thing about Santiago's films is that he really understands what fans want: a ton of action. One Man Army buzzes past a breakneck speed, hurtling from one fight scene to another with little regard for plot or nuance. It's like the motto of the film was, "we got it, we're moving on." At one point Pelt gets caught breaking into official police records and thrown in jail. This is never brought up again and apparently a pending felony charge in no way disqualifies him from running for sheriff. Characters are killed and there is no time to mourn before more characters are killed or become embroiled in yet another street fight. Pelt has a dog that functions as a Deus ex machina, always saving the day in the nick of time. The dog gets a credit during the opening credits which I naturally scoffed at but by the end of the film I could understand why: he's a miracle worker and without him, Pelt would have died many times over.

One Man Army gives you what you crave in a low-budget action flick and doesn't waste your time about it. It isn't even 80 minutes long and still delivers the goods.

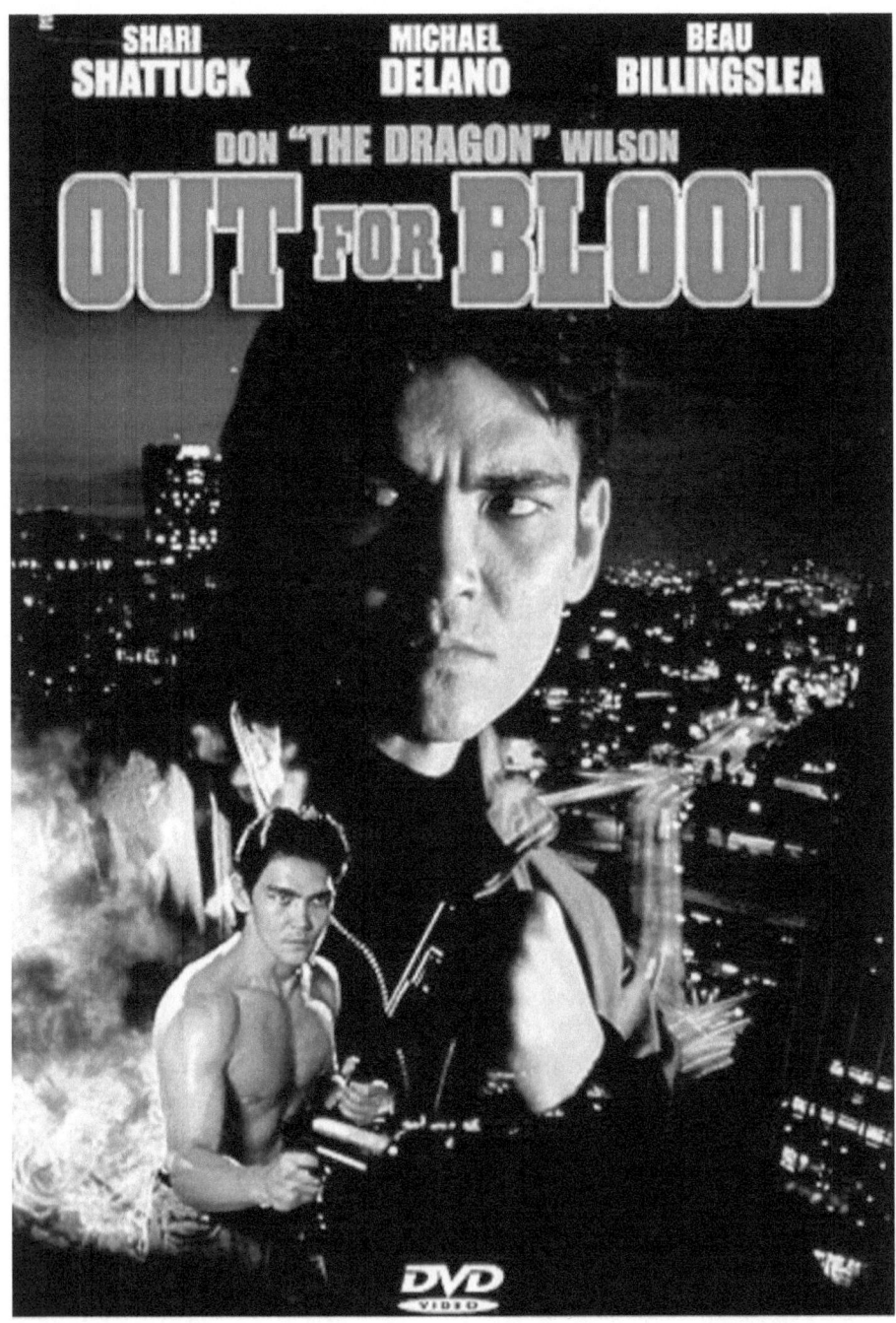

Out for Blood (1992)
Runtime 85 minutes
Directed by Richard W. Munchkin

Out For Blood begins with John Decker (Wilson), shadowboxing on the beach in slow motion. A good start. We then get flashes of some sort of brutal crime committed with Decker the victim. He's covered in blood, and we don't know why. Decker is a successful lawyer who has amnesia. He can remember most of his life, just not the part where his wife and daughter were brutally murdered by a drug cartel before his very eyes. The police think he did it, despite the injuries Decker sustained in the attack. He's seeing a shrink to help him remember that fateful night but so far, he can't piece it together. He's put into a dangerous situation by some no-good lousy punks and Decker fights back, killing them. The violence sparks new memories and also pumps his heart full of machismo. He enjoyed taking on the criminals and now he's OUT FOR BLOOD. The trouble is the cops are still sniffing around and when a witness to the vigilante acts says the guy was a "regular Karate man," their suspicions grow stronger: Decker knows martial arts! Now Decker has to keep his nightly payback on the down-low, otherwise the cops will discover the truth and throw him in the klink.

Out For Blood, being an earlier PM effort, tries very hard to be a legitimate film. It feels very close to Death Wish, which makes sense because the story concept came from Wilson after he watched some Death Wish flicks. The film is moodily-lit, using monochromatic gels that really add a nice touch of style to the movie. There are moments of total cheese like when Addison Randall (The Killing Zone (1991)) shows up with a mighty perm to beat up Decker in a bathroom with a curly –mulleted goon. Also, the last twenty minutes are total PM action with shootouts, fist fights, and explosions. Out For Blood almost manages to be a serious vigilante flick and not an Awful Awesome movie. The subject is taken seriously and it's obvious the film was meant to be more like Death Wish than Death Wish 3. That being said, it's still a PM flick and has little flashes of over-the-top action. I wouldn't say it's a must-watch unless you are a Wilson completist and, in that respect, you could do a lot worse. It's a fun flick but its serious tone doesn't lend itself well to a night of goofy action with friends. It's too good to be truly Awful Awesome, if that makes sense.

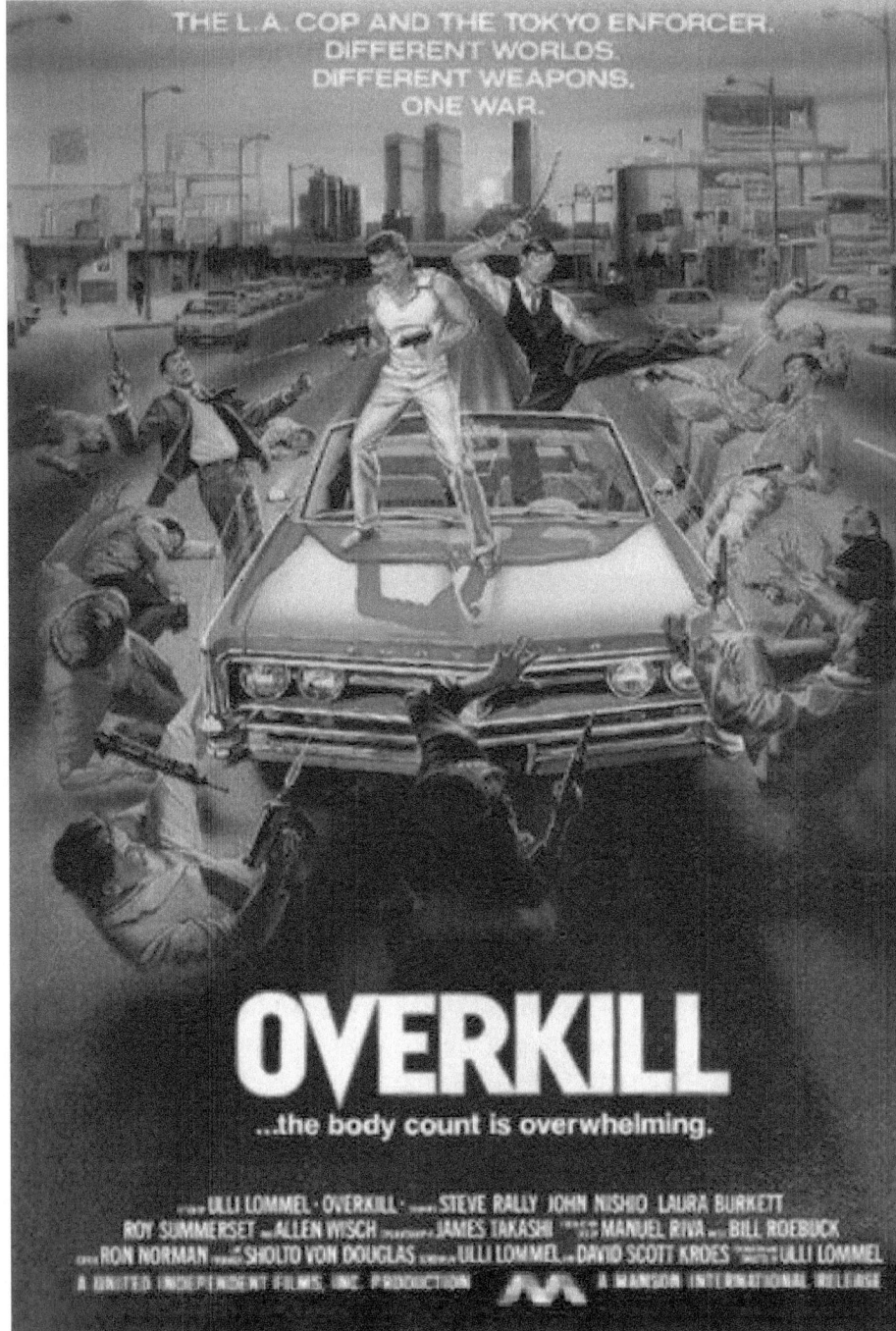

Overkill (1987)
Runtime 81 minutes
Directed by Ulli Lommel

Overkill takes place in Los Angeles, the city of sin is being overtaken by Yakuza (Japanese gangsters) and the only one to see it coming is our hero, Mickey Delano (Playgirl model Steve Rally). He's a detective that sports a man-perm, mustache, and spends most of the movie shirtless. He drives a big old blue convertible and chases a lot of ladies. Dude has a serious bone to pick with the Yakuza, and minorities in general. He doesn't like them. He also knows nothing about Japanese culture. In fact, at one point in the film, another character says, "Sayonara," and his reply is, "what the hell does that mean?". It's hilarious. After some bloody shootouts and confirmation of his theory of a West Coast Yakuza takeover, he joins forces with a Tokyo cop to bring down the Yakuza, even if that means tearing the police department apart. Or becoming a male exotic dancer. He does both.

Overkill is a fantastic cop action flick that delivers on the action and the laughs in equal measure. The lead is so macho and sleazy, he's impossible to take seriously. The shootouts are poorly choreographed, leaving characters spraying what can only be described as ketchup. Numerous characters refuse to wear shirts throughout the film (even if they should). A katana is used to decapitate a dude. At one point, a character suggests to our hero that he can infiltrate the yakuza by posing as an erotic dancer. He refuses for about five seconds and then gives in. The film then cuts to him doing an exotic dance to the delight of an ocean of women. Let me say this, he's WAY too good at his dance number to be an amateur. Overkill has lots of action, bad acting, worse dialogue, and a whole lotta macho posturing. The runtime is lean, leaving it little time to get flabby. It almost feels like a vanity film, akin to Rock House (1988). I love the fact that a Playgirl model was cast as the hero of the movie. Cuz that'll get the fellas to rent the video in '87, right? Overkill has laughs around every corner and delivers on just about every element I love in a bad action flick. In short, Overkill is pantheon awfully awesome.

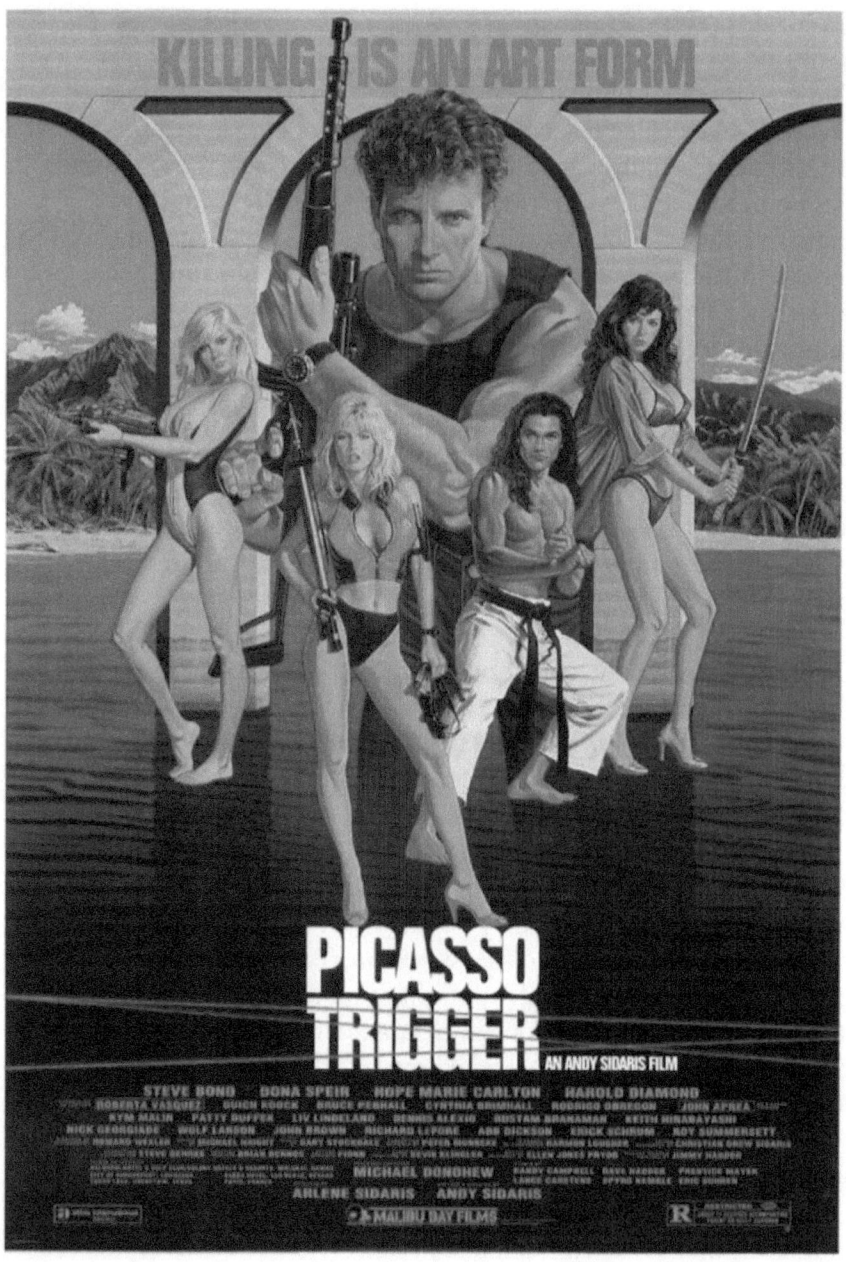

Picasso Trigger (1988)
Runtime 98 minutes
Directed by Andy Sidaris.

Picasso Trigger is the third film (Malibu Express (1985) and Hard Ticket to Hawaii (1987) being the first two) in the "Malibu Universe." It features returning characters (if not all the same actors) from the first two films, and as you might suspect there are ample opportunities for nudity and explosions.

Picasso Trigger begins with the assassination of a former criminal turned rich dude and art aficionado. Then an assassination attempt on a Texas tycoon by the same shadowy criminals spurs the Texan to hire some help to track down the killers. Travis Abilene (from Malibu Express) is hired to help out sexy agent Pantera to do just that. Donna and Taryn from Hard Ticket to Hawaii are also called in to help along with Jade (Harold Diamond). Professor (?) from Hard Ticket to Hawaii is also on the case as are other various familiar faces/characters. Together they travel the world trying to find out just who is behind these killings and bring them to sweet, sweet justice.

I kept wondering what the hell was going on, and who this person was or what was happening in that scene. The characters are in different places doing different things, so their connection becomes confusing. It would be a good idea to watch the previous two films before checking this one out (if you want to have any semblance of what's going on). Of the first three films it likely features the most nudity and the most explosions. It does however suffer from a lack of action during the first half of the film. Once the movie finally kicks into high gear it stays there until the very end of the film. If you can hang tough through the amusing but somewhat dull beginning, you'll be rewarded with plenty of action on the back end. The film even features goofy weapons like a toy airplane used as a bomb, a crutch that doubled as a shotgun, and a boomerang bomb which is almost as cool as the bladed Frisbee. So, is it as fun as Hard Ticket to Hawaii? No, it isn't. It doesn't have as much action and isn't as over-the-top or ridiculous. It delivered on what I expected: cheese, bad acting, explosions, machine guns, silly weapons and fancy cars.

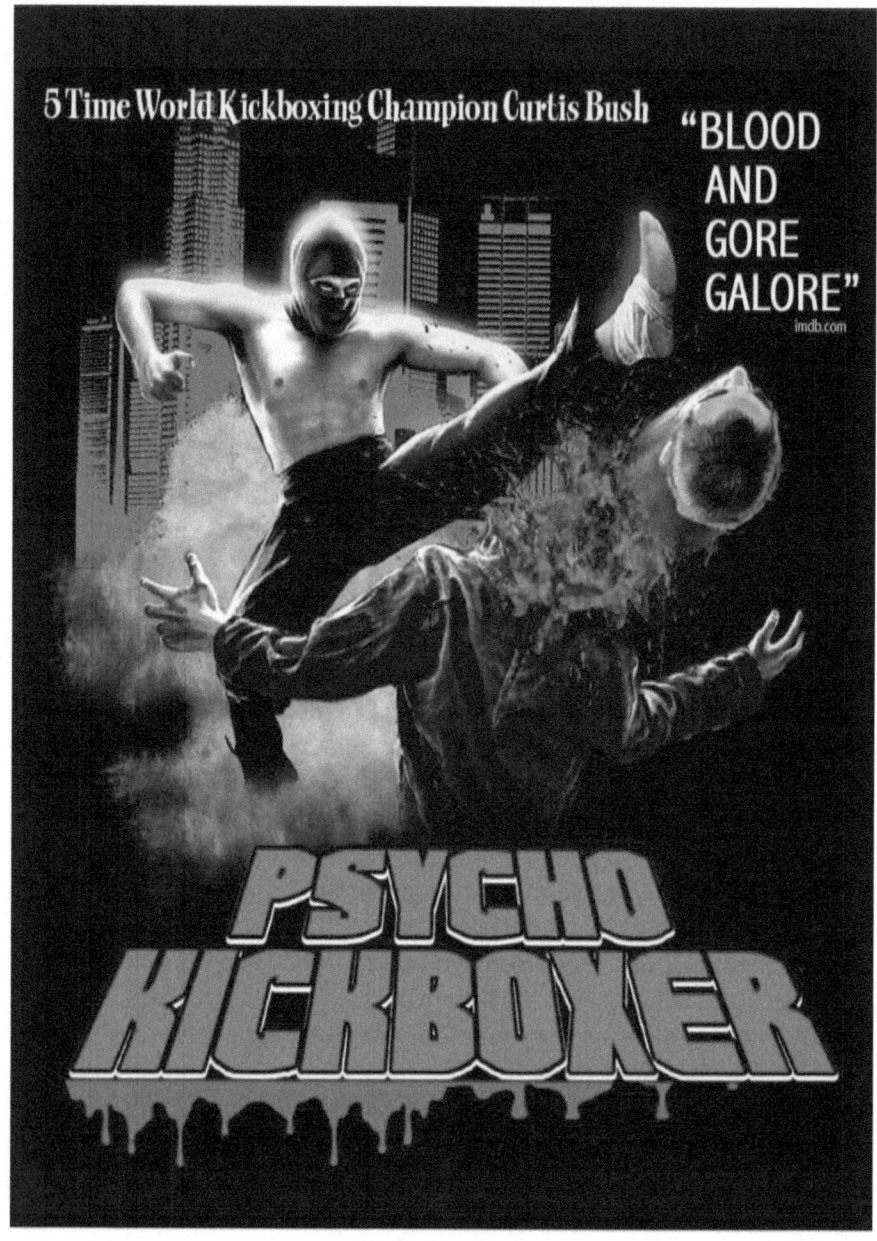

Psycho Kickboxer (1997)
Runtime 87 minutes
Directed by David Haycox & Mardy South

Psycho Kickboxer is about local fighter Alex Hunter. Things are going great for Alex, he's got a great fighting career, a sweet mustache, and a little lady he's about to marry. His daddy is a big shot lawyer intent on taking down the city's criminal kingpin. This plan doesn't work out too well when Alex, his daddy, and his lady are kidnapped by the thugs. Things go from bad to worse when daddy gets his head blown off, literally. His lady gets murdered, and Alex is left for dead. He's discovered by a wheelchair-bound homeless dude who decides to train Alex for REVENGE! Although Alex knows how to kick some serious ass in the ring, he doesn't know how to handle himself on the street. That's where his new buddy/trainer comes in. Alex is hungry for justice and "trains" by beating up thugs that apparently infest their corner of town. He wears a ski mask, sweats, and a black shirt. He's dubbed the "Dark Angel" by the press as a do-gooder vigilante who dishes out some well-deserved comeuppance for the nogoodniks everywhere. Finally, Alex is ready to take on the cabal of bad dudes and give them what they deserve: a serious beating.

Psycho Kickboxer is a lot of fun. It's cheap, action-packed, and poorly choreographed (one helluva combo there). Alex's finishing move is to simply speedbag his opponents. It's pretty funny. Everyone involved is earnestly trying to deliver the best performance they can and most of them succeed, except Curtis Bush who is admittedly pretty bad. The cover art for this movie features a drawing of Bush kicking off some poor sap's head, and although this never happens in the movie (bummer), a few overly gory scenes that are both cheap and highly entertaining are featured. The middle of the movie is chock-full of fight after fight, shot in broad daylight, with a clumsy vibe. I had a good time watching Psycho Kickboxer. While I don't think it's required viewing, you could certainly do a lot worse. It's fun, short, and full of action and questionable decisions on the part of the characters and film makers. It's even got a few gory scenes that push it into a territory of bad taste rarely seen in cheap 90's action. I only wish the film makers had continued to make cheap flicks but reportedly this one took 5 years to finally get completed and released, so I can understand.

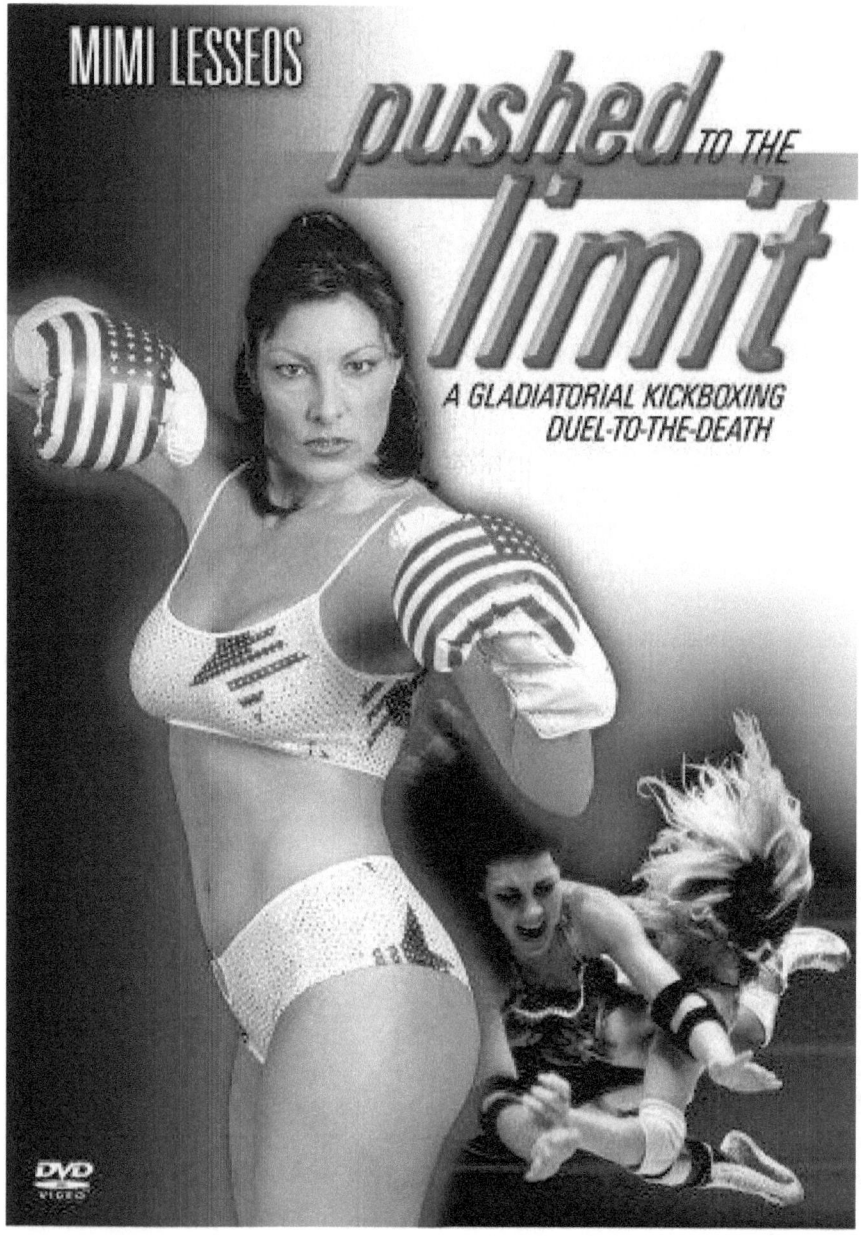

Pushed to the Limit (1992)
Runtime 100 minutes
Directed by Michael Mileham

Magnificent Mimi is a certified star in the wrestling circuit, she knows how to wear a leotard and pin her opponents with style... She's also an interpretive dancer on the Vegas strip. She's living life at the top of her game, when her brother gets mixed up with dangerous drug dealers and kingpin Harry. He has a cocaine habit and skims a bit of blow off the top. Bad move, his bosses don't like that, so they shoot him. Enraged when she finds out about her brother, Mimi decides to seek revenge. She finds out that said drug kingpin Harry also runs super illegal full-contact fights in a crappy warehouse. The fights sometimes go all the way to the death, but she still wants to infiltrate the fights to get close to Harry so she can bring him down. She asks local fighting training master Vern to help her prepare for the fights. He begrudgingly agrees and so begins a very long and drawn-out act involving her training. Finally ready she must defeat Inge, a giant German woman who loves lifting weights and cracking necks. She also has a particular affinity for off-the-shoulder fighting attire and G-strings.

Pushed to the Limit has many things I love: odd music, long-butt leotards, training sequences, wrestling, martial arts tournaments, and guys named Vern (knowwhatimean?). The trouble is the film feels rather sluggish. The training involves a lot of meditating and talking instead of you know... actual training. The interpretive dance is also embarrassingly long and just when you think it might be over, we're treated to more. Sadly, there is very little wrestling in the movie which, for me, was a bummer. Mimi herself is a solid lead but Vern is pretty dull. All is not lost however, the film does feature a plethora of sloppy fights, bad lighting and the aforementioned long-butt leotards. We get plenty of dated outfits and hairstyles, silly lines of dialogue, and an earnest vibe that makes the film fun. The trouble is it's at least 10 minutes too long. In the end, Pushed to the Limit is fun for martial arts tournament fanatics and people who have already seen the bulk of Cynthia Rothrock's oeuvre. It's a shame the two never teamed up.

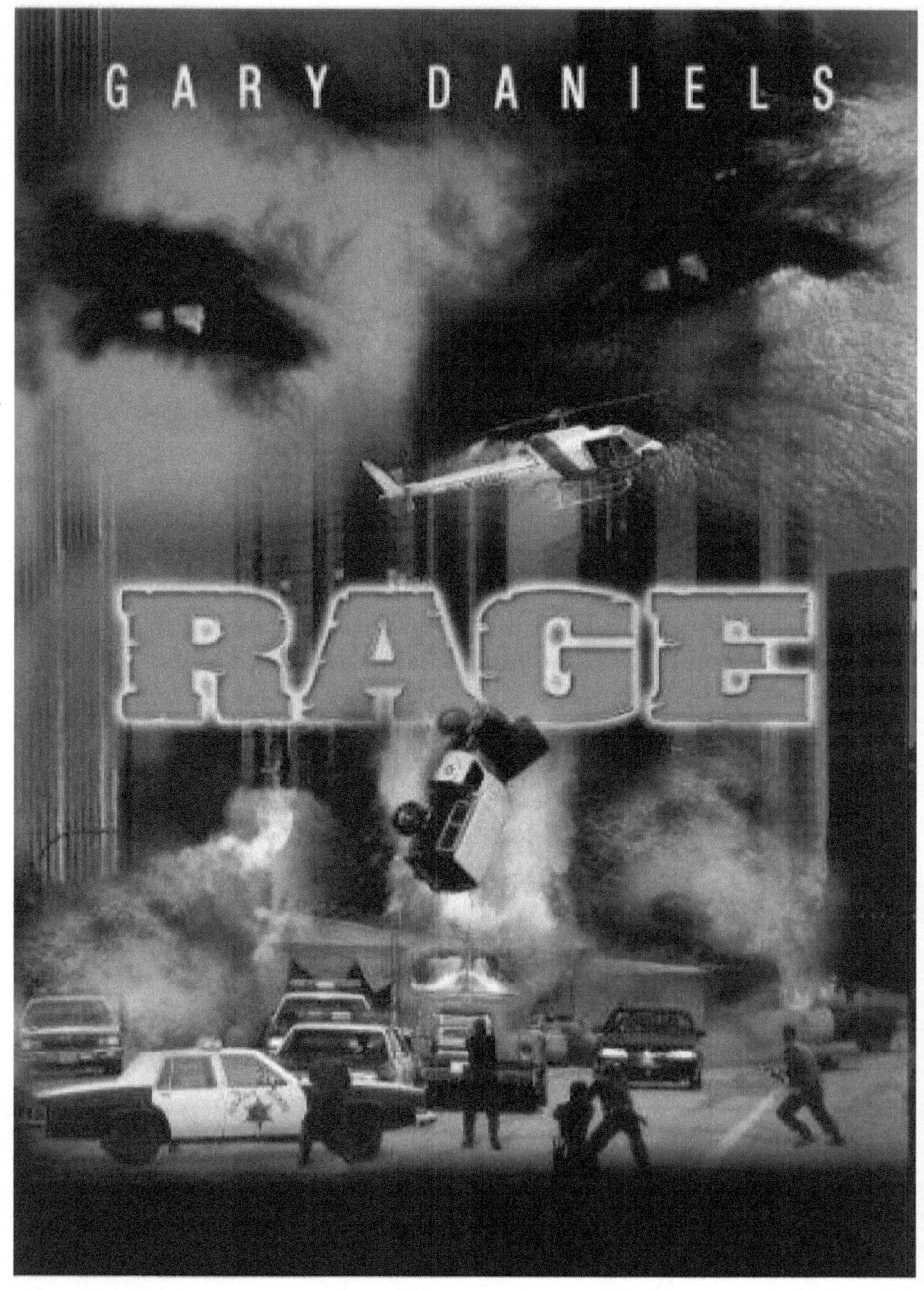

Rage (1995)
Runtime 90 minutes
Directed by Joseph Merhi

PM Entertainment film Rage stars Gary Daniels as a second-grade teacher/consummate ass kicker. He's captured by the police after an armed man car jacks him. The police beat Daniels to a pulp after which he's transported to a secret shadowy research lab where they inject him with some special sauce that makes him even more badass. Before they could wipe his brain and turn him into a super solider, he stomps the ill-prepared doctors and geriatric guards and breaks loose. He spends the rest of the movie on the run from the corrupt police and the shadowy scientists who all want him dead to keep their evil plot quiet.

This movie had the least amount of plot of any movie I have ever watched. That isn't a slight, it's a compliment. Nothing kills the fun faster than emotional subplots, needless expository dialogue, and unwanted plot twists... we came for the action. Rage delivers just that in a tidy 90-minute runtime. The setup takes about 10 minutes or less and for the most part, after that it's one big chase sequence. We are instead treated with a very long (and awesome) car chase involving a semi-truck, an extended fight scene in a shopping mall (complete with video store that stocks nothing but PM Entertainment VHS tapes), and a skyscraper stunt extravaganza involving a helicopter. Director Merhi pulls out all the stops in this flick with some of the most eye-popping action sequences in PM history. Seriously if you're going to watch just one PM flick, Rage would be an excellent choice. Some of the stunts looked so dangerous, they didn't even look legal. Gary Daniels is solid in the film too. Hell, he even manages to keep his shirt tucked in THE WHOLE MOVIE, despite surviving explosions, car wrecks, fights, and shootouts. I need to know his shirt tucking secret. It's impeccable. Rage is a blast. It delivers everything you could want in a low-budget, direct-to-video action flick. There's almost no fat to trim here. We've got martial artist Gary Daniels kicking major ass in denim jeans, ubiquitous use of machine guns, unbelievable car crashes, and a very silly plot. It's impossible to take seriously but it can't be written off either, it's too much fun to ignore. Rage is a pantheon Awful Awesome movie.

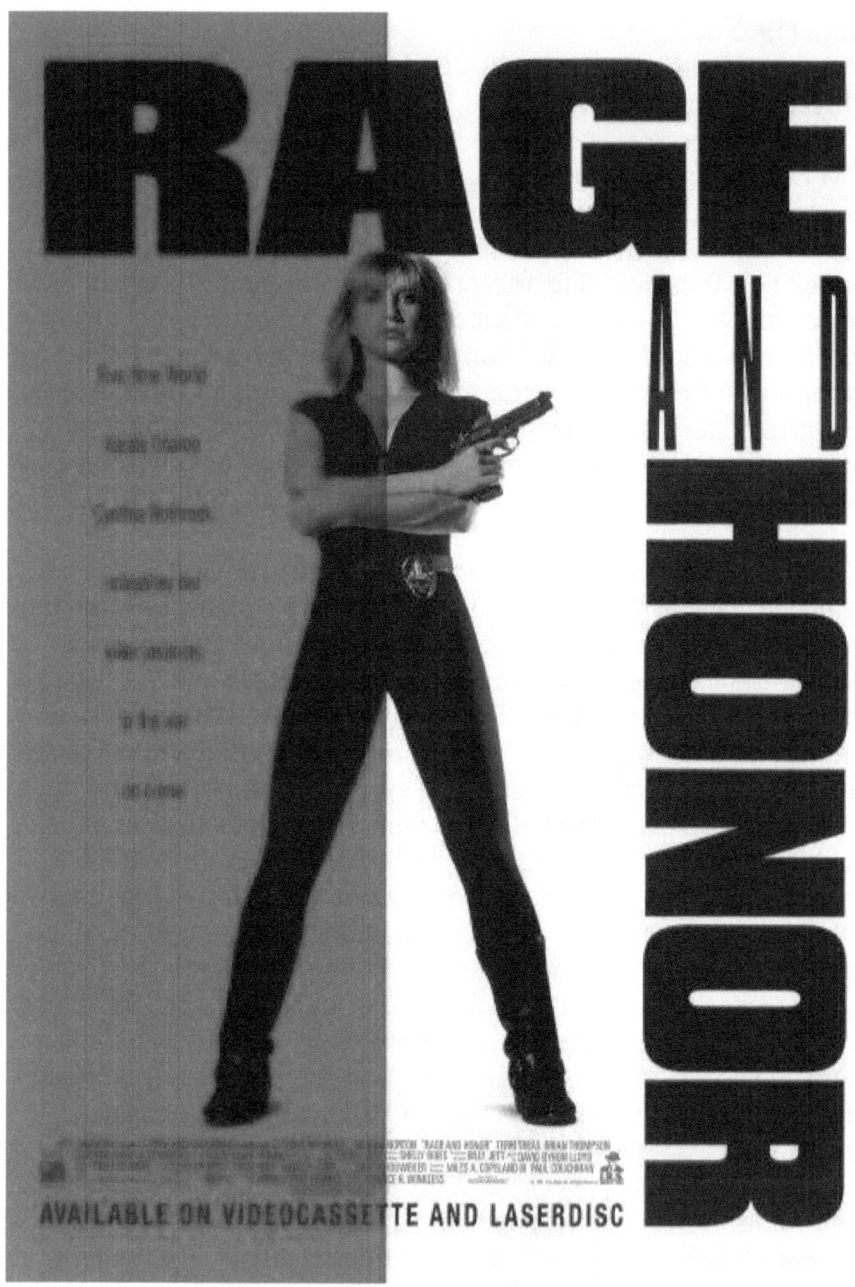

Rage and Honor (1992)
Runtime 88 minutes
Directed by Terence H. Winkless

Richard Norton stars as Preston Michaels, he used to be a cop in Australia but now he's a bodyguard for a trashy rock band (still not THAT bad of a job, right?). He gets involved with a crime syndicate when he witnesses a drug deal/murder. He kicks some major ass but some of those involved are cops, of the dirty variety and they blame the murder on Norton. Now he's public enemy #1. As it turns out a teenager filmed the entire fiasco and handed his tape off with a mysterious street person right before he's nearly beaten to death. Now Michaels has to find the tape to clear his name. Rothrock stars as Kris Fairchild, who's a martial arts instructor who Norton asks for help in recovering the tape, because she knows the mean streets and the denizens of skid row. The leader of the drug cartel is Conrad Drago (Brian Thompson). He's got big muscles; an incredible mullet and he loves to punch ice and deal drugs. He too wants the tape because it was one of his soldiers that did the killing. He wants her guilt to be hidden and Michaels to do the time for the crime. They're both after the tape, but who will get it first?

Rage and Honor is a cheap, direct-to-video action flick that delivers solid action and cheese in even doses. Alone Rothrock and Norton struggle to carry an entire film, but together their combined martial arts might light up the screen, in a town where everyone knows martial arts but nearly no one owns a gun. We travel the mean streets and watch as the pair fight their way through town to get their hands on the tape. We all know that won't be enough, however. The duo has to face the head of the cartel, it's a forgone conclusion. It's a lot of fun to watch Rothrock go toe-to-toe with Brian Thompson with his magnificent spiky mullet and hammy performance. There's plenty of questionable early 90's fashion on display as well as some seriously cheesy music. The film could have had more action for my taste, it does lag in places but overall, I had a good time with it. If you have fun watching Norton and Rothrock beat up bad guys, this one is a solid entry.

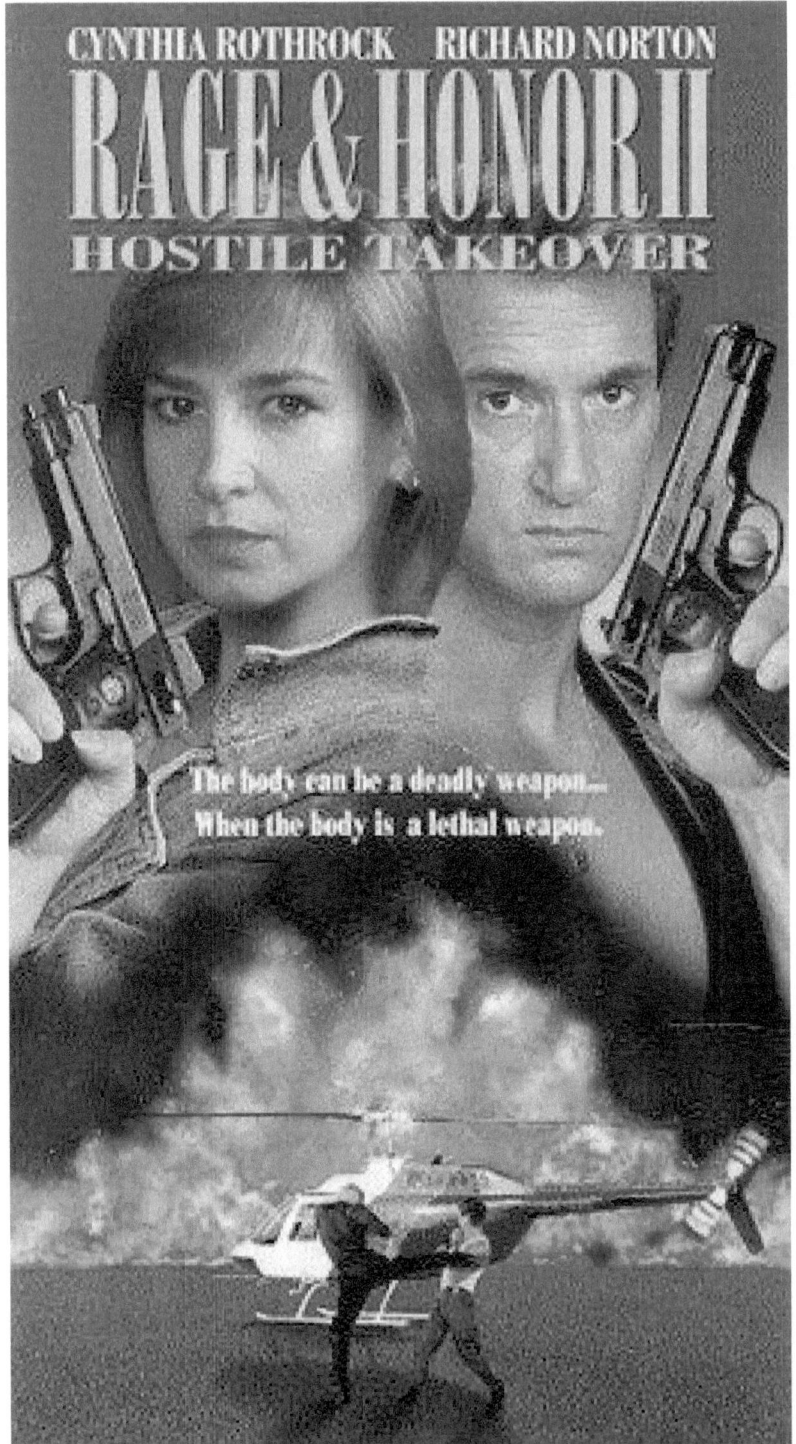

Rage and Honor 2: Hostile Takeover (1993)
Runtime 97 minutes
Directed by Guy Norris

Kris Fairchild (Rothrock) is now working for law enforcement as a special operative. She's sent to Jakarta to work at a bank, where she is to look for information that will support the theory that the bank manager is as dirty as a thrice-worn pair of underwear. There she meets Tommy Andrews, the son of the bank manager. He's sorta hunky and knows it. He's got eyes for Rothrock, but he's also got eyes for Preston Michaels (Norton) albeit in a different way: he wants Preston to train him. Tommy hates hanging around the bank but loves to learn how to fight. He's heard that Preston is the best (he is) and so he strikes off a friendship involving getting punched by Preston. Meanwhile, Preston gets invited to a company party after all his sweaty instructing, and there he meets Kris. They pretend to not know each other and meet up later to trade notes. Together they want to take out the bad dudes and roundhouse kick their way to justice.

Rage and Honor 2 starts off with a solid bang: Norton beats up a bunch of dudes in a bar and Rothrock beats up a (different) bunch of dudes in a house. It's a good start, but unfortunately this flick suffers from a lack of action. The characters talk a lot and do plenty of investigating but there just aren't enough fight scenes. The training sequences are pretty good, but they just aren't enough to satisfy. Rothrock wears some very awful pants and Norton loves his black trench coat with the sleeves rolled up (so the fashion is a plus). The locations are great and the action (such as it is) is solid and well-choreographed, this flick just needed more for it to be a proper awful awesome film. That being said, I enjoy flicks like this and love Rothrock and Norton so for me, I had a good time watching it. I just wouldn't recommend it as a first foray. After you've watched the first film, and both China O'Brien's, you might want to check this one out. Maybe.

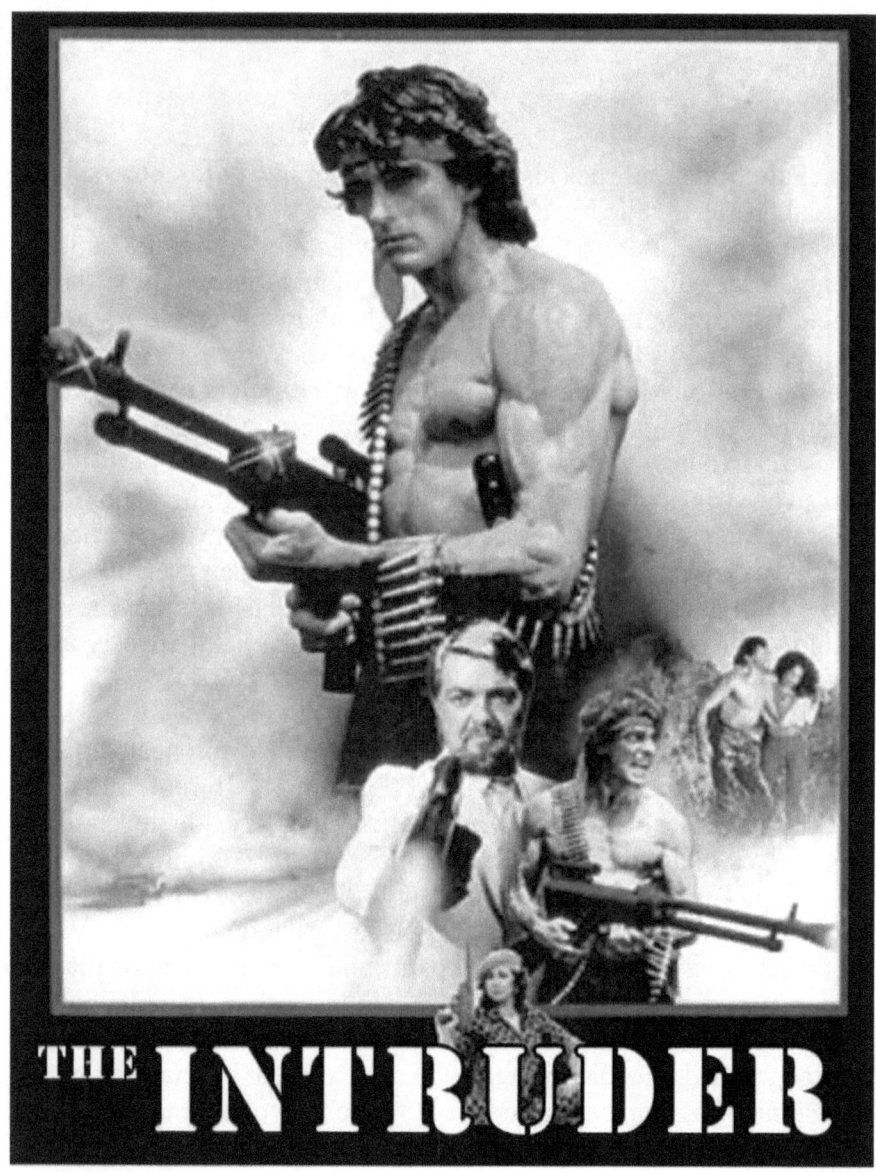

Rambu: The Intruder (1986)
Runtime 80 minutes
Directed by Jopi Burnama

Rambu: The Intruder is an Indonesian rip off of, you guessed it, Rambo (if not any of the Rambo films specifically then at least the character of Rambo). It stars Indonesian favorite Peter O'Brian (The Stabilizer (1986), American Hunter (1988)). Rambu is a normal guy who loves kicking major ass. Unfortunately, he doesn't have a job and so he just lives with his lady in shame. This doesn't stop him, however, from being a defender of the weak and managing a fantastic perm. At the beginning of the film some local thugs nearly run down a woman in their car. She's uninjured but the thugs do manage to destroy her livelihood, a cart. She begs for compensation but instead gets slapped around, enter Rambu! Using only an apple as a weapon (I'm not joking) he defeats the thugs and sends them away. They are, unfortunately for Rambu, connected to the local crime syndicate and tell their bosses about Rambu. Later Rambu rescues a woman being held hostage by the same thugs. The syndicate boss, Mr. White doesn't like all this interference and so they decide to make Rambu pay: they kidnap his girlfriend and livelihood (she IS his sugar momma after all). They beat, rape, and murder her, hoping Rambu will leave them alone. They were wrong. Now Rambu has a vendetta against them, and nothing will stop him from getting his revenge. The film begins with a spectacularly silly fight, followed by a sloppy bar fight (great start so far!) but then the movie slows down. Lots of talking among villainous types ensues and the movie loses its momentum. The kidnap and rape in the film are pretty gnarly too. They are (thankfully) not super graphic but they aren't fun either. Rape is something that, understandably, really kills a fun mood in a cheesy flick like this. The middle of the film is punctuated by a fantastic brigade of dirt bike riders vs. a horde of tuk-tuks (3 wheeled taxis used in southeast Asia). It's hilarious and awesome. I loved it. It feels like the end of the movie but alas it isn't. More talking follows.

Even at only 80 minutes, Rambu felt a bit long. The movie peaks too early. How could anything beat dirt bikes vs. tuk-tuks? If you're a fan of Indonesian craziness, there is plenty here for you to enjoy, just have a tempered expectation.

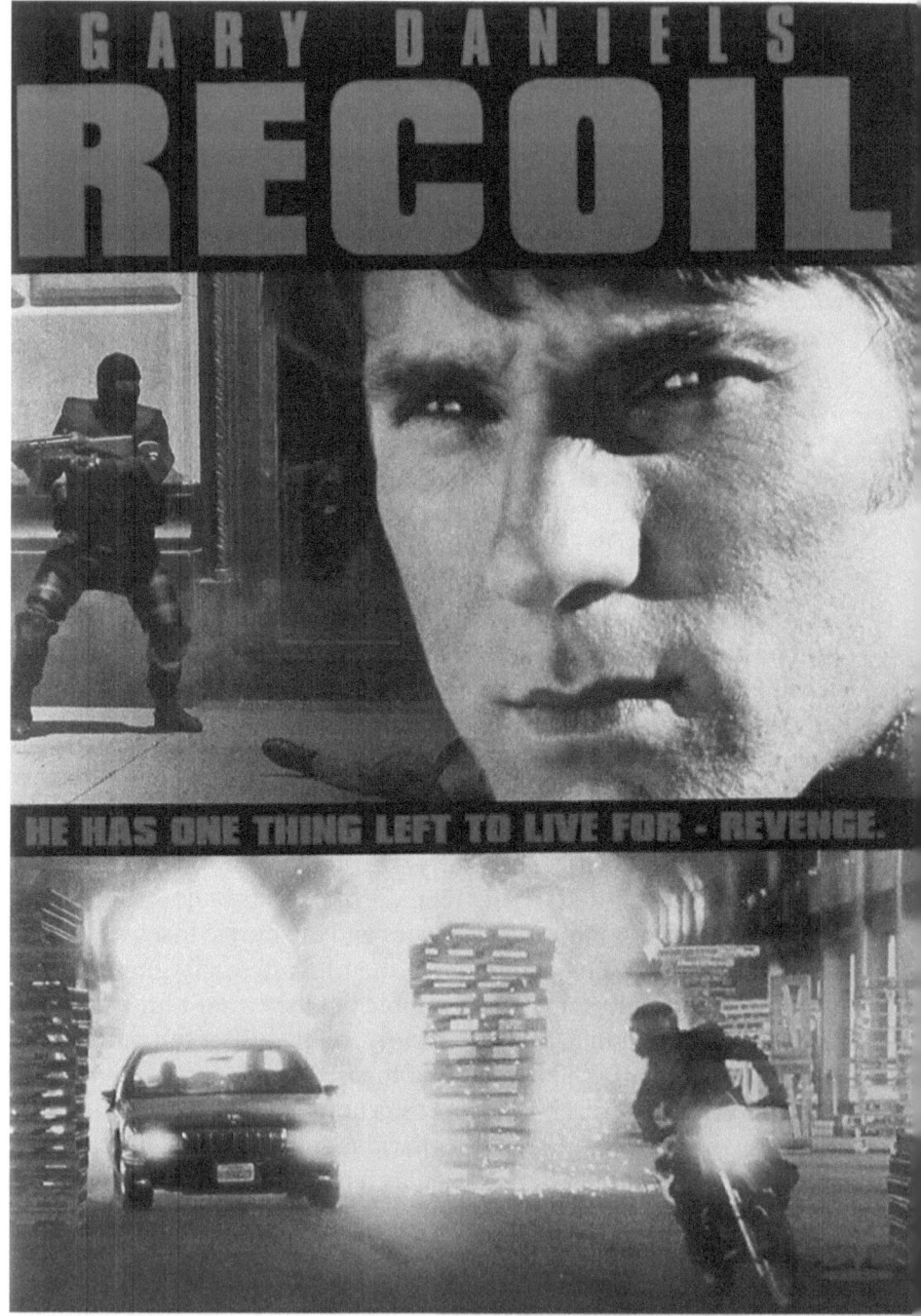

Recoil (1998)
Runtime 93 minutes
Directed by Art Camacho

Gary Daniels stars as Detective Ray Morgan, a tough as nails cop who knows how to handle a pistol (or two) better than any cop on the force, as evidenced by the explosive opening scene in which he dispatches some bad guys robbing a bank after "normal" cops seemingly couldn't hit the broad side of a barn with the same munitions Daniels had (apparently, they were taught by stormtroopers or something). After the amazing opening scene, the bank robbers are left dead and one of them was the son of a mob boss. Now the mob is after Morgan and his family. Spoiler: eventually they get Morgan's family and Morgan spends the rest of the flick taking out the mob one by one to get his sweet revenge. The "beginning "of the film is intense. I used quotes because the beginning action scene in the movie is about 20 minutes long filled with shooting, explosions, a car chase in what could be the longest warehouse in the world, and so much action I needed a nap afterwards. It also constitutes nearly 1/3 of the movie so calling it an opening scene is a bit of a misnomer. The film is clearly influenced by the late 80's work of John Woo, with Morgan sporting guns akimbo throughout the runtime. Everyone gets shot a bunch of times and the general sense of savage action that permeates Woo's films, is seen here. There are some other great action sequences sprinkled throughout that give justice to the PM trademark style of "more is better", but to be honest this movie has too much flab. It may sound morbid, but my friends and I kept expecting Morgan's family to get axed (and there are many opportunities) but frankly it took too long to get there. The beginning sets up the viewer for a rollercoaster ride but instead the middle of the movie delivers the cinematic equivalent to a carousel: the movie goes around and around but never really gets anywhere. Finally, the action picks up and thankfully delivers the goods in the back 1/3 of the movie.

Recoil is a PM action flick that delivers the action but unfortunately the beginning set me up for a movie I didn't really get. The movie tries (and in places achieves) the stylized violence found in Woo's movies, albeit in a cheaper and sillier manner.

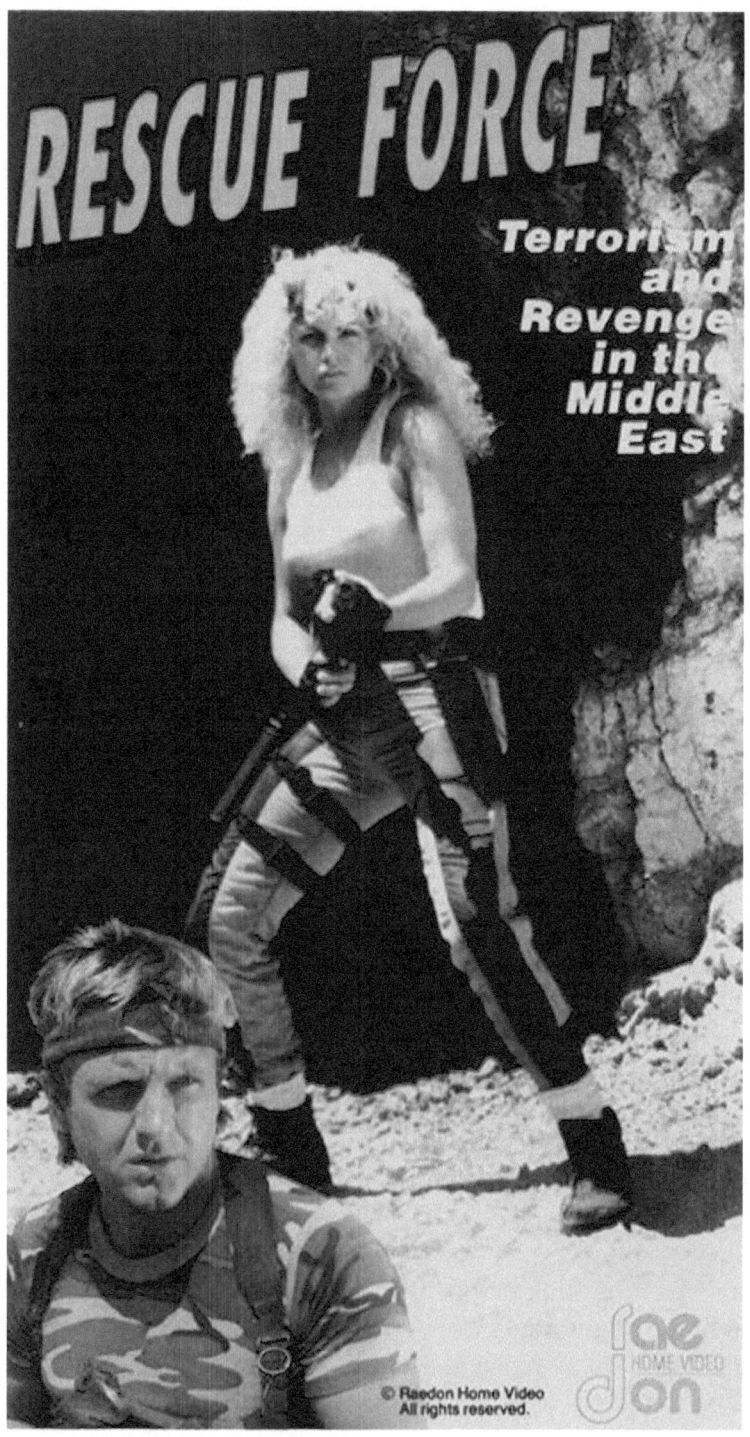

Rescue Force (1990)
Runtime 82 minutes
Directed by Charles L. Nizet

Rescue Force is about a governmental agency that has lots of special agents that do dangerous special forces work around the globe to fight terrorism. When one of their agents is kidnapped as well as an American diplomat working with Israel, the crew is assembled, and attacks are planned. In a nutshell that's the whole movie. What I didn't mention was that a significant portion of the film is spent on telephones and walkie-talkies. Often times the mouths of the callers are obscured by a hand or the phone itself so that anything could be dubbed in later. Maybe they forgot their scripts on those days? When the lines are delivered unobscured, it's obvious the actors are reading their lines from a sheet of paper in front of them. Rest assured though, when the action hits, it's mighty cheesy.

Rescue Force is a flag-waving, anti-Middle East film that stars a bunch of dads and their mustaches. Much of the movie either takes place in a room on a phone or in the desert blowing stuff up. Richard Harrison (Ninja Terminator (1986)) shows up briefly to nod and agree at a board meeting, and later he pops up seemingly magically shooting a machine gun in the desert. He also has trouble manning his machine gun, visibly losing control and grimacing. The film also features some bizarre and hilarious lines like "You better get the job done before I give you a hot fudge enema". It sounds delicious and gross all at the same time. Later during a briefing, the agent in charge warns, "if you're captured or killed, you'll be fired". What a bummer, so if they die in action, their family will be notified of their death *and* their termination. Way to kick the family when they're down, dad boss. The film manages to have several action sequences with lots of explosions being delivered by cannons made out of PVC pipe and bottle rockets. Rescue Force is indeed an inept piece of exploitative action trash. The writing is terrible, and the line delivery is more wooden than George Washington's teeth. The action is underwhelming, and the plot is needlessly complicated. The film ends with the female stars taking a bubble bath together nude. Because that's what all attractive ladies do (...right?). If you love Dad action, this one might tickle you. It really depends on how much you enjoy poorly-executed phone conversations and action.

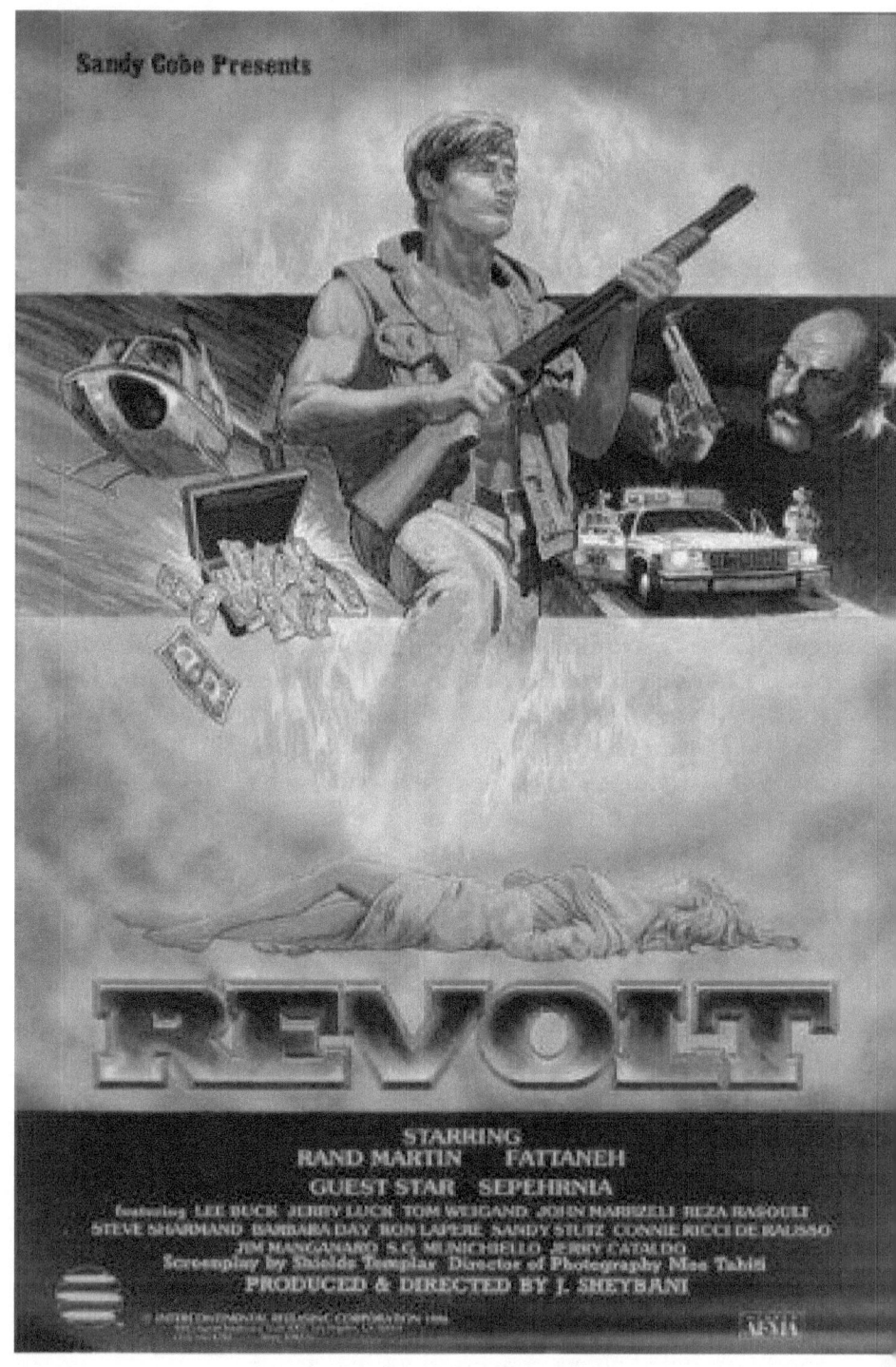

Revolt (1986)
Runtime 72 minutes
Directed by J. Sheybani

The film begins with an extended voice-over narration telling us how awful drugs are and how soulless drug dealers are. The voice sounds like a low-rent Johnny Cash, the dialogue sounds like something out of a D.A.R.E. manual that was taken out because it was too ham-fisted and blatant. Macintosh is the local drug kingpin in the nondescript town the film takes place in. He likes wearing ostentatious clothing and a Tom Selleck mustache (like a REAL man). He hires a plucky young man desperate for a job to drive for him, though he doesn't say that he'll be smuggling drugs. The new drug mule has a brother who also drives drugs for Macintosh. He gets shot by the cops and gets away. He alerts Steve Brown, who also sports a Tom Selleck mustache. Steve HATES drug runners and plans to take Macintosh down with the help of the plucky young drug mule. Macintosh sends his goons to rough up the staff at Steve's Persian restaurant, but it doesn't work because Steve is a badass and earned his upper lip flavor-saver. Steve has had enough and decides to arm himself with a revolver while his young sidekick arms himself with the best armor on earth: a Denim vest with no shirt. He also sports a sweet shotgun. Together they want to destroy Macintosh with hot lead.

Revolt is one of those rare treats in a sea of mediocrity that brings the laughs and the action. Every actor gives it their all, but all of them have 0% subtlety. Everything is yelling, pointing fingers, and mustache twirling. Given the film's scant runtime, there isn't much time for any fat and Revolt does a good job of shoehorning in action around every corner, which I approve of greatly. The ending is appropriately action-packed, with a great shootout that involves "tactical" vertical jumps while shooting. It's great. The film also manages to end on a total bummer, contrary to the tone of the rest of the film, ending with a giant THE END in cartoony text. Revolt is a blast of cheese with no subtlety in sight.

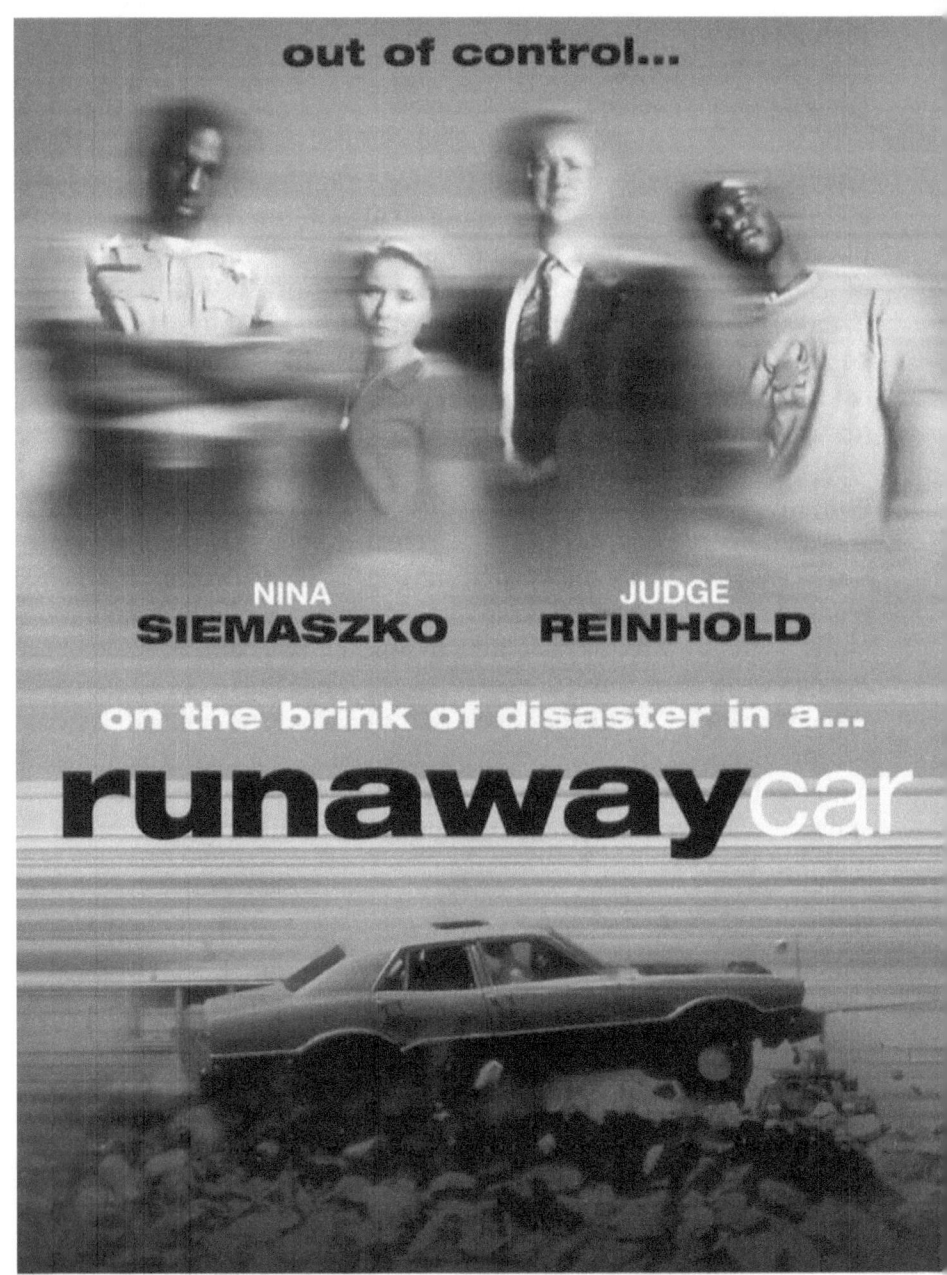

Runaway Car (1997)
Runtime 86 minutes
Directed by Jack Sholder

Jenny is a nurse who kinda sucks at her job. Despondent over her poor performance in the operating room, she picks up her '78 brown beater from the mechanic, ready to have a relaxing weekend. There she meets Ed Lautner (Judge Reinhold), he's there to pick up his car before an important business meeting but it isn't ready. Jenny, being the helpful sort she is, offers to give him a lift to his meeting (what a gal!). However, she has to pick up her sister's baby on the way. After the baby has been lovingly deposited into her back seat, she hits a skateboarder. He too needs a ride. Now she's got a full car. What could go wrong? Everything of course! She gets on the highway, but her car won't stop accelerating! Her brakes don't work either! Now she and her passengers are stuck in a speeding crappy car with a nearly full tank of gas and peril at every turn.

Runaway car is very silly. The suspense is dialed to 10, none of it believable. The characters scream and fret while the police try to figure out how to stop the hurtling lemon before she reaches a city full of citizens for her to mow down. The fever pitch of the movie reminds me of a PM Entertainment flick, only without all the explosions and shooting. I laughed aloud many times at the sheer ridiculousness of the movie while watching it. I wouldn't want to spoil the movie for you, but there are many attempts to stop the car and save the baby and none of them work. Nearly every character shouts their way through the film, the excitement level being pushed to the max. It takes a solid 20 or 30 minutes to get to the point where the car goes bananas but it's totally worth the wait. Cliches abound in the film, from the soulless police captain to the dispatcher who is one day from retirement, the noble patrol officer, and the jerk (Reinhold). Each character is cookie-cutter and lacks any kind of humanity or nuance. It's great. The situations become more and more extreme and thus the film gets more and more funny as it goes on. Runaway Car is a silly, inoffensive, over-the-top 90's screechy fun flick worth checking out. Because it was made for tv it sadly never pushes the envelope as far as it could have had it been a direct-to-video flick but it's still a fun way to spend less than 90 minutes.

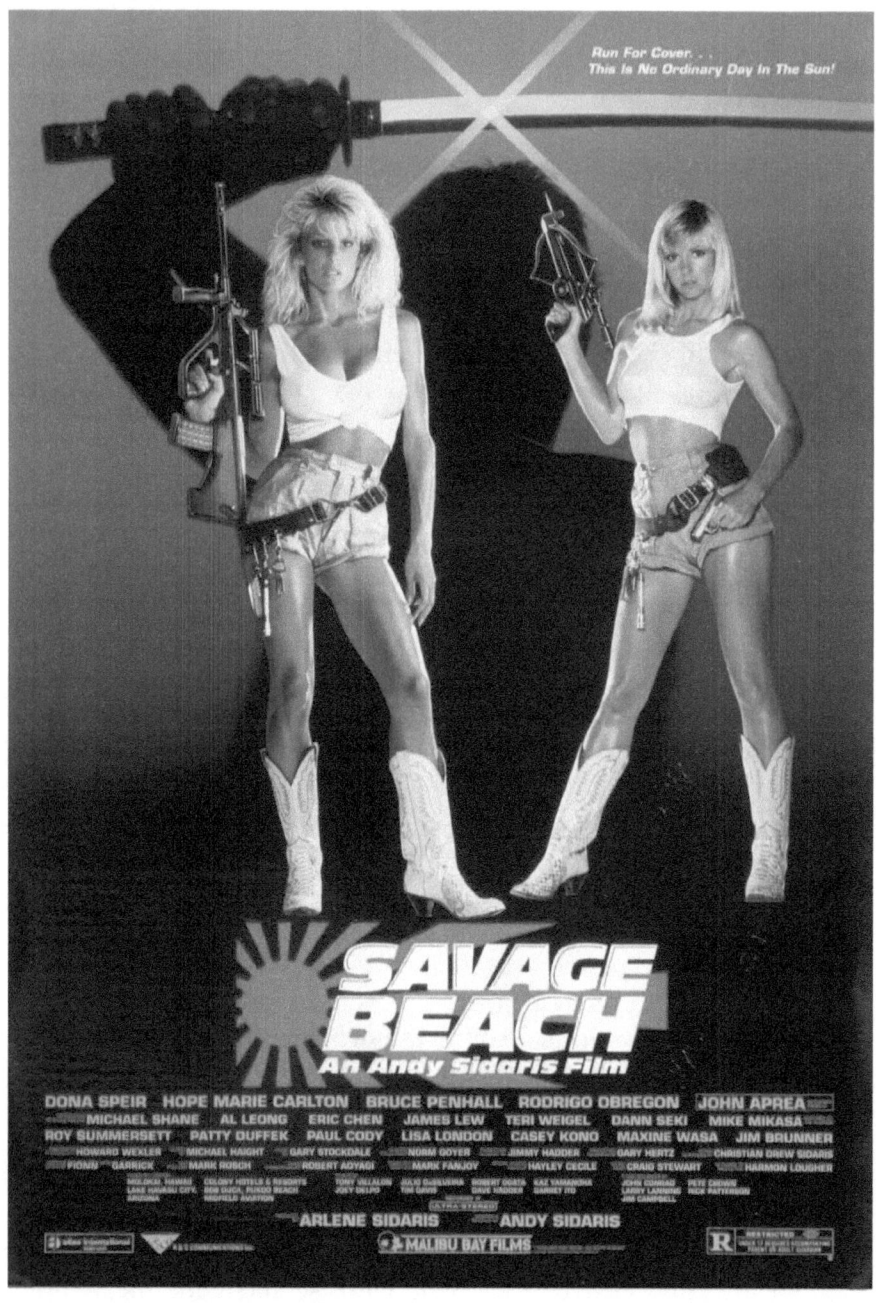

Savage Beach (1989)
Runtime: 90 minutes
Directed by Andy Sidaris

During the 80's and 90's, Andy Sidaris cranked out action trash films starring Playboy Playmates almost on a yearly basis. Typically, it involves nudity, explosions, and machine guns (no real complaints thus far...). These are the movies your mom warned you about and your dad rented. Savage Beach is the fourth entry into the official Sidaris universe, having followed Picasso Trigger (1988), and precedes GUNS (1990).

Savage Beach follows a nefarious plot involving dirty military officers from multiple branches and their hunt for WWII gold pilfered from the Philippines by the Japanese. The gold was put onto a boat... which almost immediately is sunk. Now the military guys have finally tracked down where they think the stolen gold ended up and they want to get it. A group of militant communists also want the gold and will stop at nothing to get it in order to fund their revolution. As it turns out, the island in which the gold is buried (I know, how did the gold get end up BURIED on an island when it was lost at sea? No clue.) is the place where our heroes Donna and Taryn have crash landed. Our heroic ladies have to figure out a way to get off the island without getting killed by the warring factions.

Full disclosure: this one's not as much fun as Hard Ticket to Hawaii (1987), which could be the high-water mark in the Sidaris oeuvre. It lacks the mutant snake and silly weapons, but it does feature the requisite nudity and action found in any of these films. Picasso Trigger had some dull spots but ended with fantastic action. Savage Beach has slightly more action spread around the movie, but it too suffers from too much talking and not enough action. There are long stretches where characters are talking, and frankly that's not what I signed up for. Savage Beach lacks the over-the-top ending or inventive methods of destruction of Picasso Trigger, but the pacing is a bit better.

Savage Beach is a solid entry into the Sidaris universe, but it isn't a highlight. It's like a jeep (which is always featured in these films): it gets the job done. It has *just* enough action, nudity, and cheese to make it a fun, if middling, watch with friends.

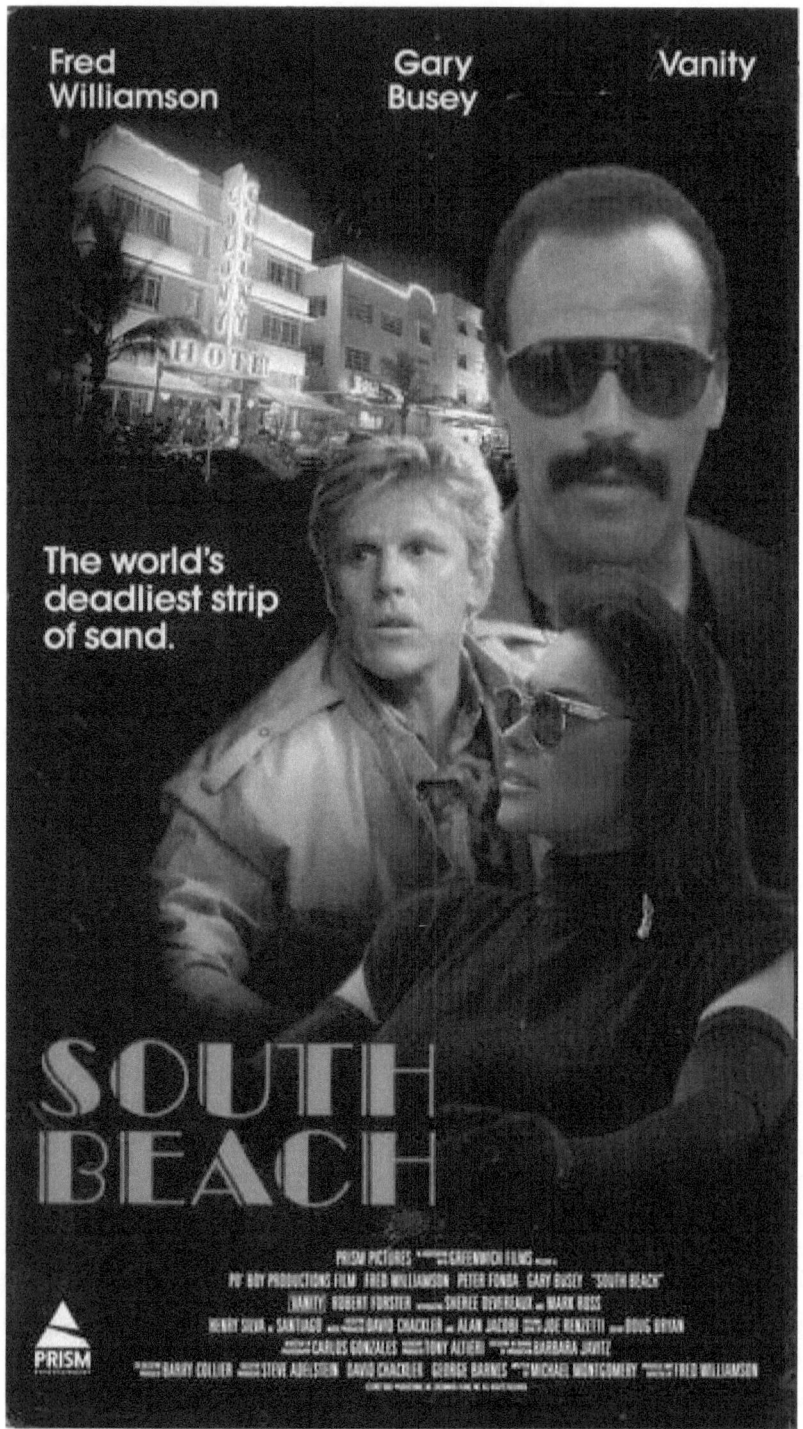

South Beach (1993)
Runtime 93 minutes
Directed by Fred Williamson

Starring Fred Williamson, Gary Busey, Peter Fonda, Robert Forster, Vanity, Sam Jones, and Henry Silva, the cast of South Beach cannot be ignored (and was the main reason I watched the movie). Fred and Gary star as ex-NFL stars that are over the hill but not done being studs. They are private detectives always on the prowl for privates they can detect. Vanity stars as Fred's MUCH younger ex-wife that still loves him. She works for a phone sex company and keeps getting freaky phone calls from someone named Billy. She hires Fred to check into it while Gary is on vacation. Fred looks up his old buddy and also former NFL star played by Peter Fonda. Now, I don't want to body shame, but I found it TOTALLY unbelievable that Fonda's scarecrow-esque physique could have ever made it to the NFL (maybe he was a kicker?). He sports a greasy ponytail, a pervy mustache, and sunglasses so the audience won't know he's actually inebriated (we're talking Peter Fonda, NOT his character). His performance however doesn't leave anything to hide. At one point he tries to reach for a file cabinet's handle and misses. Yikes.
Later in the film Fred is hired to be a bodyguard for a pretty lady, again MUCH younger than him. He stares at her butt and says, "didn't your mama ever tell you to wear underwear?" to which she replies "yes in case of accidents, but I don't believe in accidents". So, I guess that means if she pees herself, it was intentional? There isn't much action in the movie aside from a few shootouts and sloppy fights. South Beach isn't an action flick per se, but more of a neo-noir written by a person with limited conversation skills. The dialogue is hilarious in the movie and so is Busey (in general). He's acting like a hyper 12-year-old and breathes energy into the film every time he's on screen. The plot makes little sense and left me confused but I didn't care. I had a great time with South Beach, watching some of my favorite actors chew the scenery and spout nonsensical lines with total seriousness. Given the lack of shoot em up action in South Beach I hesitate to whole-heartedly recommend it. I had a blast with it and laughed my face off at the hilarious dialogue and confusing plot, but mileage may vary depending on your love of the actors in the film.

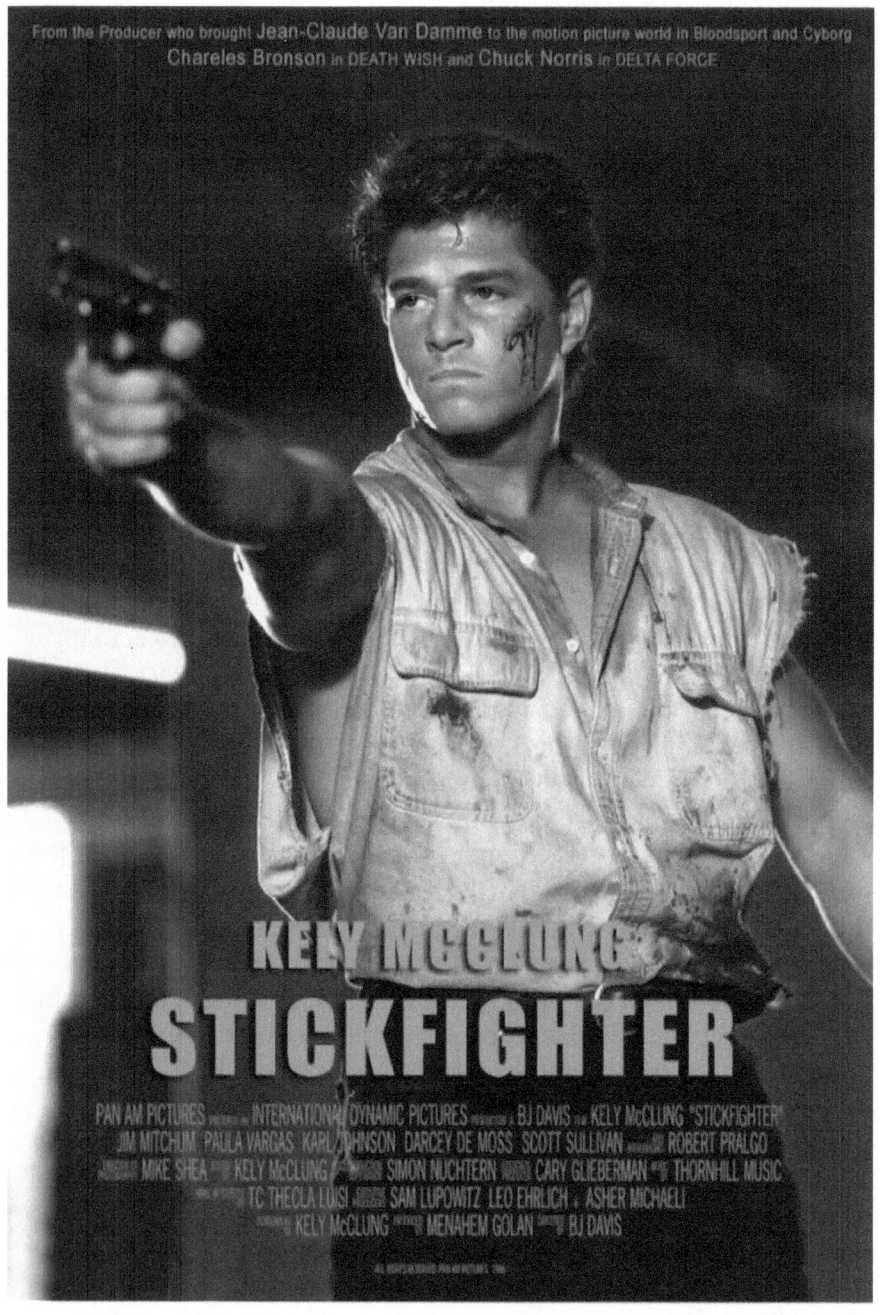

Stickfighter (1994)
Runtime 90 minutes
Directed by BJ Davis

Stickfighter (already a great start with the title) is about a hunky, tanned, and toned cop who's a loose cannon but gets the job done (the cliché that keeps giving!). He and his partner bust a gang of heroin dealers in their sleazy lair, but the action gets hot, really hot and our hero's partner gets his chest filled with buck shot. Sure, our hero lays waste to the ne'er-do-wells and they all end up in a body bag, but no amount of bullet spraying will bring his partner back. Only one bad guy escapes and he sports a bleached blonde flat top. Our hero's boss tears into him, as cop bosses frequently do in these movies, and our hero quits. That, however, does not stop our now ex-cop from tracking down the last lingering bad dude to put him six feet under as well. He tracks the bad guy to California where he meets his partner's highly attractive sister (what a coincidence!). Turns out little sis has been targeted by the crime syndicate that our flat-topped baddie also belongs to (double coincidence!). Now our stickfighter and his pretty lady friend have to take out the trash before the trash takes *them* out!

Uniquely, the film doesn't star any recognizable actors with the exception of James Mitchum (who looks so much like his father Robert Mitchum, it's eerie). Stickfighter won't win any awards for its plot; It's pretty cliché and clearly didn't tax the screenwriter much. What makes the movie stand apart is how over-the-top and simultaneously silly it is. Comparisons to films like Parole Violators (1994) would be apt and welcome. Our hero barely acts in the movie, filling his dialogue with awkward pauses and unconvincing tough guy posturing. In reality he really was a stickfighting champion, which is pretty amazing considering I didn't even know that was a thing before watching this movie. Much like Action U.S.A. (1989), this film was directed by a stunt man and so he wanted to showcase his regular profession extensively. I absolutely recommend this movie. It has tons of action, over-the-top villains, questionable decision making by our protagonists, and numerous memorable moments. Stickfighter is a pantheon movie.

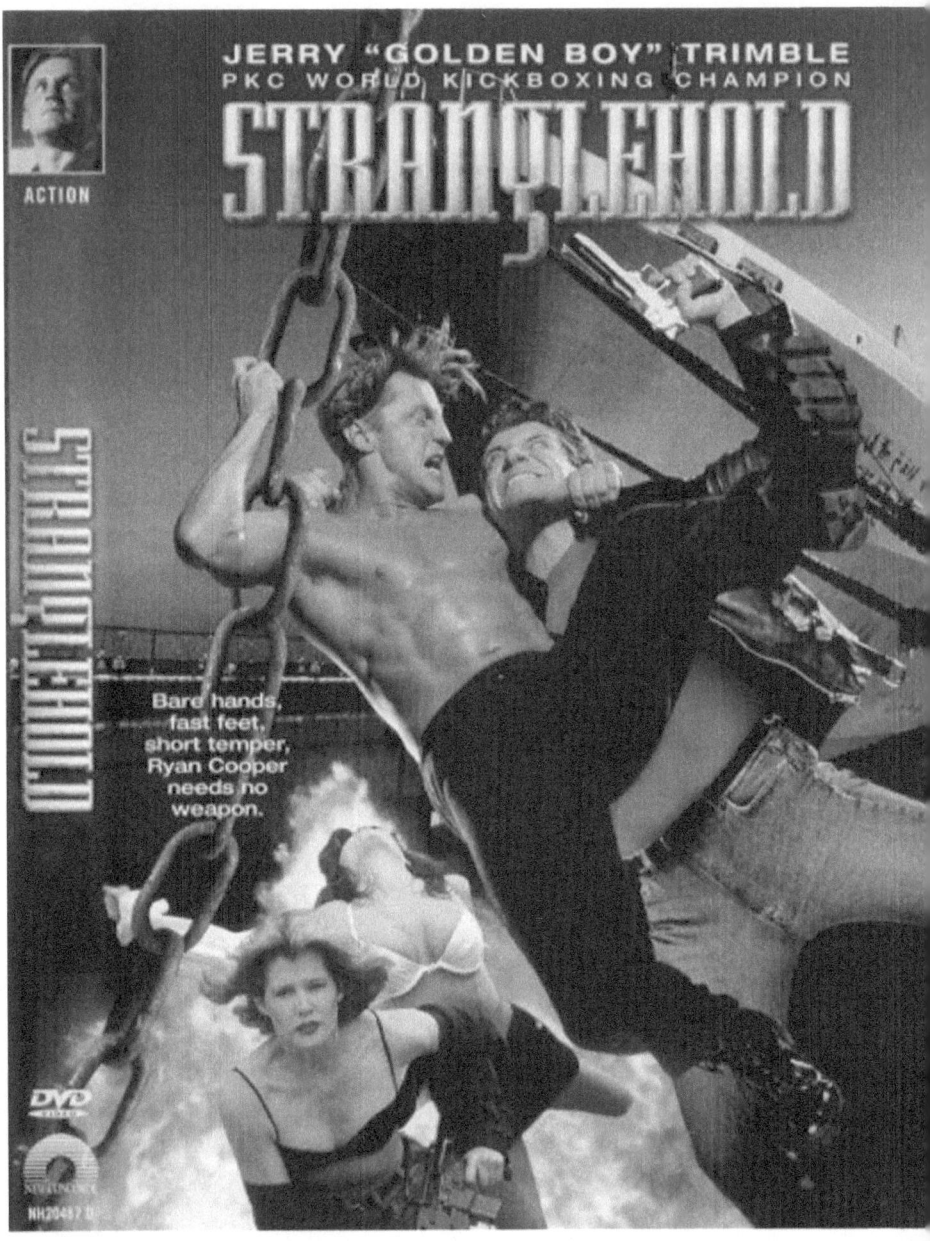

Stranglehold (1994)
Runtime 73 minutes
Directed by Cirio H. Santiago

The film begins with a group of dignitaries from the U.S. visiting a chemical plant in the Philippines. Senator Filmore is there to check out the plant which hopes to revolutionize the world of manufacturing. Her bodyguard Ryan Cooper (Jerry Trimble) isn't so sure, he smells a dangerous situation brewing. A news crew is there on site, with Gerald Richter (Vernon Wells) reporting. While the dignitaries are examining the plant, Filmore sends Cooper out to get sodas. Mistake. While our yuppie ponytail-wearing hero is trying to get a Pepsi a double cross is revealed! As it turns out our friendly news crew are actually terrorists who plan to use the Senator as a hostage for ransom. That's not all though: as it turns out the U.S. has been using that chemical factory to make a highly deadly nerve gas! The plant currently has 10,000 gallons, enough to wipe out the entire world! Now it's up to Cooper to get the hostages away from the villains and take out the bad guys before they can escape with their loot of deadly gas. Good thing Cooper is a loose cannon who always gets the job done! The film begins with every character sweating profusely (it's the Philippines y'all) and ends with everyone sweating profusely. Within five minutes the action has already begun, and it doesn't let up the rest of the runtime. There is no needless melodrama. There's no moment where Cooper grapples with his own mortality or what it means to be a man. He's sweaty, he kicks, punches, and shoots everything on two legs for over an hour, blows some shit up, and then the movie ends. There is zero fat to trim in this flick, every second counts here. If this movie was a band, it would be the Ramones. Vernon Wells chews the scenery with gusto, and it makes me wonder why he wasn't used more frequently in his career. The movie is so cheap they couldn't afford to blow up real stuff, so they blow up models of real stuff and that only adds to the fun factor. The music is a fantastic representation for the film: it's simple and doesn't waste your time with unneeded guitar solos or flim flam. Everything in this movie is streamlined for maximum action in a minimum amount of time. Stranglehold may not be the most memorable movie out there, but it'll kick some ass and won't waste your time. It may not be pantheon but it sure is fun and lean.

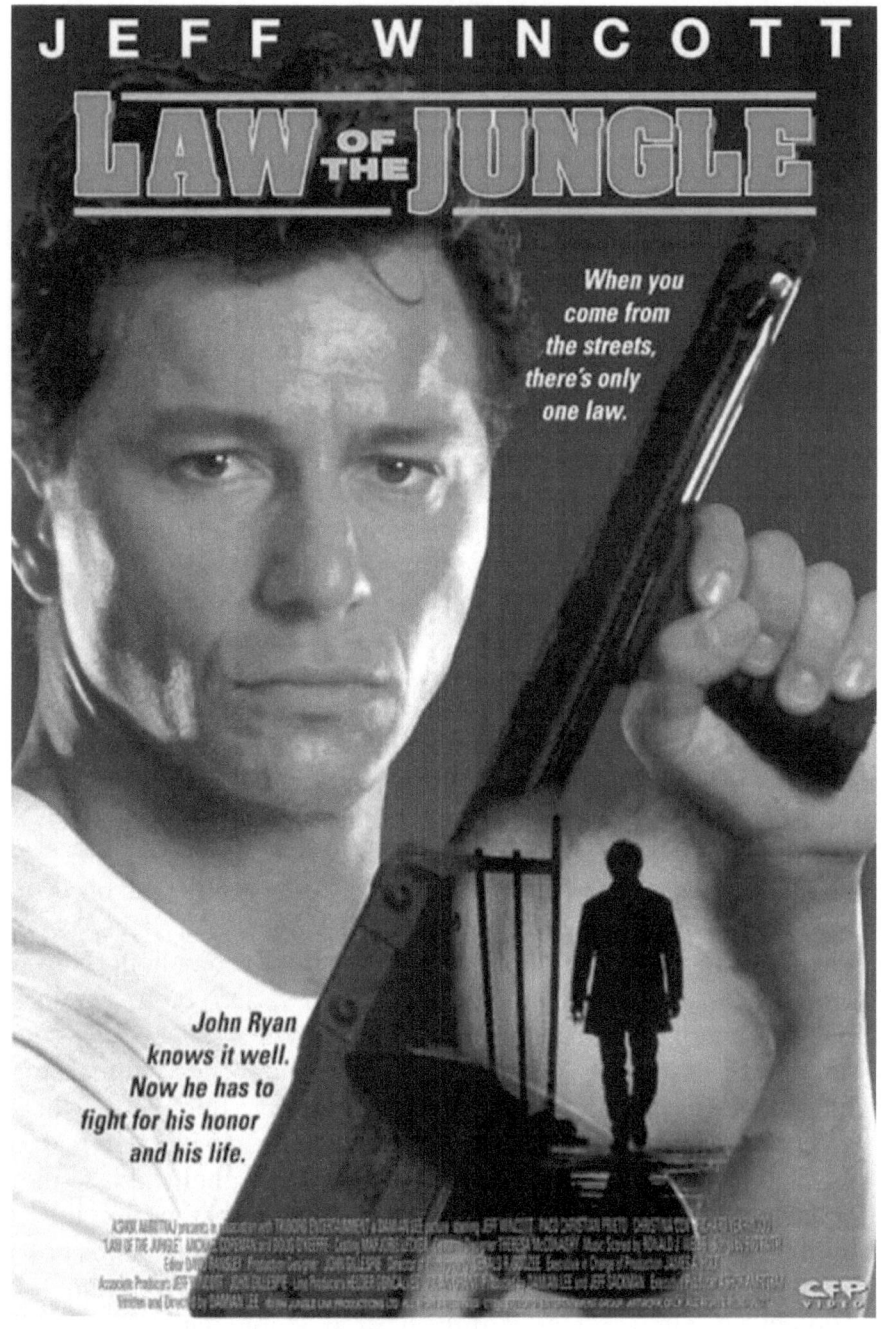

Street Law aka Law of the Jungle (1995)
Runtime 97 Minutes
Directed by Damian Lee

Jeff Wincott stars as John Ryan, an ass-kicking martial artist lawyer. Yes, you read that right. When he's not busy practicing his spin kicks, he's punching the law in its metaphorical face. He works for an expensive firm that offers defense services for those that can pay. Ryan however likes to take the cases of "the little guys" and does pro-bono work, much to the chagrin of his employer. He even owes money to loan sharks due to his big ole bleeding heart. The loan shark is an old friend turned foe, Luis Calderone (Paco Christian Prieto), who likes having Ryan in his debt because he wants to settle an old score, the one that soured their friendship. Meanwhile Ryan's employer set him up defending a rich scumbag with a fetish for beating up prostitutes. Ryan gets the guy set free but learns that his client was indeed guilty. Ryan decides to set things to rights by setting up the client to get beaten up with a baseball bat by the woman he abused. Ryan then finds himself kicked out of the firm, broke, and homeless. Now he owes Luis and has no way to pay except to fight in illegal underground fighting matches. What he doesn't know is that Luis and his ex-boss are in cahoots and the whole thing was a setup! Now Ryan has to fight his way out of this sticky situation, a job he's well suited to do!

Street Law has many of the tropes that make awful awesome action movies fun. It has bad fashion (Wincott's hair is at an awkward length that makes his head look like a mushroom), hammy over-acting by the villain, low-rent fight scenes, and an explosive conclusion. It also has the unique twist of a law drama which is a strange mix with illegal fighting. I thoroughly enjoyed Paco Christian Prieto's accent and performance and its presence in the film that helps to elevate it to a memorable level. Wincott does his best in the film, which I can appreciate. Wincott may not be the most electrifying action lead, but he never sleepwalks through his films, no matter how cheap they may be. If you're a fan of his, this one is worth checking out Street Law is not a must-see film, but it is solid and will provide you with plenty of entertainment for an awful awesome get-together.

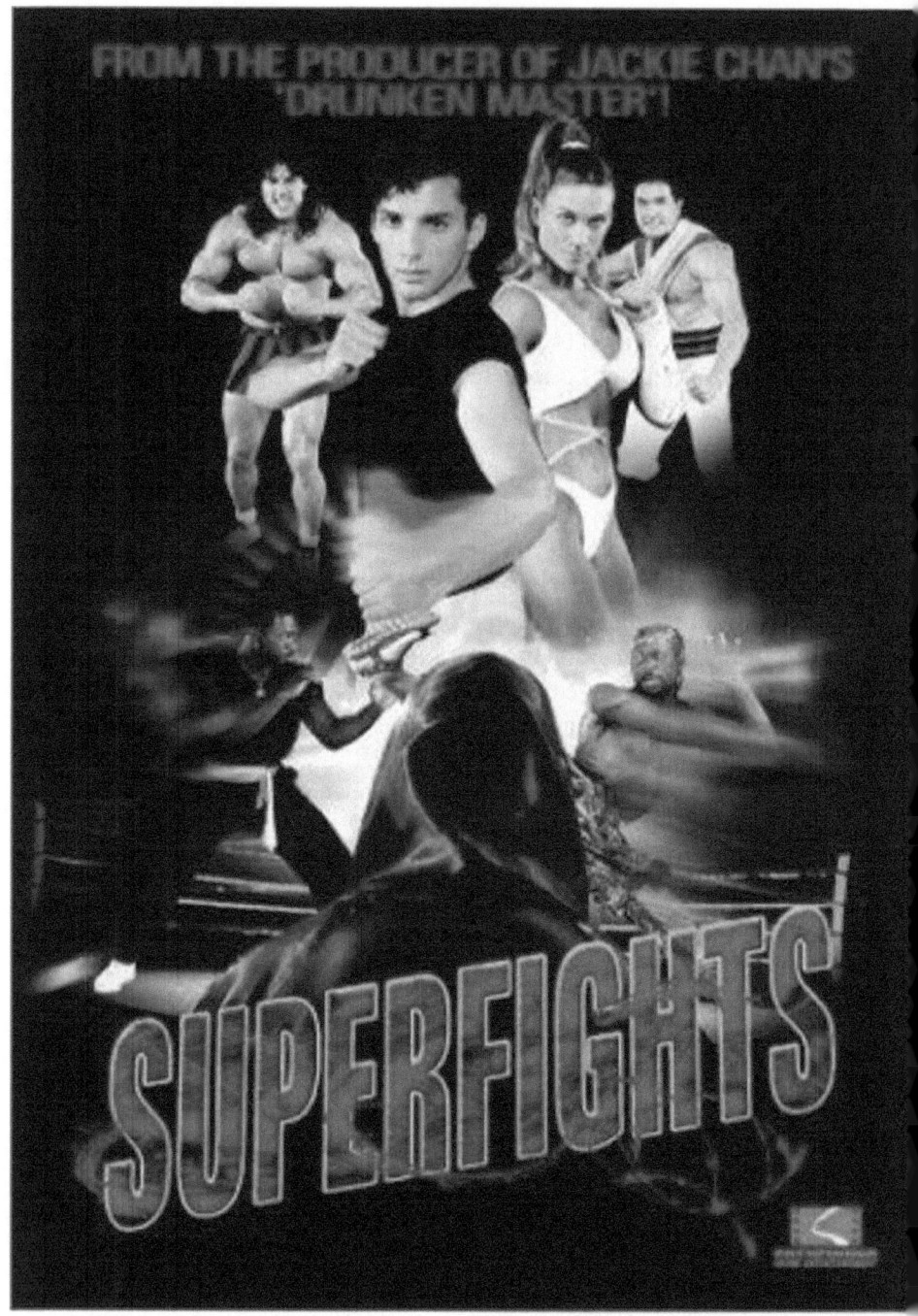

Superfights (1995)
Runtime 94 minutes
Directed by Siu-Hung Leong

Superfights is about a diminutive young man with a dream: to be a star fighter on an ultra-popular weekly fighting show. He spends his days training in an empty box factory until one night when he saves a young woman from being mugged. The entire event is caught on a security camera and this footage launches him into local stardom. Smelling an opportunity, the sleazy owner of Superfights offers the young man a contract. Life is good for him: he gets his place on his favorite show, he gets paid to train, and the girl he saved is interested in him. Plus, she has a tie-chi master for a grandfather. That is until he finds out his televised fights have been works; he didn't actually win any of them. The fighters, aside from being dishonest, are also involved in extortion and assault, a world he now finds himself in. He has to find a way to get himself out of the Superfights and bring down the sleazy owner.

Superfights is one of a handful of films created for the U.S. Audience by a Hong Kong-based film company The result is a bizarre mix of Americanisms through the lens of Hong Kongers. Although our hero is a full-grown man with very impressive martial arts skills, he looks like a pubescent boy. Dude is tiny. The film features a theme song that uses that title of the movie and it's catchy, cheesy, and wonderful. The movie also stars Chuck Jeffries, professional wrestler Rob Van Dam (who doesn't have any lines), and a final villain with the fanciest footwork I've ever seen in a direct to video action flick. The film is very earnest but feels like it was written by a child, in the best possible way. The dialogue is very heart-on-sleeve and hilarious. The action is intense, well done, and frequent. The colors in the film are loud and very 90's, just like the characters themselves. We get some serious mullets, sweaty dudes, and a very masculine female trainer. Superfights is a great Awful Awesome film to throw on for friends. The plot is very simple, the action nearly non-stop, the hero is uncharacteristically short, and the stakes very high. This is a great entry-level flick to show friends because although it does have a limited budget, it's still professionally executed and a ton of fun.

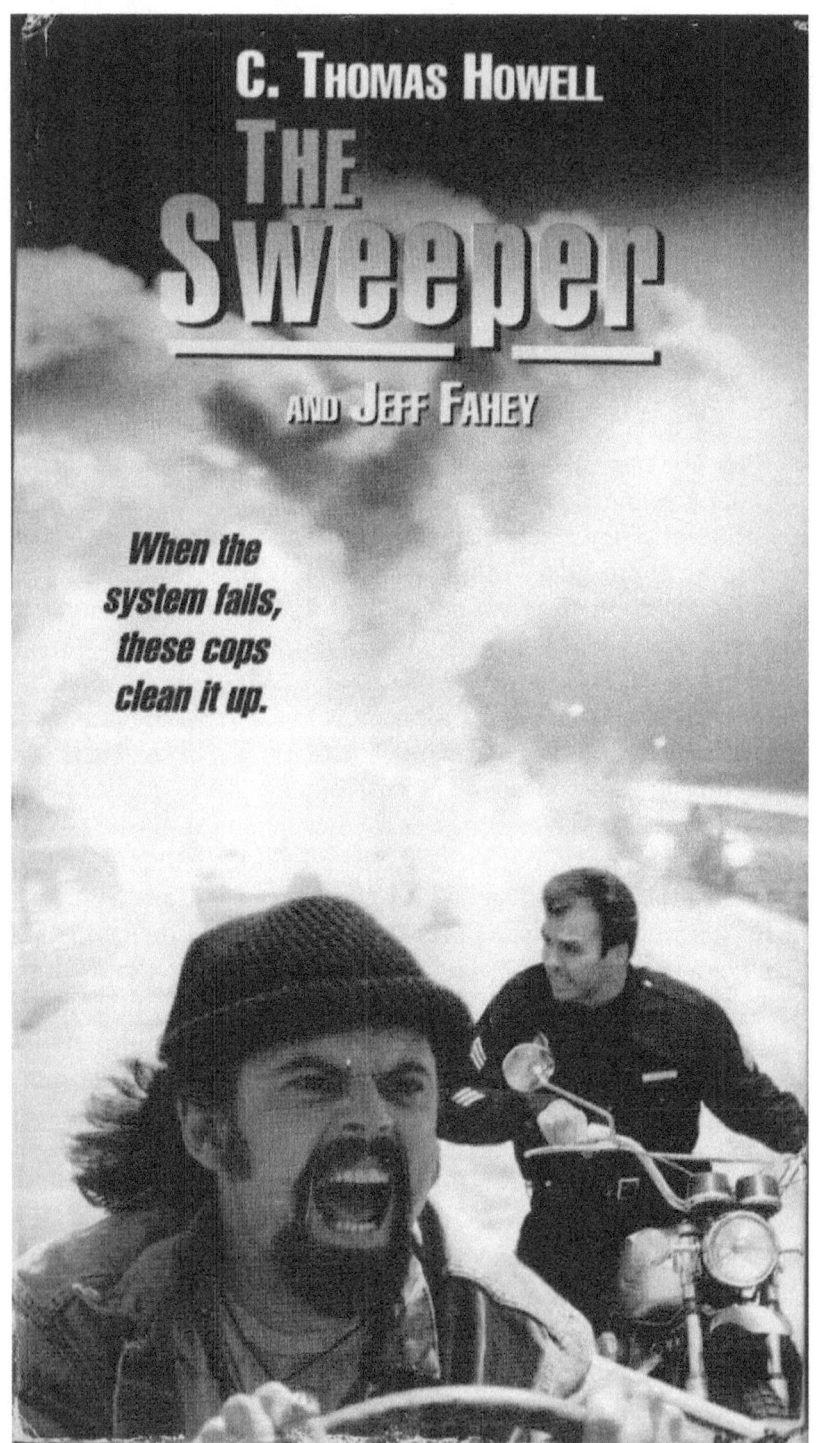

The Sweeper (1996)
Runtime 90 minutes
Directed by Joseph Merhi

PM Entertainment film The Sweeper begins with a beat cop (Jeff Fahey) who decided to take his son on a ride along on the wrong day. He tries to bust some pimps on a pier but one of them hijacks the car (along with his son) and drives down what could be the longest pier in the world. The cop hijacks a motorcycle, does some sweet wheelies and brings the crook to justice. That's not the end of it though, the cop gets a home visit from some thugs and gets murdered along with his wife and daughter. His son, however, survives. Fast forward fifteen years and we meet the grown-up version of the kid who has become a cop himself (Howell). He's a loose cannon but he gets the job done. He's invited by a shadowy law enforcement agent (Ed Lauter) to join a secret branch of law enforcement with a license to kill. He joins the group but soon finds it's as corrupt as the criminals they're trying to take out. Now he's a one-man wrecking crew hell-bent on taking everyone in the world down, even if it means having a fist fight on a biplane.

The Sweeper is exactly what I look for in a PM Entertainment flick: The action is consistent, over-the-top, and very memorable. We get some of the biggest car-splosions I've ever seen, numerous shootouts, a fist fight in a mall where no folding table is safe, stunts involving jumping off of buildings, and C. Thomas Howell wearing a House of Pain hat and a necklace with a medallion that looks like a slice of pizza with a chicken foot on it. Chicken foot pizza? Who knew? The "plot" takes a long time to finally kick into gear, but it doesn't matter because the movie dishes out the action frequently and it never disappoints. Who cares about things like plot, character development, or realism when you've got guns that don't need to be reloaded, 90's fashion, and some highly-disposable cars? I watched this one with my bad movie buds and we had a fun time joking about the bad fashion and marveling at the crazy action. We've all seen several PM flicks, so we know what to expect and even we were impressed by its zany antics. Is it the best PM flick? Probably not. Rage (1995) still has the most action and the least amount of plot, plus it has Gary Daniels. The Sweeper, however, is an excellent entry in their filmography and shouldn't be missed.

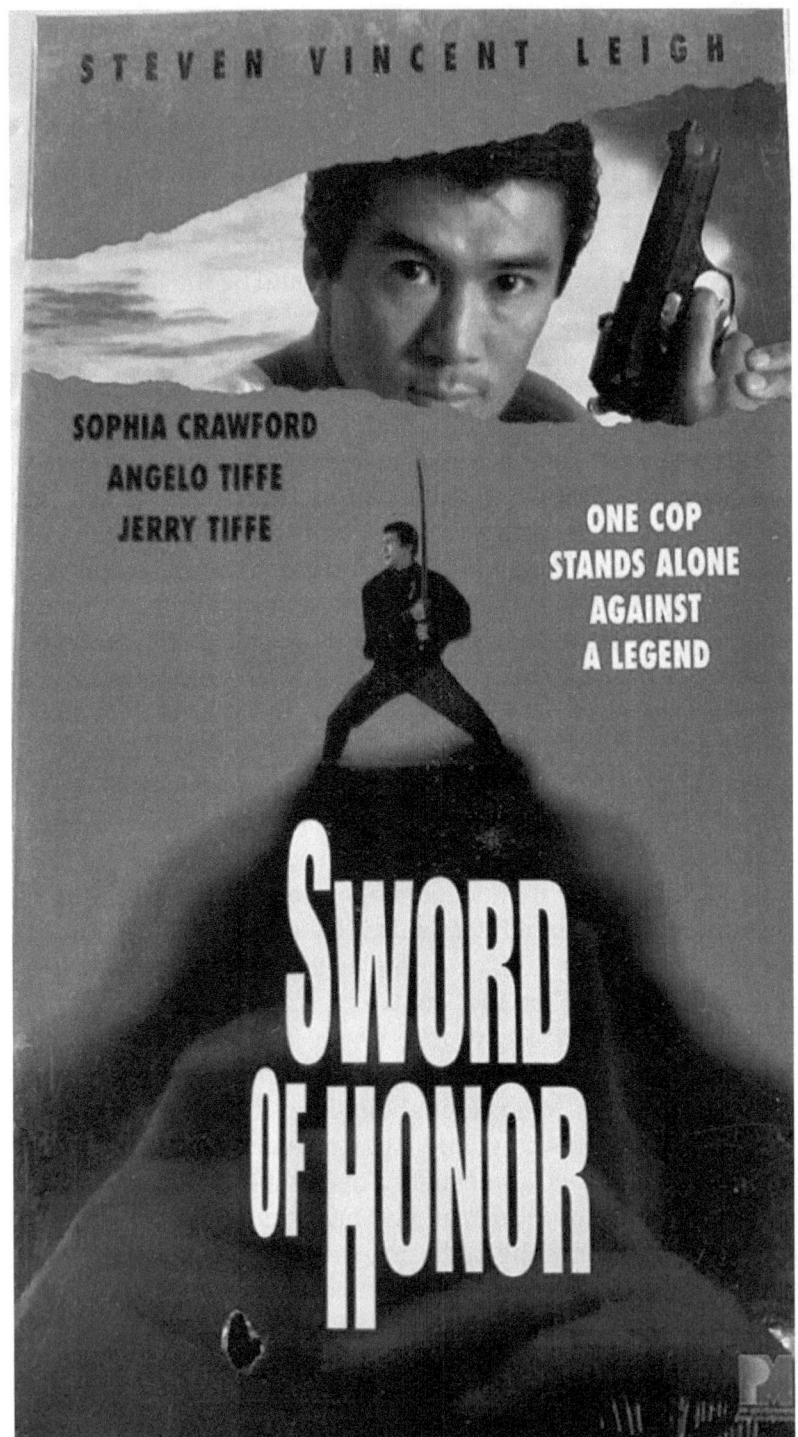

Sword of Honor (1996)
Runtime 96 minutes
Directed by Robert Tiffe

PM Entertainment film Sword of Honor takes place in Las Vegas, where a famous sword that slayed many foes is up for auction. It's worth a pretty penny due to its deadly pedigree and it attracts the interest of a local crime boss. He hires a crew to steal the sword at night from the auction house, but the trouble is the goons attract the attention of the police. Our hero Johnny (Steven Vincent Leigh) responds to the call and so does his partner, despite it being his last day on the force (uh oh...). He's retiring early so that he and his sister can run a martial arts dojo. Of course, the partner gets plugged and now Johnny wants to find the criminals responsible and bring them to sweet justice. The crime boss who steals the sword decides that instead of selling the blade once, he will try to sell it multiple times by killing the buyer and stealing his money. Surprisingly his plan works, but it leaves a trail of dead bodies for Johnny to follow until he finally pinpoints the perpetrators and hatches a plan with his partner's sister/his-new-lover to get the bad guys once and for all.

Sword of Honor is a solid PM flick. While it doesn't have the high levels of destruction and stunts, I expect from a PM film, it does feature action every 7-10 minutes in ingenious ways. I marveled at how the writer was able to convincingly shoehorn fight scenes and shootouts throughout the film's runtime. What this means is the film never has a chance to get dull. Steven Leigh does a good job of carrying the film, I can't understand why he wasn't a bigger star as he's both charismatic, an impressive physical specimen, and seems to know how to fight as well. The subplot involving the love affair between Johnny and his partner's sister is nothing but a ploy to sneak in arbitrary nudity and sex but doesn't distract from the main plot. While the film isn't highly memorable, it doesn't let the viewer down either. We get what we came for: lots of action and not a lot of thinking. If you enjoy PM Entertainment films, this one is worth your time. If you haven't seen any, this wouldn't be a great place to start as it lacks the over-the-top car crashes and stunts that I've come to expect. I'm glad I watched it, but this isn't a "must see" flick.

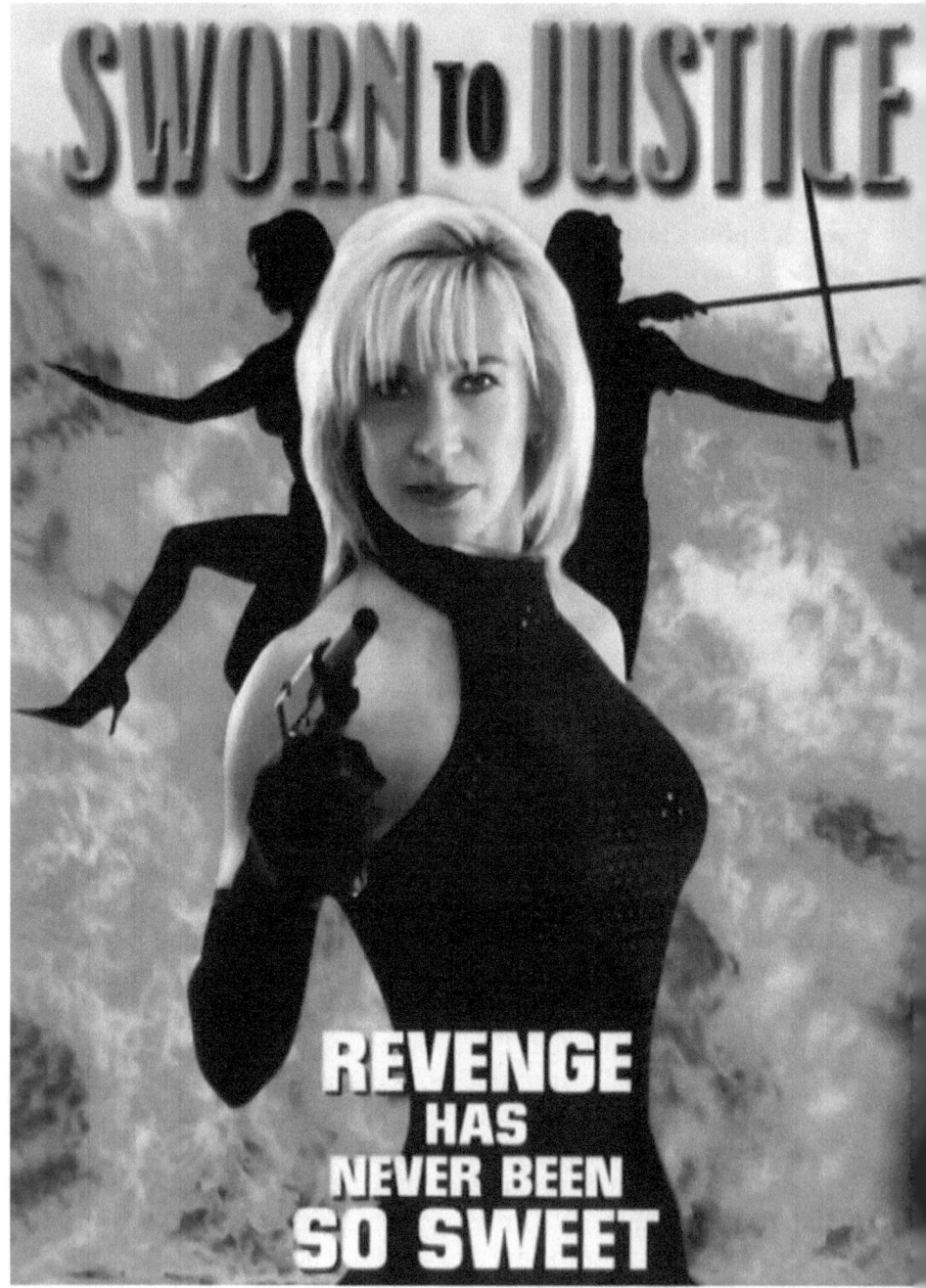

Sworn to Justice (1996)
Runtime 97 minutes
Directed by Paul Maslak

Cynthia Rothrock stars as Janna, a psychologist that specializes in court cases involving weird-o's. The film begins with her sister and nephew being brutally murdered when a robbery goes very wrong. Janna is crushed and angry, she wants to lash out... and lash out she does. She's also a martial artist (naturally) and starts doing some vigilantism on the side while trying to find her sister's murderers. She's also psychic. When she touches things, she gets memories associated with the item. Why? Because psychics were popular in '96 apparently. The detective on her case stops by her house often to ask questions. Instead, they end up arguing while Janna gives the detective a load of crap even though he's the only guy looking. Some thanks, right? She meets a hunky lawyer, and they begin a love affair which doesn't enter much into the plot. Really, it's just an excuse to get Rothrock nekkid and sweaty with him. He also knows martial arts because everyone in these movies does, right? Mako plays a blind guy who is way too interested in Janna; his whole role is sitting on a stool selling newspapers and giving her mysterious warnings from some vaguely prescient dreams he has. Brad Dourif plays a small role as a guy on trial for murder. Walter Koenig is in the movie for about five minutes, he's a parapsychologist and helps to establish Janna as a psychic.

This movie is a mess. It's overstuffed with plots and doesn't know what the hell it is. Is it a vigilante flick? Is it a martial arts flick? Is it a thriller? Is it a bad episode of the X-Files? Is it a steamy lifetime movie about a woman trying to make it in a male-dominated world? It's all of these things, which means it's none of these things. It's a big ole bag of bad and I had a hoot watching it. We get to see Rothrock throw a tantrum at Brad Dourif, and it was so funny I rewound the movie and watched it twice. Rothrock is trying to act her heart out, but the director was too ham-handed to know when to reel her in. We do get to see her hunky lawyer boyfriend kicking ass in some denim pants (with belt) and no shirt. It's pretty ridiculous. I loved that part. Watch some of her other films first to grow an appreciation for Rothrock, then jump into this one.

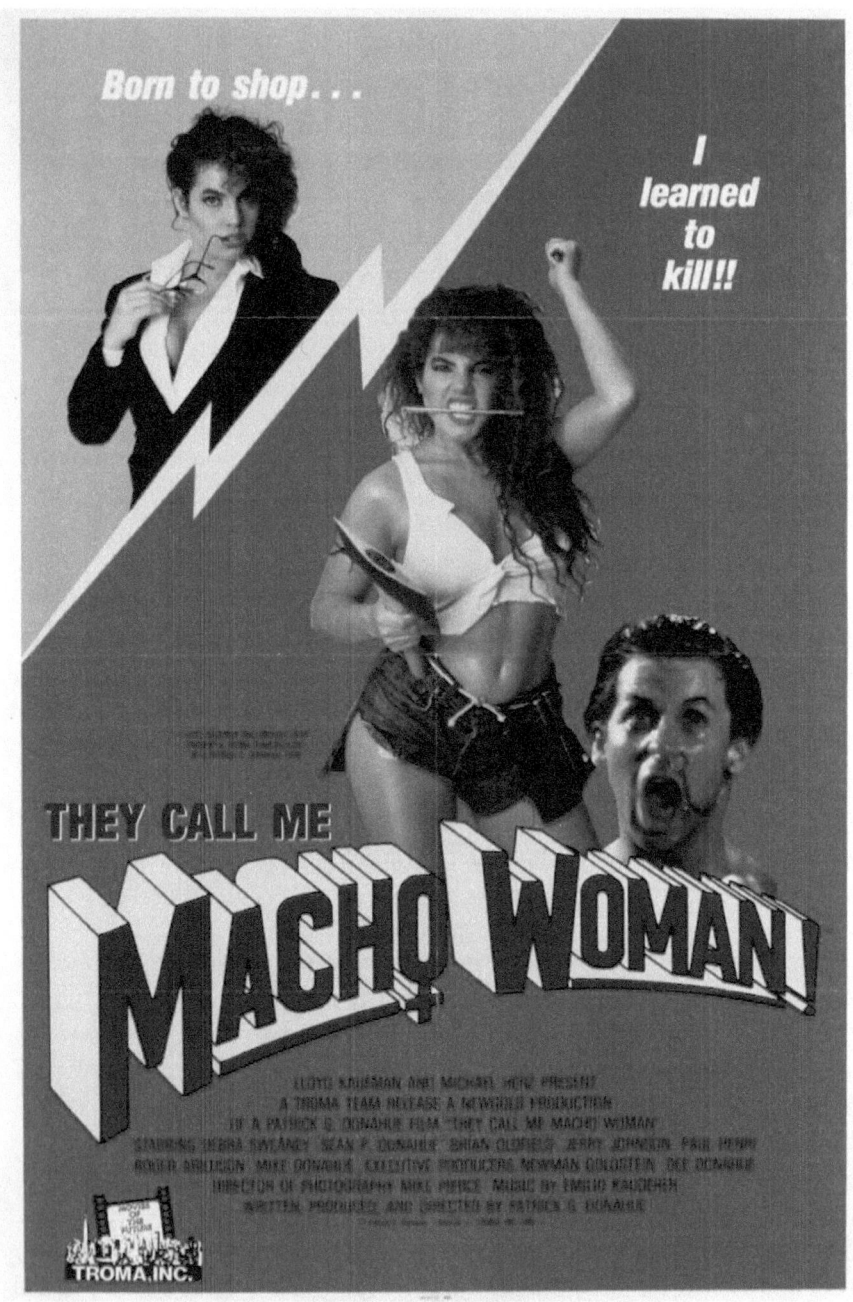

They Call Me Macho Woman (1991)
Runtime 85 minutes
Directed by Patrick Donahue

They Call Me Macho Woman is about a woman (duh), Susan, who travels out to the country looking for a house to buy. She's traveling with her real estate agent Cecil, who wears a jacket that looks like it was skinned from a cheap couch. What they don't know is that the area is controlled by a vicious gang of drug distributors, and they don't take kindly to outsiders. The gang, run by Mongo (Olympic Shotput star Brian Oldfield) sets out to capture or kill the duo so that their dirty little secret doesn't get leaked to the cops. The gang runs Cecil and Susan off the road and quickly dispatch Cecil. Susan on the other hand is captured by the gang where she is beaten and tied up. She escapes and throughout much of the first hour of the film is either being chased, beaten, or is escaping from capture. The last 30 minutes or so are dedicated to Susan finally kicking some serious drug peddler ass in an over-the-top way only Patrick Donahue could provide.

Although the movie doesn't feature any nudity, it does feature a lot of attempted rape. It seems that everyone, man or woman, in this film finds Susan irresistible. They all get their comeuppance before things go too far, this isn't a rape revenge story after all, but those sensitive to material like this will not have much fun watching it. For others who can stand some sleaze as long as it has an over-the-top payoff *will* enjoy this flick. We get feet spiked, eyes poked out, chrome hatchets thrown, booby traps, and very mild car crashes that I'm sure were meant to look very intense. They don't. For the first fifteen minutes of the movie Susan says the name Cecil probably a hundred times. It's hilarious. The dialogue in the film is unnatural and the acting is poor for the most part. The music consists of metal clanking sounds except, oddly, when she's building her sweet armory to take on the gang. It seems like the time to use anvil smacking music would be when weapons are being made, but maybe I just don't understand the subtleties of the composer. While not as much fun as Donahue film Parole Violators (1994), They Call Me Macho Woman is still an enjoyable if not pantheon Awful Awesome flick, so long as you understand the nature of the film going into it.

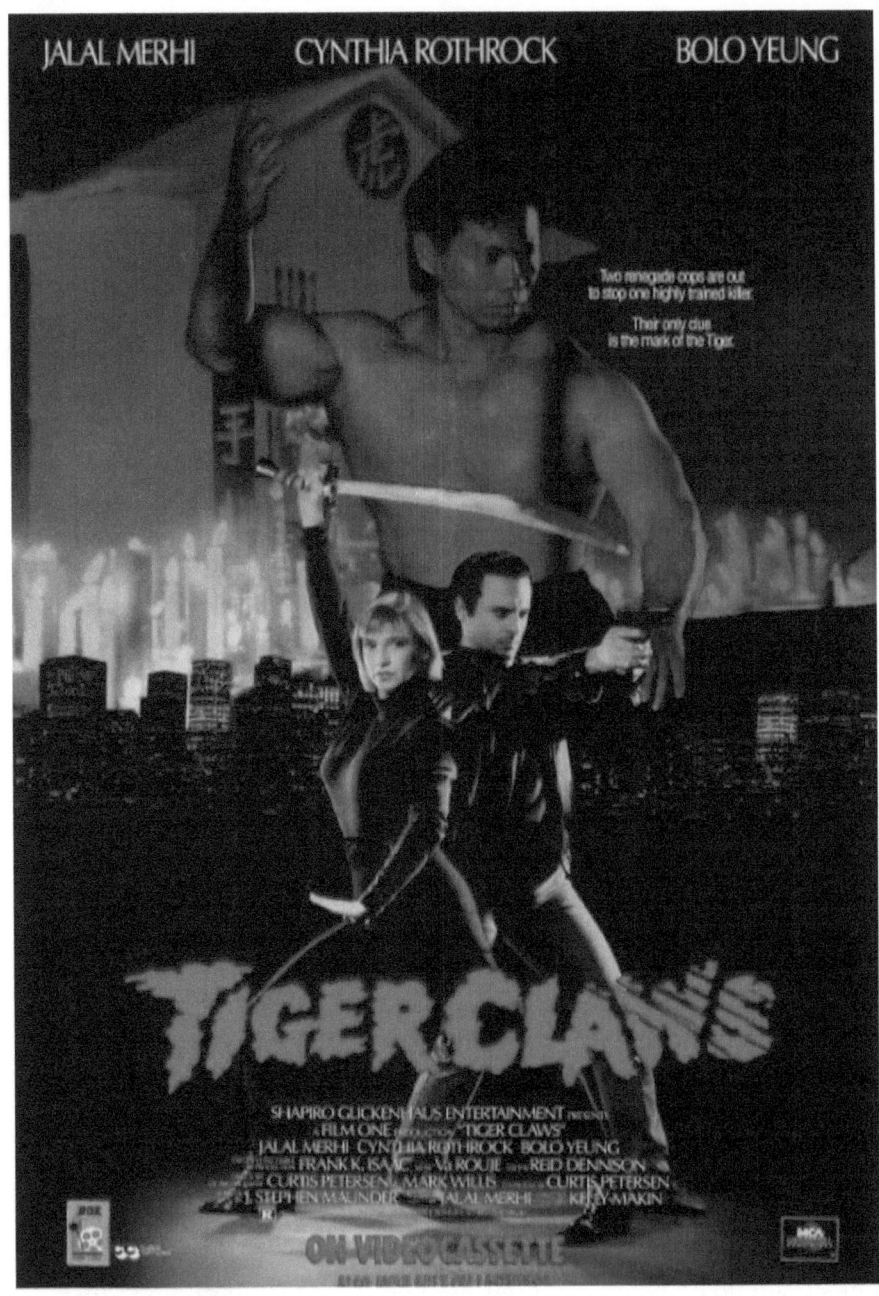

Tiger Claws (1991)
Runtime 96 minutes
Directed by Kelly Makin

Cynthia Rothrock stars as Linda Masterson, an undercover cop tired of dressing like a hooker to bust bad guys (sounds reasonable). Jalal Merhi stars as Tarek Richards, also a cop, he's the obligatory loose cannon, but he gets the job done. When a series of martial artists are murdered and left with mysterious scratch marks on their faces, Masterson and Tarek team up to find out who this serial killer is and bring him to justice. The two use their impressive martial arts skills and knowledge to deduce that the killer must be someone who uses the ultra-rare and secretive tiger style to kill the victims. Tarek infiltrates a clandestine Tiger training dojo to further investigate. Bolo Yeung plays Chong (also his name in Bloodsport), who trains with the tigers and paints murals. He might be the killer (of course he is) and he may be too powerful for the pair to bring him to justice. Despite the film's impressive cast and awesome plot (a serial killer martial artist?! Amazing!) Tiger Claws still manages to feel very middle-of-the-road. Jalal's fashion in the movie is nothing short of hilarious and the Canadianisms are also cute. The film features some solid martial art action, but there isn't much here that is memorable. I had seen this movie before and couldn't remember anything about it and now I know why: there are few moments that I can remember about the movie, and I just watched it the night before I wrote this review.

Bolo isn't in the movie enough, there aren't quite enough action scenes, and despite one giant car explosion the film feels underbudgeted. Of course, the budget isn't hilariously low, just low enough that the film leans on dialogue a bit too much. If you're looking for another Undefeatable (1993) with great fights and a bonkers plot, look elsewhere. While it isn't a total waste of time for Rothrock and Yeung fans (and Merhi fans if they exist), it isn't a must-see movie. Tiger Claws is mostly the cinematic equivalent of shrugged shoulders. It's ok but nothing impressive.

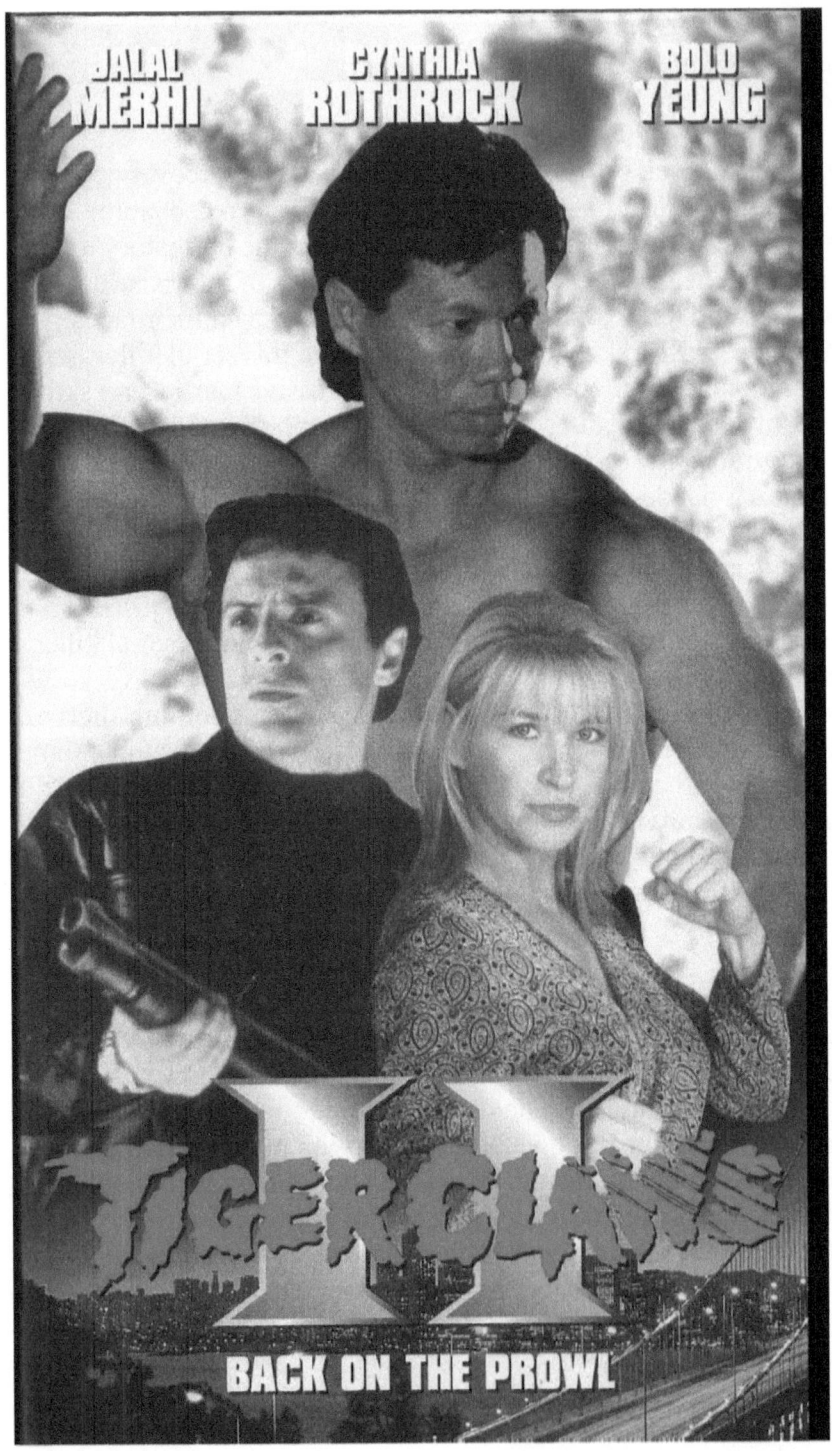

Tiger Claws II (1996)
Runtime 90 minutes
Directed by J. Stephen Maunder

Once again, we return to the world of Tiger Claws. Serial Killer Chong is sprung from the klink by an evil Triad leader that trained with Chong. They both belong to the same dark style of martial arts, but the Triad leader is even darkerer. Tarek (Jalal Mehri) and Masterson (Cynthia Rothrock) are reunited when a fresh rash of killings matching Chong's trademark face scratching start popping up around San Francisco. In truth the Triad leader has a diabolical plan that involves utilizing Chong's dark martial arts power and his own in order to open an ancient pathway deep in the bowels of San Francisco's catacombs from our world to ancient China. His plan is to bring in loads of modern weapons to China to change history in his clan's favor, forever! The Triad leader needs the fresh power of many martial artists, so he's also invited the best of the best to a clandestine death match near the portal. Tarek and Masterson must find the fight and stop the plot!

I really enjoyed the mystical qualities of Tiger Claws II, but the real neat portal-opening spookiness only happens at the very end of the film. Most of the film is centered around Chong and the Triad leader arguing about evil kung fu, and Tarek & Masterson trying to track them down. Evan Lurie gets to play a smaller role as a heavy, and he wears a blue silk Gi which is pretty fantastic. The set of the "catacomb" is totally cheap and has lots of Fulci fog and what look like cardboard sets. The tournament also involves evading various traps as combatants work their way through the maze-like catacomb and that's a lot of fun too. Of the three films, this might be the best in terms of how strange it is, and the solid amount of action delivered by the third act. The preceding two acts however have very little by way of action and feel like a slog. Tiger Claws II is an uneven movie that thankfully gives a fair amount of screen time to Bolo and Evan, and thankfully not a ton for Mehri who is as always, void of charisma. I would have liked more Rothrock in the film or perhaps more of her fighting, as she doesn't get to do much here, but to be honest I always want more Rothrock in my movies. Her cheerful plucky attitude is always welcome on my screen. Tiger Claws II is a mixed bag, the third act is great, the preceding two are not.

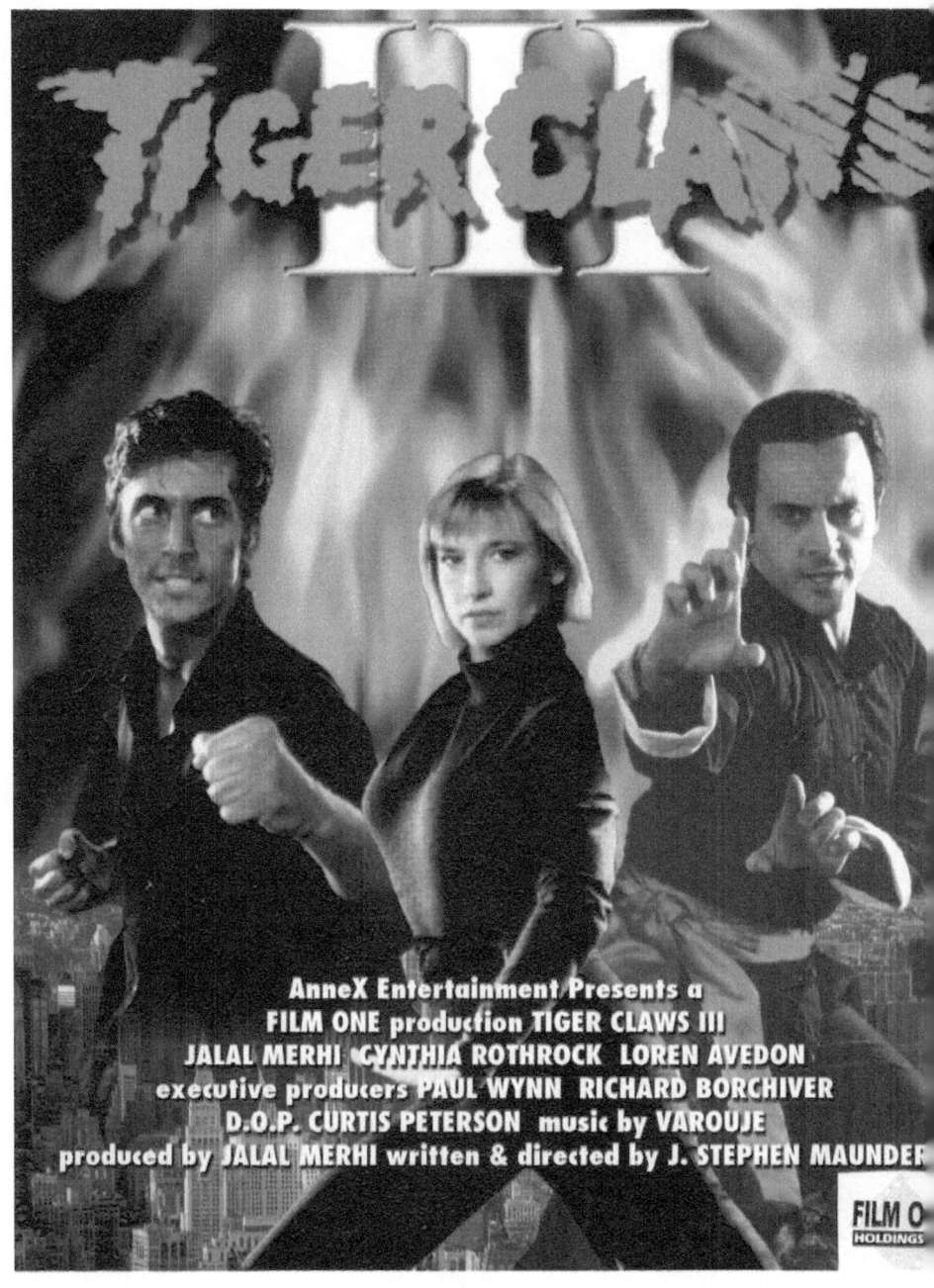

Tiger Claws III: The Final Conflict (2001)
Runtime 95 minutes
Directed by J. Stephen Maunder

The third installment of the Tiger Claws saga finds Tarek (Jalal Mehri) and Linda (Cynthia Rothrock) resting after the events of Part 2. They're invited to a super chic party where some sacred and ancient garments of 3 notoriously brutal martial artists from China's distant past will be revealed and a super special ceremony will be performed by Stryker (Loren Avedon), a mysterious martial artist himself. Tarek resignedly agrees and he and Linda hang out. The mysterious Stryker performs the ritual and suddenly the three martial artist butchers are resurrected and under his command! They can shoot lightning bolts from their hands ala Raiden in Mortal Kombat. The entire party is decimated by the evil butchers much to Stryker's joy. Linda is mortally wounded and somehow Tarek is spared. Elsewhere in the city we find Master Jin (Carter Wong) who knows all about the evil masters and their deadly fighting style. He agrees to train Tarek to take on the supernatural villains while Stryker and his evil minions begin to take over the underworld crime syndicates through force.

Tiger Claws III: The Final Conflict is a very late cycle direct to video action flick that didn't really know what to be. It's a post-Matrix film so the villains wear a lot of leather and ridiculous outfits. Loren Avedon has a bad guy goatee and likes to smoke cigars. His real-life martial arts prowess is almost completely unused in the film and that's a shame. He feels like a jerk you must work with occasionally that you try to avoid because he's tiringly smug. The minions have zero character at all. One is tall and big, another is smaller, and the third is a woman with cleavage. That's about it. They don't even have different evil martial arts powers, they all zap people. Carter Wong is fun in the movie and despite his accent, he's more emotive and engaging than Mehri. A very early role for comedian Russell Peters is featured here too and every time he's on screen the film becomes 100% more entertaining due to his goofy improved banter. I had a solid amount of fun watching this due to the low-rent locations, silly outfits, Avedon trying very hard to inject energy into the film, and the lightning zapping baddies. Had the film at least had a fun sidekick for Mehri, it would have been much more entertaining.

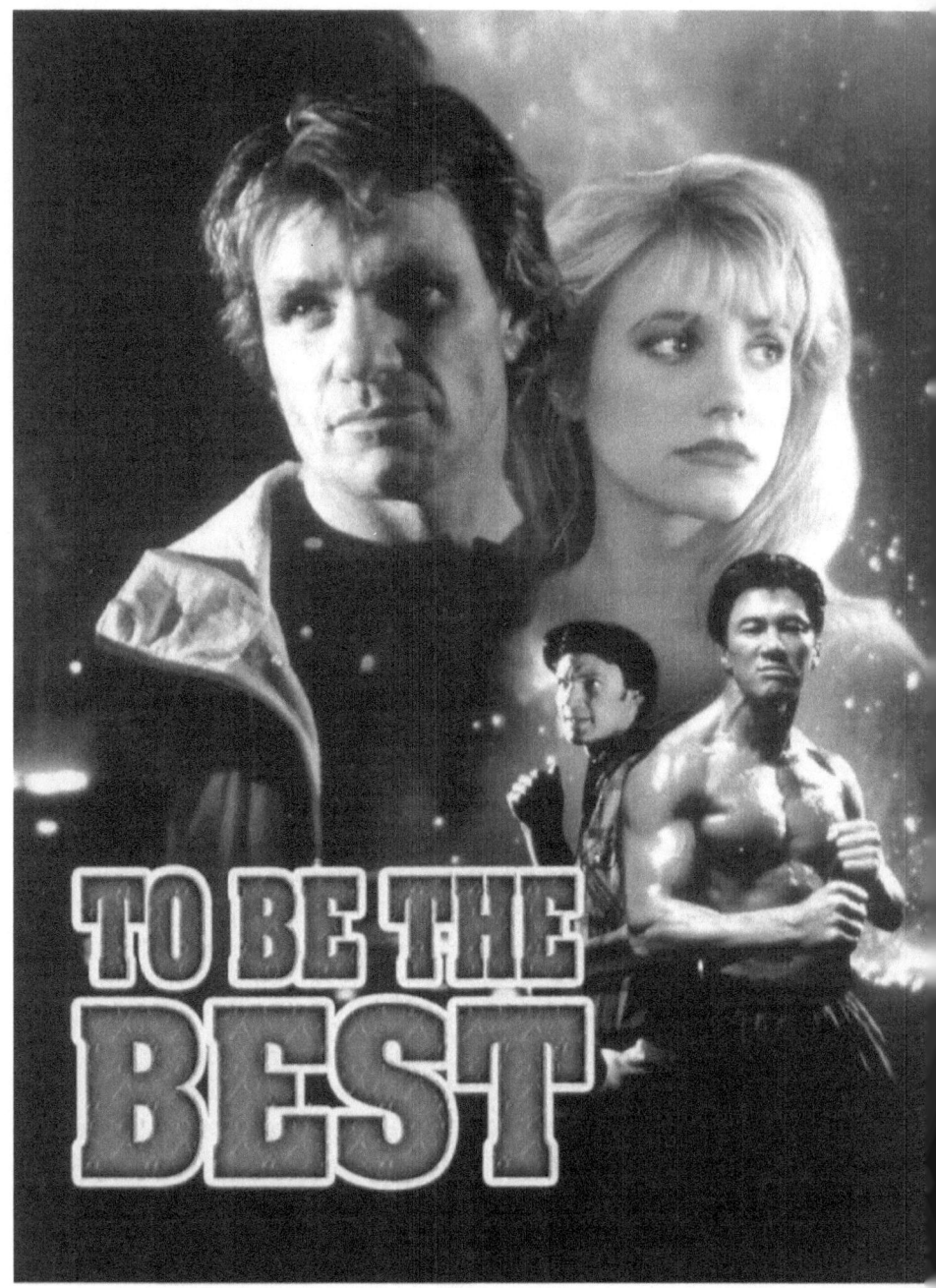

To Be the Best (1993)
Runtime 98 minutes
Directed by Joseph Merhi

PM Entertainment film To Be the Best is about two brothers (whom I kept getting confused) who are kings at kick fighting. Their dad (Martin Kove) is assembling a team for the Kickboxing World Championships. One son spends his time competing in illicit back-alley fist fights while the other has retired from competing but decides to join the team for one last go-around. They both hate their daddy-o because he can't stay off the booze (or keep from using Raiders branded merchandise) but they decide to compete anyway. The younger brother, the one who likes to punch dudes in alleys, has a girlfriend, she's blonde, pretty, and from a fabulously rich family that don't like his nogoodnik ways. He wants to prove them wrong by winning the competition, but he's tempted by a high roller who wishes to bet against the American team, betting on the rival Thai Team. It must be noted that the Thai team seemingly has 0% Thai people on the team, I guess they figured the audience would accept anyone from Asian descent as Thai. The high roller has offered to pay 100k if he throws the fight. As if that isn't enough motivation, if he doesn't throw the fight, it's likely his little lady will be killed. What's he going to do? To Be the Best starts off with a magnificent bang typical of PM's films. We get a fistfight on top of a building, followed by an attempted murder via helicopter, followed by said helicopter crashing into a building and exploding. Later we're treated to a dirt bike chase scene that ends with a spectacular car crash on a little league field. I've never seen a car crash onto a little league field and explode so the film gets bonus points for originality. The trouble is the movie is mostly downhill from here. We get reams of exposition from the characters and honestly, I didn't give a damn about them. We do get a five-on-five fist fight at a bowling alley with dudes wearing some fantastically 90's acid washed clothes. Again, I don't think I've seen a movie that involved a martial arts fight in a bowling alley. Bonus points. The root problem with the movie is that there is simply too much flab. We get far too much exposition and not enough action. The tournament fight scenes are underlit, poorly choreographed, and repetitive. The ending unleashes some great action and provides a glimpse to what is to come from PM. This one is for big fans of their output only.

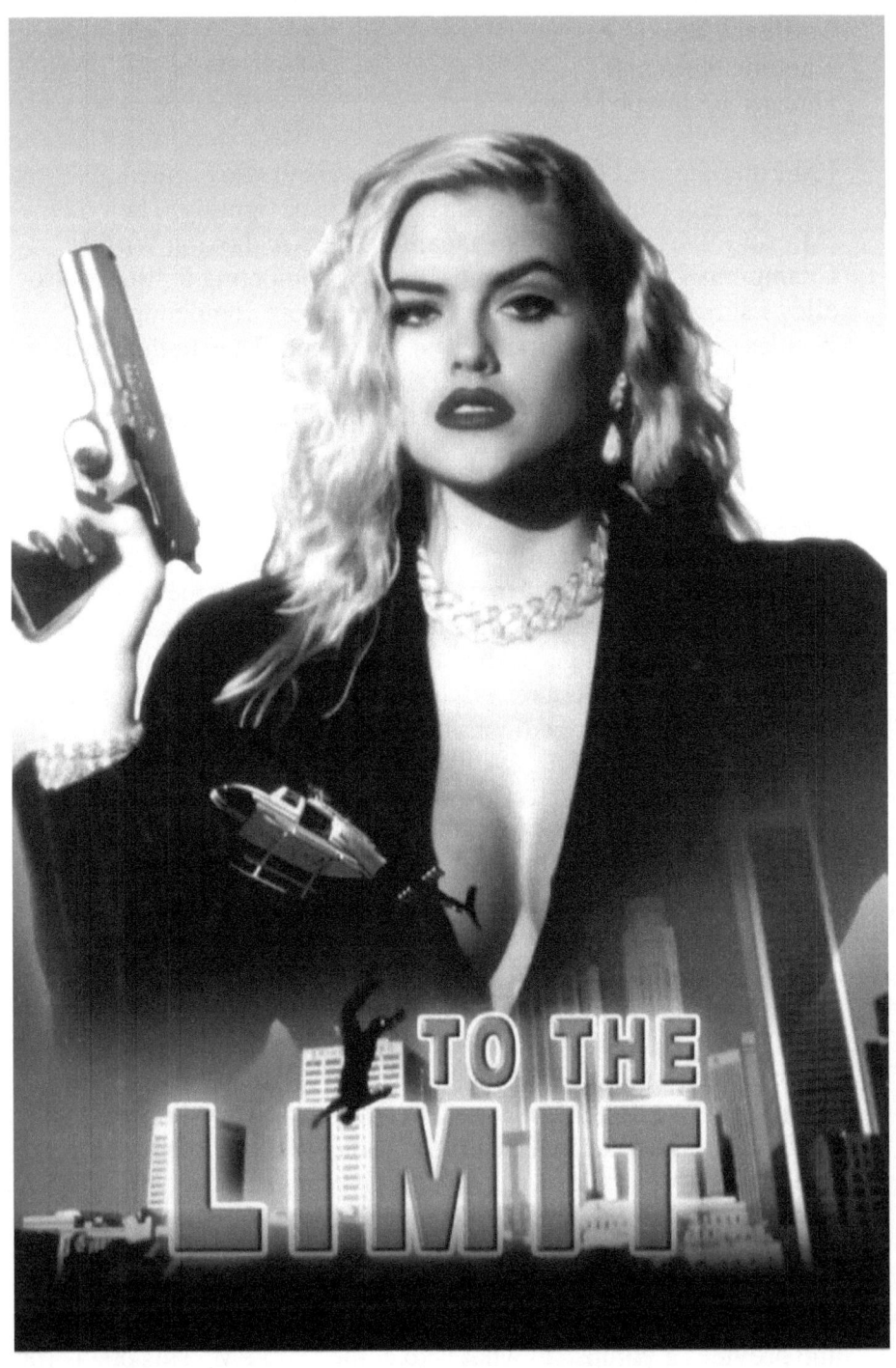

To the Limit (1995)
Runtime 96 Minutes
Directed by Raymond Martino

After Anna Nicole Smith's career blew up because of her involvement with Playboy and well before her personal life melted down into a drug-fueled train wreck that E! Entertainment callously cashed in on, there was a moment when someone thought it would be a great idea for her to star in films. PM Entertainment film To the Limit stars ANS as the wife of a sleazy older fella (hmmm life imitates art sometimes...). Said older fella dies suddenly via car bomb, while simultaneously his compatriot Frank DaVinci (Joey Travolta, John's much older brother) is gunned down at a wedding. He's also a mob boss. ANS' husband was a CIA operative. Frank survives the shooting but must escape further attempts at his life while ANS is also on the run due to secret codes on a CD-ROM she has in her possession thanks to her deceased husband. From here the two must evade a cavalcade of ninja-esque killers sent to murder them both. The plot was unclear as was the nature of the relationships between the characters. I didn't really care, all I wanted was what I came for: over-the-top PM Entertainment action. To the Limit delivers on the expected stunts, explosions, ridiculous fights, and eye-popping action sequences. The trouble is that the film is either about 10 minutes too long or at least one action scene too few. The movie is flabby in the middle with lots of needless dialogue and also features a much higher level of sleaze than I was expecting. Just about every actress goes topless in the film at least once and ANS is in the buff frequently and at length. Every man she sleeps with in the movie is at least 10 years her senior and Joey Travolta in particular looks grandfatherly. It's pretty clear the intended audience for this flick: over the hill dads in need of nudity and action and not a lot of stories.

To the Limit is not one of PM's greatest films, but it isn't one of their worst either. It's certainly middle-of-the-road PM with an extra dose of gratuitous nudity. The film features some very memorable action sequences involving explosions and helicopters, and one scene where a CD is used as a weapon that's worth the boredom endured during the drawn-out dialogue scenes.

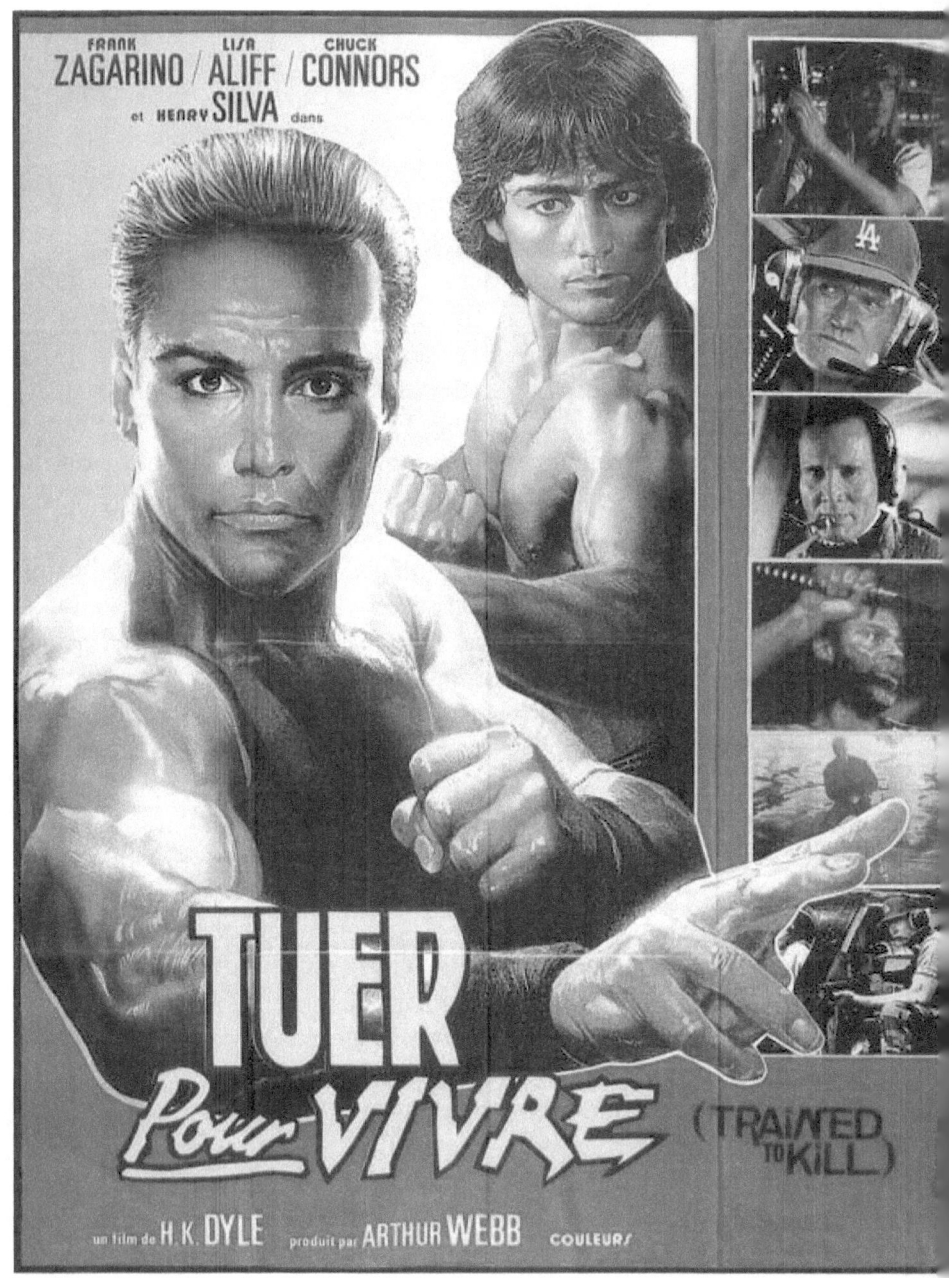

Trained to Kill (1990)
Runtime 90 minutes
Directed by H. Kaye Dyal

Trained to Kill begins in Cambodia where a young man named Samnaug (Glen Eaton) is running to escape some military types who clearly want to kill him. He runs to a helicopter waiting for him with a big machine gun to take out the dudes chasing him (hell yeah!). Inside the helicopter is a pistol-wielding older man named Ed Cooper (Chuck Connors). As it turns out this older gentleman is the refugee's father, during the Vietnam War this dude didn't keep his dingus in his pants and sired a son. Reunited after more than 20 years, he takes his new son back to the states to start his new life. Miraculously he can speak perfect English despite growing up in a straw hut in rural Cambodia. Unfortunately, Daddy-O has some old enemies (Harold Diamond and Robert Z'dar) that are broken out of prison by Ace Duran (Henry Silva). They track Cooper down to get sweet revenge and Z'dar kills him with a flame flower in what could be the most amazing full body stunt man burn I've seen. Ed's (other) son Matt (Frank Zagarino) comes for the funeral and along with Samnaug, they hatch a plan to track down the crew of criminals that killed their father. But first they have to do a lot of slow-motion training that involves pushups, running on the beach, and sparring.

Trained to Kill is a lot of fun. There is never a dull moment and that by itself would be worth championing, but it also has the stellar cast which helps to push it up into a higher echelon of fun. The movie has some sweet dirt bike stunt scenes, lots of fighting and shooting, and implausible ending involving a giant wooden tower with a blonde actress tied to it ala King Kong. Henry Silva is sorely underused in the movie, but he does get to steal a few scenes. Z'dar is dispatched too soon in the movie but he gets some memorable scenes in the film as well. We get a very slow car chase with what could be the longest timer on a grenade in cinema, lots of cheesy music, and a homeless man who trains the brothers in an abandoned restaurant. The movie is so much fun I hardly noticed how dull Frank Zagarino is, which is really saying something. Trained to Kill is a rock-solid choice to watch with friends. If you love Z'dar and direct-to-video action flicks, it will leave you plenty entertained.

AUTHOR NAME

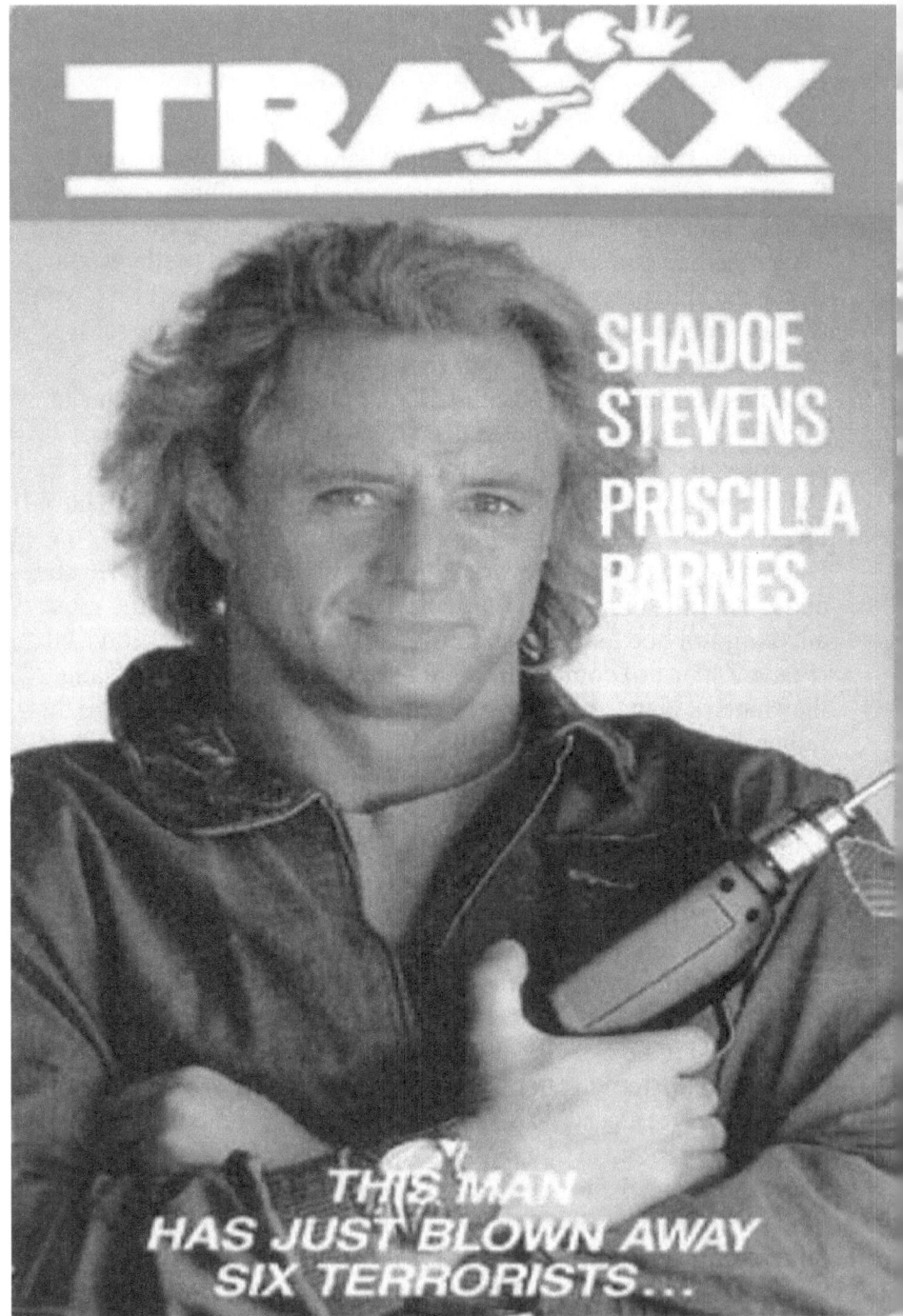

Traxx (1988)
Runtime 84 minutes
Directed by Jerome Gary

Traxx is about Traxx (Shadoe Stevens), 'nuff said right? He's a bad ass with a great physique, blown out blonde hair, and honeyed voice. We are introduced to Traxx as a sheriff's deputy taking out a bad guy that had killed an old lady and a puppy. His boss doesn't like Traxx's style, so Traxx quits and becomes a mercenary for a few years until he quits THAT to become a cookie baker. His cookies are awful (it's a running gag throughout the ENTIRE film). While baking a batch, he sees on a news report that a city nearby is overrun with criminal scum. He talks to the police chief offering to take care of the problem for $10,000. The chief doesn't agree but he doesn't say no either. Traxx, armed to the teeth, begins his crusade of taking out the trash in town along with the help of Deeter, a sidekick of sorts. Robert Davi plays the local drug kingpin, and he wants Traxx dead, so he hires 3 tough hombres to take him out.

The movie is intentionally goofy which sometimes works, and sometimes doesn't. Shadoe commits himself to the role very well and he oozes charisma and charm. The action in the film is appropriately over-the-top. I watched this with my awful awesome buddies and for us, it was fun in parts but mostly a drag. The problem with the film is the pacing, there is almost no forward momentum. Traxx just hangs out baking cookies and occasionally takes on the thugs in town. Those scenes are great, it's all the in-between that ruins the movie, and because of this the pacing is pretty bad. Even though the runtime is only 84 minutes long it still feels like a drag. The movie throws out plenty of jokes and some of them land big time but a good chunk of them just falls flat. The film at times feels like a legit action flick and at other times a parody. This confused vibe kinda kills the fun too. While not terrible, there are many, many other action flicks to dig into for an Awful Awesome evening before you catch Traxx. Its pacing issues and flat jokes nearly ruin the fun completely. I will say though, that it is likely the only movie that has a cameo by Famous Amos (the cookie mogul). So, there's that. In 2014 Shadoe Stevens released a re-cut version of Traxx to YouTube and perhaps this version fixes the pacing issues found in the original release... As of this writing, I haven't seen it.

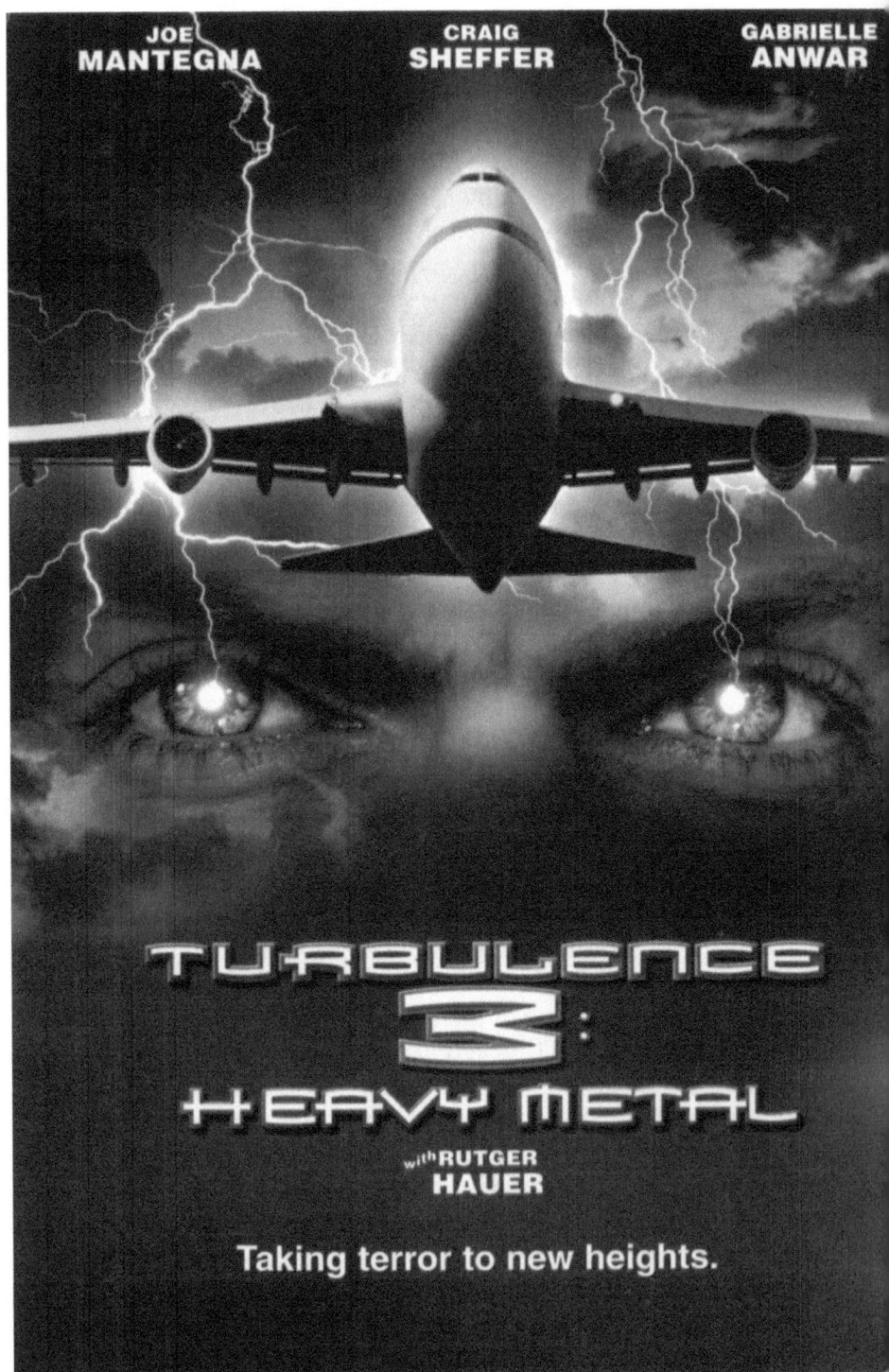

Turbulence 3: Heavy Metal (2001)
Runtime 94 minutes
Directed by Jorge Montesi

Turbulence 3: Heavy Metal is about a super edgy and highly popular "metal" icon, Slade Craven. He's decided to hang up his pleather jacket and shiny boots and retire but not before one last concert. This final concert won't be on the ground however, apparently that's too "safe." Instead, the concert will be held on a 747 with the largest interior I've ever seen on a commercial plane. A selection of lucky fans gets to witness the event in person, and the whole thing is streaming live on the interwebs. There also happens to be a hacker with mad skillz who has hacked the website's mainframe. This hacker has been tracked down by an FBI Agent and she gets into his apartment and starts to arrest him just as things take a turn in the plane. Slade has produced a gun and is waving it around raving. Uh oh. He's a part of a plot by a satanic cult to begin the end times and apparently it involves playing terrible music and having no eyebrows. Now it's up to air traffic control, the FBI and our hacker to figure out how to stop the mayhem before everyone on the plane crashes to their death.

I've gotten over my self-importance and identity as a metalhead (mostly) so the inaccuracies in the movie as they relate to metal culture are merely entertaining now. That said Turbulence 3: Heavy Metal is a mess and not in a good way. The film takes far too long to get going, the characters only get into the air about 30 minutes into the film. Before that we're "treated" with numerous character moments that are at best cliché and at worst grating. The actor playing Slade tries very hard with a bad script and poor characterization. Also, all that pleather must have been a strain (post-Matrix (1999) style on display here) but still he's unconvincing and worse: uninteresting. Rutger Hauer shows up for a bit in a sit-down role that would have made Cameron Mitchell proud. Our hacker looks like a reject from a boy band, which is amusing but really that's about it. The whole film lacks life and feels dull. The actors try their best with the material, but the material is the equivalent to the color beige (the most boring of colors). The movie feels safe, predictable, and boring. I really wanted to enjoy this, but I just couldn't. It was a strain to pay attention and that is never a good sign.

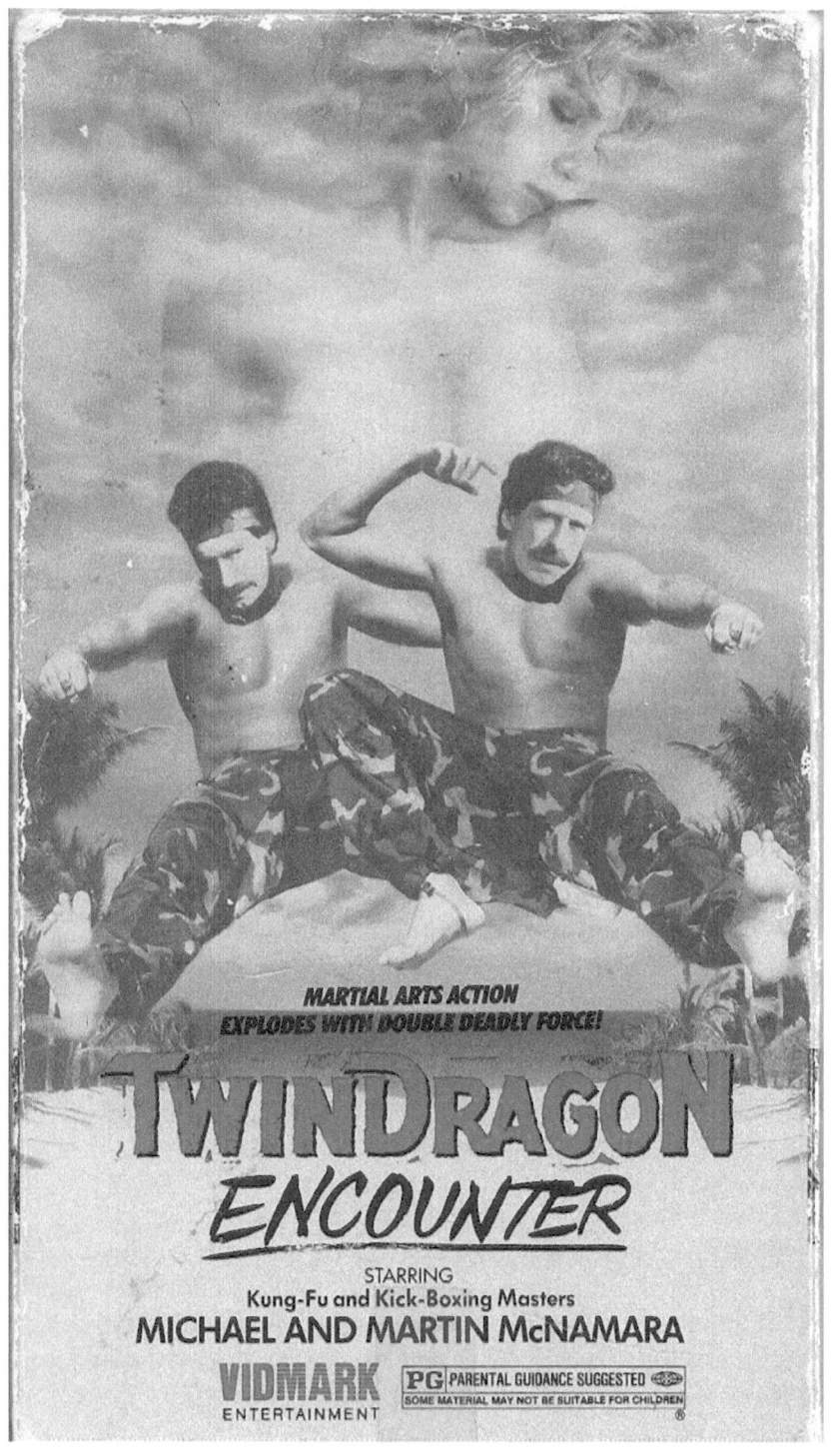

Twin Dragons Encounter (1988)
Runtime: 73 minutes
Directed by Paul Dunlop

Twin Dragons Encounter stars twin martial artists Martin and Michael McNamara. They run a martial arts studio, have matching mustaches, and matching physiques that they love to show off constantly. We're talking Van Damme-levels of bodily pride. They grab their girls (who also train at their studio and could easily be young enough to be their daughters) and head up to a shanty cabin in the woods far away from the prying eyes of the city. Along the way they beat up some truckers which provides the opportunity for one of the twins to spout, "Confucius say when fighting truckers, nail the suckers", in a faux accent. Yikes. Moving on, the twins grab their girls and supplies and head to the pier where they plan to take the world's largest/slowest/squarest boat up to their cabin. They get hassled by a clan of paramilitary mouth-breathers, but the twins trained their ladies well: they beat up the ne'er-do-wells handily without any help from their studly companions. Embarrassed, the quasi-revolutionaries spend the rest of the movie plotting their revenge.

The twins don't change their names for the movie, and they own matching twin vans that have their kung fu studio name (Twin Dragons Kung Fu Club) painted on the side. With their names. So, is this really a fictional film or is it a ridiculous man fantasy film meant to impress the viewer into thinking this is what life is really like for the twins? These two guys have the combined charisma of one Chuck Norris, which clearly isn't saying much. The intro title sequence/fighting montage scored to a song called, "Fight for Your Right to Fight" is pretty priceless. Whether it's more training, chopping wood, getting gear together, or fighting the bad guys, this movie has montages aplenty. The villain is also a lot of fun. He chews a cigar, has a bleached blonde Mohawk-esque hairdon't and barks orders throughout the film. We also get to see the twins do just about every manly thing you can think of, except bed their ladies. In fact, there seems to be zero chemistry. It's almost as if they merely wanted an audience to their badassery with no interest in boot-knocking. Overall, however it is a fun flick with enough bad dialogue, and over-the-top action antics to keep Awful Awesome fans happy. It's followed up by a sequel called Dragon Hunt (1990).

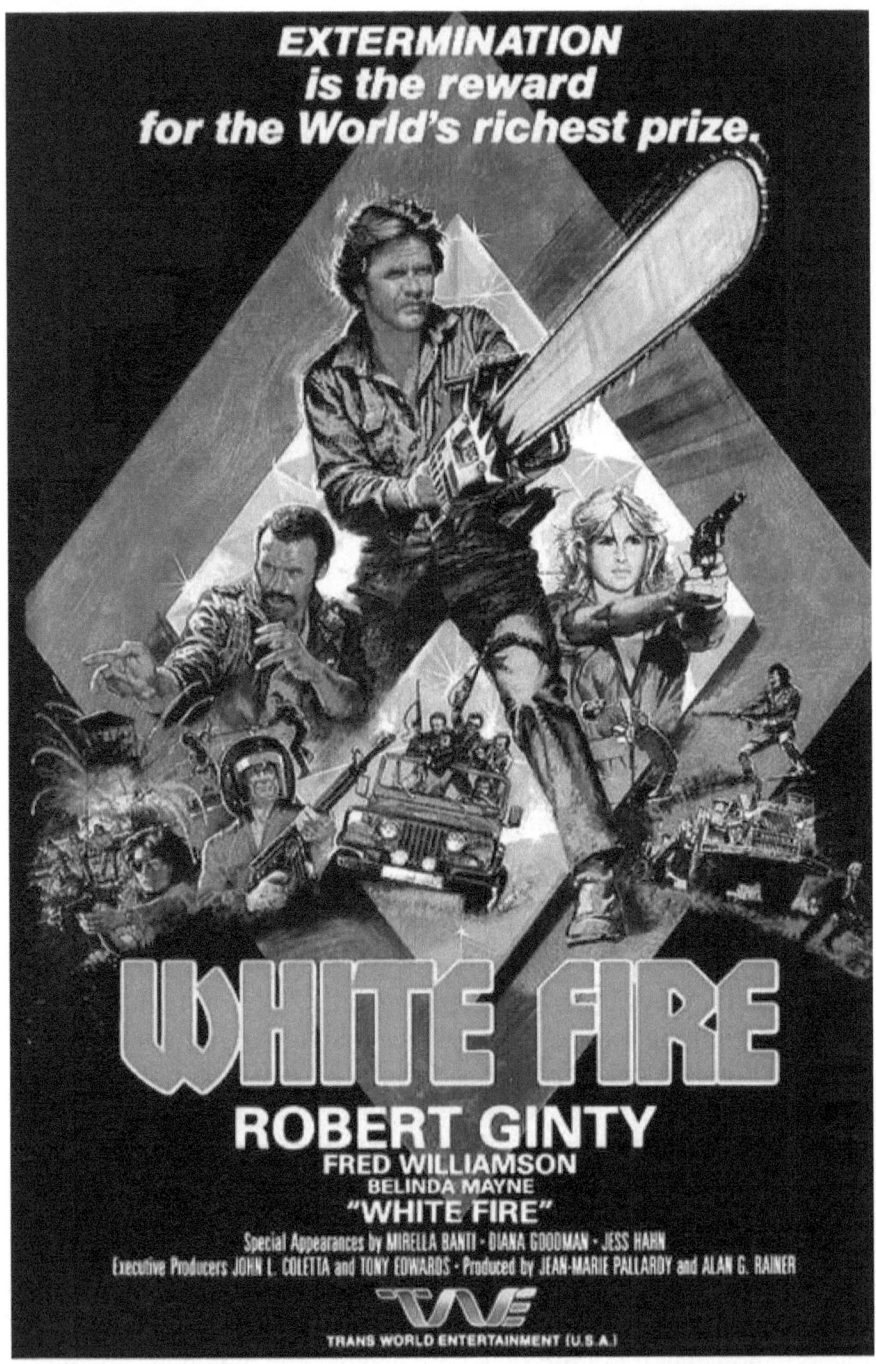

White Fire (1985)
Runtime 101 minutes
Directed by Jean-Marie Pallardy

Largely filmed in Turkey, White Fire begins with a family fleeing in terror from a madman bent on killing them. He catches up and kills the parents but before he can take out the children, he's dispatched by a kindly old smuggler. The brother Bo (Robert Ginty) and sister Ingrid (Belinda Mayne) grow up as orphans, but develop a very strong and very inappropriate bond. As adults they work for a diamond mine and hear about a mysterious and potentially dangerous super diamond called White Fire. They decide to track down the diamond, but Bo is crestfallen when Ingrid is murdered suddenly, He gets drunk at a bar and meets a woman that looks strikingly like Ingrid... he saves her from being hassled from a belligerent drunk guy and she takes Bo home. Bo decides to train her to become his new diamond-hunting buddy and together they try to find the mysterious White Fire. What he doesn't know is that she's the main squeeze of a very important and rich man who pays Noah (Fred Williamson) to track her down. Lots of fights, including one with a chainsaw, car chases, and opportunities for nudity abound in White Fire. During the course of the movie Bo falls in love with the woman who looks very similar to his sister. Earlier in the film Bo taunts his sister by ripping off her towel, revealing her naked body and remarks, "hey you don't look like anybody's kid sister anymore" (...that's creepy dude). This bizarre incestuous relationship is just one example of how bonkers this movie is. There are numerous gory deaths in the movie, a convoluted plot that is tough to follow, Fred Williamson chewing the scenery, adventure, and of course Robert Ginty's stale performance and ginger mustache. The pacing of the film is just right, there are enough action scenes to keep the viewer interested and enough bizarre dialogue and sleazy situations to fill in the moments when no one is getting punched or shot at.

I had a blast with this flick. Director Jean-Marie Pallardy began directing in the early 70's, working on hardcore and softcore films like Emmanuelle 3 (1980) and Emmanuelle Goes to Cannes (1986). This explains the sleazy vibe of White Fire and the brazen nudity. Sadly, White Fire is one of only a few non-adult titles he directed.

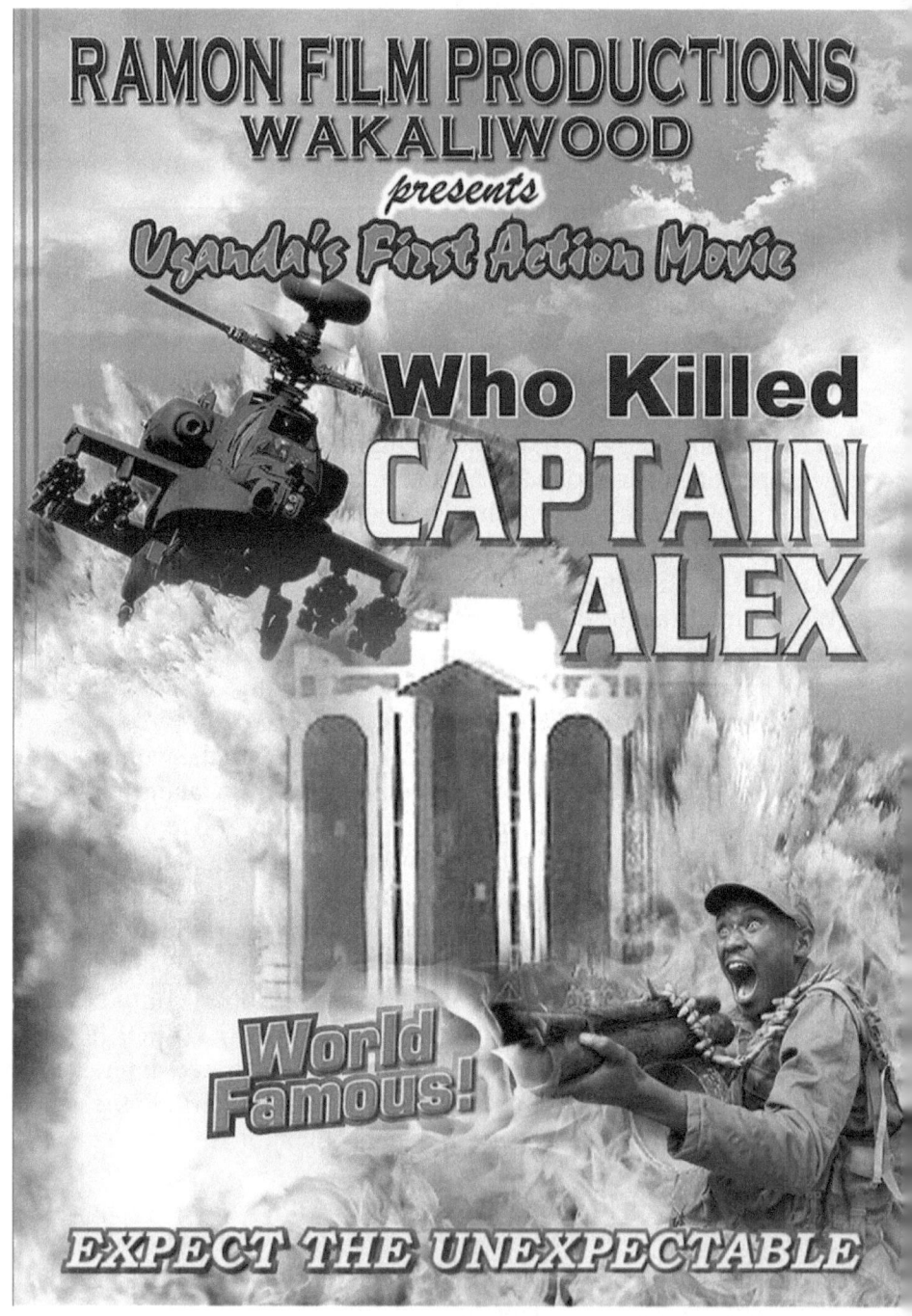

Who Killed Captain Alex? (2006)
Runtime 64 minutes
Directed by Nabwana I.G.G.

Who Killed Captain Alex? Is the very first Ugandan action movie, apparently ever. Nigerian film, or Nollywood, is wildly popular in both Nigeria and Uganda and, not wanting to be left out, Nabwana I.G.G. set out to make a name for himself and Uganda. This man of vision set out to do the unthinkable: make an action movie in Uganda to compete with Nollywood movies. Who Killed Captain Alex is his first attempt.

Who Killed Captain Alex is about a police raid gone wrong. A police force led by the beloved Captain Alex raids some bad dudes to put the hurt on them and help the citizens from their badness, but during the scuffle, Captain Alex is killed ...but no one knows how. An investigation is launched that includes elite law enforcement, more bad guys, shootouts, yelling, fighting, and general mayhem.

I approached Who Killed Captain Alex with some trepidation. I'm up for any kind of low-budget detritus, so the lack of budget and skill didn't bother me. I simply didn't want to watch a movie made in a very poor country within Africa and make fun it. It felt like being a bully or perhaps even racist. As it turns out, it's common in Uganda to release a movie with additional commentary that either explains what is going on or makes fun of the movie for you! Such is the case with this film. This made me feel like it was totally ok to cut loose and have fun with this in the normal Awful Awesome way. In fact, the commentator is actually pretty dang funny himself. The film's short runtime and quantity of action helped to move things along nicely. I will however disagree with the rampant hyperbole found online about the film and tell you that it is not the best movie ever or even a pantheon Awful Awesome movie. It's fun, it's a unique experience, and certainly one worth trying out with your friends, but it isn't a world-beater. The lack of a cohesive story hurts the film in my mind as well as the bland characters. But hey it's a first try from a very passionate film maker and I'll give it bonus points for even existing (especially considering it was made on a $200 USD budget!). I would recommend Who Killed Captain Alex to Awful Awesome fans; You will have fun with this.

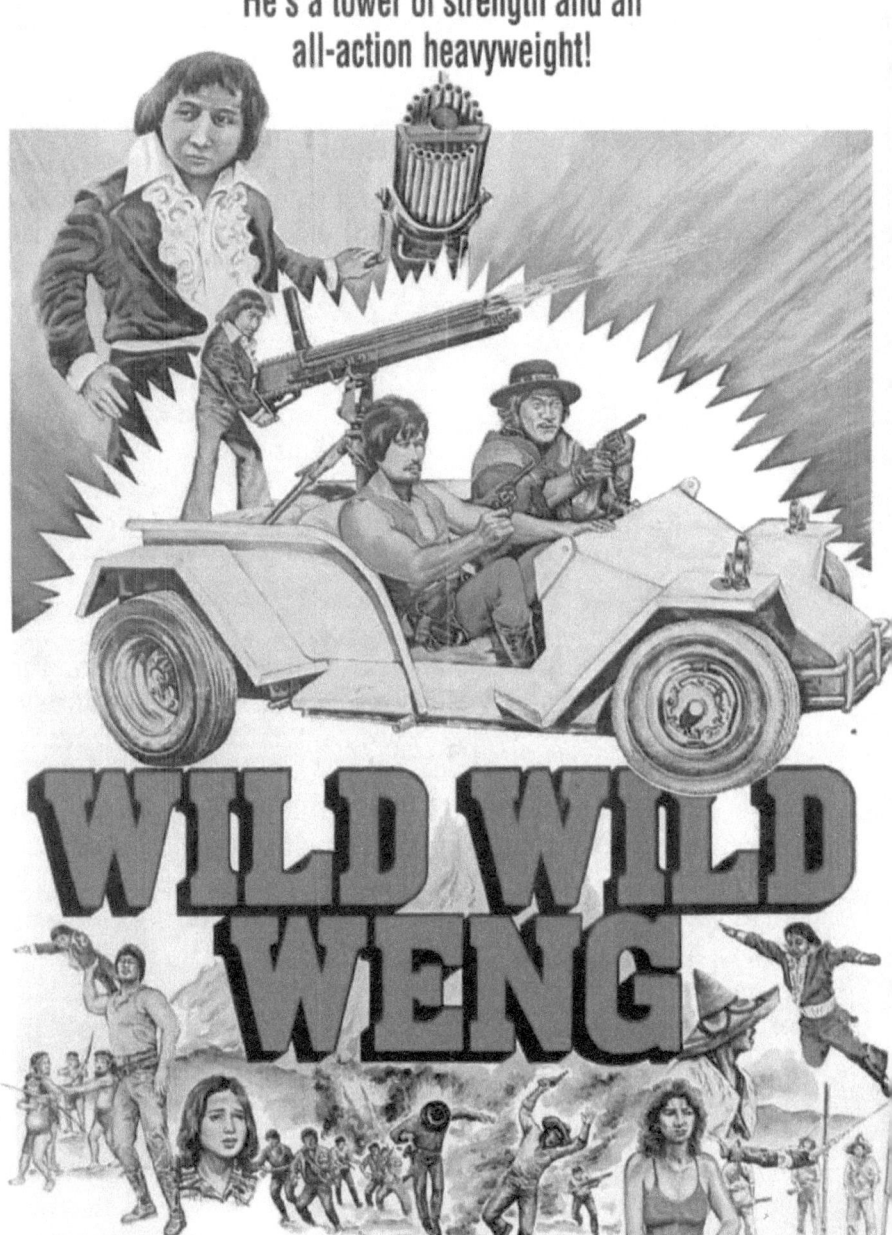

Wild Wild Weng (1982)
Runtime 82 minutes
Directed by Eddie Nicart

Wild Wild Weng begins abruptly with Weng Weng and his heavily-muscled co-star walking on a dirt path. Suddenly they hear a woman's scream and find a lady besieged by ruffians. Quickly the pair descend upon the bad guys and beat them into submission. It's clear from the beginning: this pair are a couple of tough hombres. Later we find that the town is run by a frilly-collared bad guy in charge of not only Mexican-style banditos but also ninjas (this man is nigh unstoppable!). The crime boss doesn't like do-gooders in his realm, so he sends out some goons to take care of them. Of course, the goons are the ones who get taken care of and so the villainous bad guys hatch a plan (several of them really) to get rid of Weng Weng and his handsome friend. The pair meet a man who has had his tongue cut out by one of the ringleader's minions (this one looks like he escaped from the Village People). Soon the three are working together to find a way to destroy the evil empire and free the people of the town.

But is it any good? My friends and I did enjoy watching Wild Wild Weng but not as much as we enjoyed The Impossible Kid (1982) and For Y'ur Height Only (1981). Gone are the pint-sized strange weapons (though Weng Weng does get to use a full-size gatling gun), and sure there are a couple of big stunts featuring Weng Weng, but it doesn't have the same amount of novel action or momentum found in the other films. This film features a fair amount of action but it's mostly repetitive. The locations are sun-burnt and sand –covered, which has never been a favorite of mine from a visual standpoint. I prefer Weng Weng when he's starring in a Bond rip-off instead of this sendup of the Western genre. We get some pretty hilarious fashion, and plenty of crotches get punched and kicked, but it just feels tired and at points was tiresome. It doesn't help that the tongueless character tries to speak, constantly, and the dubbing is particularly grating for his mumbling/screaming character. Still, it's a Weng Weng movie and does have its moments. If you haven't seen any of Weng Weng's movies however, this would not be a good place to start.

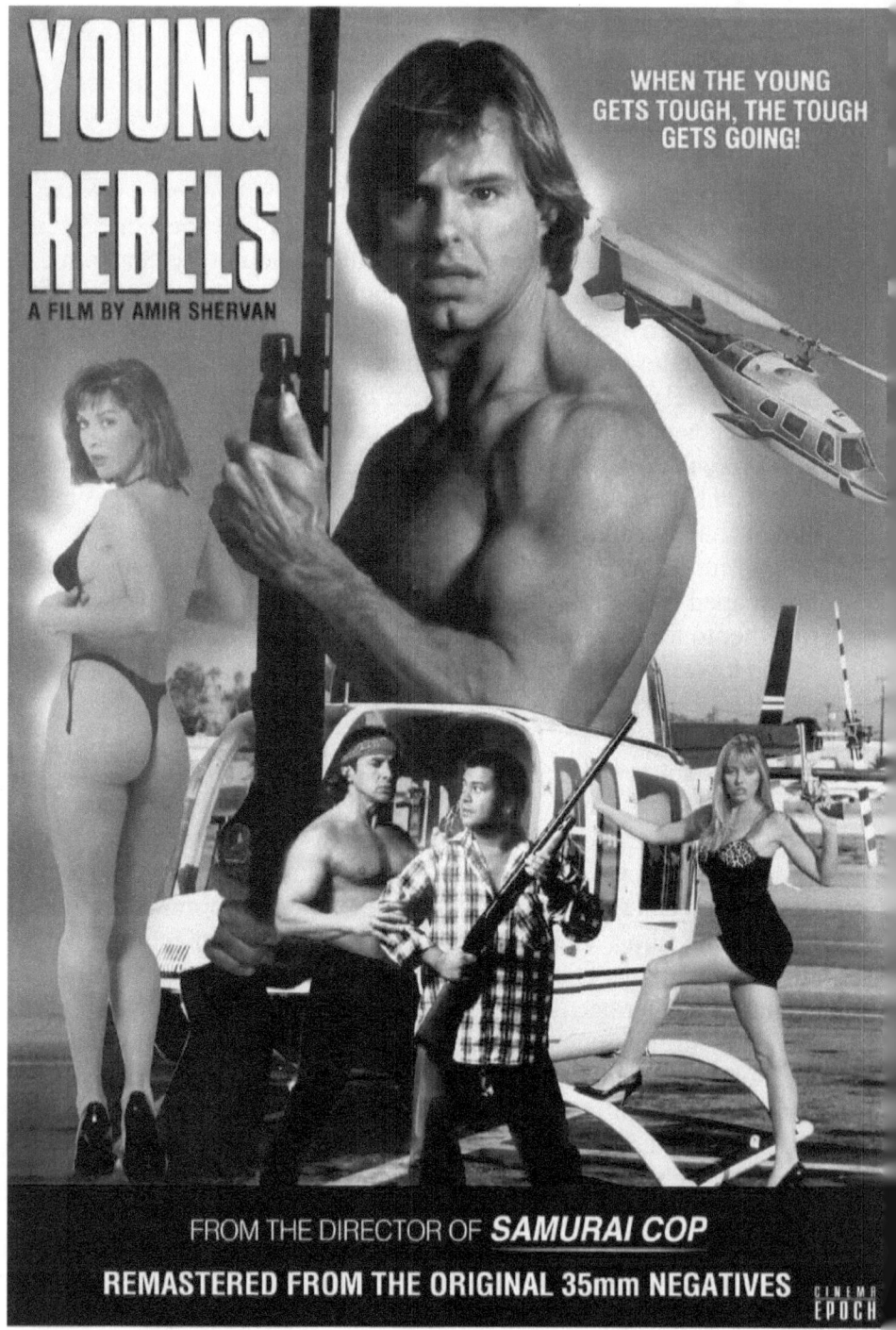

Young Rebels (1992)
Runtime: 93 min
Directed by Amir Shervan

For many of us bad movie hounds, Samurai Cop (1991) is on Mt. Olympus along with Miami Connection (1987), The Room (2003), and Troll 2(1990). That film is one of my personal favorites. Samurai Cop was not the sole film from director Amir Shervan though, he directed a handful more in the states after having a successful career in Iran. As far as I can tell, the further into his filmography you go, the less coherent his films become. Also directed by Shervan, Young Rebels was never released in the states until now!

Young Rebels is about a crime boss played by G. Alexander Vidrion (Killing American Style (1988)), who deals drugs and hates everything and everyone. His son, played by Robert Z'dar, serves as one of his enforcers... and the Crime boss hates him too. Our studly hero of the film, Charlie, has a younger brother that borrowed money from the boss, and he owes big time. The only way he can get out of debt is if he has Charlie fly a helicopter to Mexico to transport two drug kingpins to the states. Charlie shrugs his shoulders and agrees despite the risk. Predictably, the deal goes sour with the two kingpins ending up dead. Now the crime syndicate is after the brothers, and they have to fight back to survive!

I love Robert Z'dar. He's a bad guy member of a gang, a formidable foe who knows how to rock a button-down shirt with only one button at the bottom. Joselito Rescober, who played the ridiculous waiter in Samurai Cop (and the flight attendant in Samurai Cop 2(2015) as well as the doctor in Killing American Style) plays our hero's Mexican friend. He's got a sweet little ponytail, mustache, and a shirt that looks like a shower curtain. Tadashi Yamashita plays a martial arts teacher who got put out of business by the crime boss when his property was sold. He teams up with our hero to give the film some martial arts flair. I don't think it's as bonkers as Samurai Cop, but it is better than Hollywood Cop (1987) and Killing American Style. It's less competent and more action-packed. This one is chock-full of shoot em up action and good old fashion fist fighting. Young Rebels is very fun and Pantheon. I can't wait to watch it again.

ACKNOWLEDGEMENTS

Again, I must thank Chris Ewing for doing extensive editing on this book. Awful Awesome Action Volume 1 and this volume would not have been the same book without his meticulous work editing it. I also want to thank everyone that purchased Action Volume 1 & Horror Volume 1 and reviewing them on Amazon. Reviews help the books gain visibility so if you can, please review this one too! I would again like to thank my movie crew: my wife Vida, Ben, Cam, Keith, Ashley, Richard, Carl, Matt, Cody, Shane, Errol, Will, David, Tom, Suzanne, Mars, and anyone else the ever attended an Awful Awesome movie night. I'd also like to thank the Cult of Muscle podcast, The Doomed Show Podcast, and Comeuppance Reviews, and the Direct to Video Connoisseur for giving me great quotes and helping spread the word about the Action volume as well as the Horror volume.

AVAILABLE NOW!

AWFUL AWESOME ACTION Vol 1.

Over 100 reviews of Awful Awesome Action Trash. Featuring Samurai Cop, Miami Connection, Road to Revenge and more!

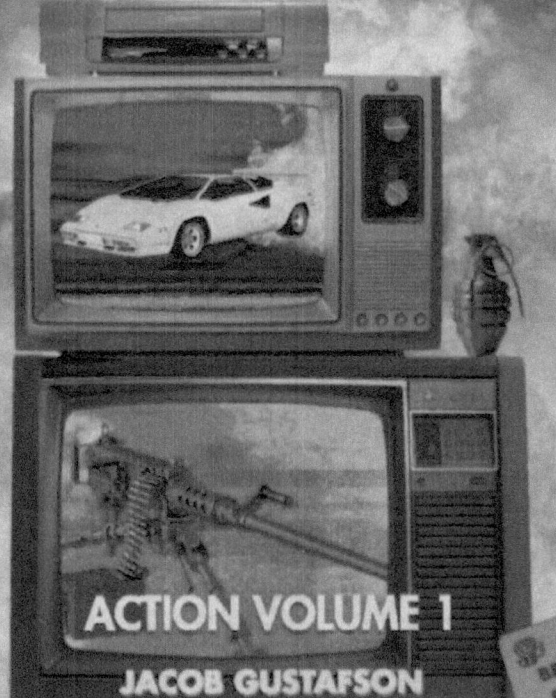

AVAILABLE NOW!

AWFUL AWESOME HORROR: VOL 1.

Featuring over 100 reviews of Horror trash like Trolls 2, Suburban Sasquatch, Demon Wind and more!

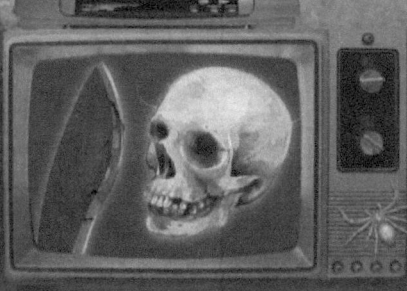

AVAILABLE NOW! AWFUL AWESOME SCI-FI VOL. 1!

FEATURING OVER 100 REVIEWS LIKE BIRDEMIC, PHOBE, SPACE MUTINY AND THE FILMS OF NEIL BREEN!

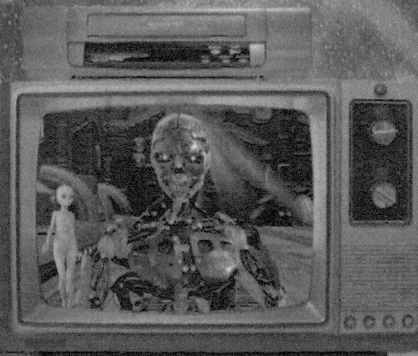
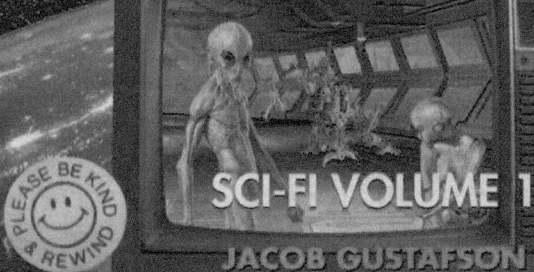

COMING SOON

Awful Awesome Sci-Fi Vol 2.

www.ingramcontent.com/pod-product-compliance
Lightning Source LLC
Chambersburg PA
CBHW020642220526
45464CB00001B/262